# BREAKING THE SKIN
## 21st Century Irish Writing

Published: 18th October 2002
by The Black Mountain Press
P O Box 9, Ballyclare, County Antrim, BT39 0JW, N Ireland
www.blackmountainpress.com

Short story Copyrights © the Authors, 2002
Introduction Copyright © John McAllister, 2002

The Black Mountain Press gratefully acknowledges the financial assistance of The Arts Council of Northern Ireland and the National Lottery Fund

ISBN: 0-9537570-1-3

The moral right of the authors has been asserted. A catalogue record for this book is available from the British Library. All rights reserved. No part of this publication may be transmitted in any form or by any means, electronic or mechanical, including photography, recording or any information storage or retrieval system, without permission in writing from the publisher. The book is sold subject to the condition that it shall not, by way of trade or otherwise, be lent, resold or otherwise circulated without the publisher's prior consent in any form of binding or cover other than that in which it is published and without a similar condition, including this condition, being imposed on the subsequent publisher.

Cover artwork by Miriam de Búrca
Layout by Tonic Design, Belfast
Printed by Easyprint, Belfast

# BREAKING THE SKIN
## 21ST CENTURY IRISH WRITING

VOLUME ONE: NEW SHORT STORIES

*Edited by*

John McAllister & Frank Sewell

## ACKNOWLEDGMENTS

Acknowledgement is made to Nigel McLoughlin, who suggested the title, and who with Matt Fluharty and Frank Sewell has edited the companion in this two book set, Breaking The Skin – 21st Century Irish Writing, Volume 2 - New Irish Poetry. John Brown, formerly of the Arts Council of Northern Ireland, is thanked for being instrumental in the publications fruition. Acknowledgement is also due to Daithí Ó Muirí and Cló Iar-Chonnachta, Indreabhán, Conamara for permission to include work from *Cogaí* (2002).

# CONTENTS

| | | |
|---|---|---|
| Introduction | | 7 |
| Taking Stock | John McAllister | 11 |
| Never Ever | Jim Meredith | 19 |
| Mystery Shopper | Brian McNulty | 32 |
| The Sky Painter | Brian Kennedy | 50 |
| Codagh / War | Daithí Ó Muirí | 54 |
| | *trans by Frank Sewell* | |
| Mobiles | Gerard Kinsella | 58 |
| As Quiet as the Grave | Kevin Gormley | 63 |
| The Price of Knowledge | Marie O'Nolan | 70 |
| Heat | Stephen McMurray | 78 |
| Objects | Gary Allen | 87 |
| Corporate Bonding | Niall McGrath | 91 |
| The Bed Bugs Bite | Jim Meredith | 102 |
| This Life | John McAllister | 108 |
| Rendezvous | Howard Wright | 133 |
| Broken Things | Katherine Martin | 135 |
| *Tace* is Latin for Candle | Marie O'Nolan | 138 |
| Cassandra | Csilla Toldy | 144 |
| New York | Sam Millar | 149 |
| Tales out of School | Claire Dagger | 155 |
| | *trans by Frank Sewell* | |
| Slow Learner | Gordon Williams | 165 |
| Furniture | Howard Wright | 177 |
| Helping Hand | Brian McNulty | 185 |
| Watching the Wind | Stephen McMurray | 190 |
| Images of Heaven | A F McKenna | 194 |
| The Value of Flames | Brian Kennedy | 201 |
| The Haircut | Gary Allen | 209 |
| Consaint / Defence | Daithí Ó Muirí | 216 |
| | *trans by Frank Sewell* | |
| The Experimental Girlfriend | Rosemary Jenkinson | 220 |
| Off the Hook | Csilla Toldy | 228 |
| Who's a Cheeky Boy | Gordon Williams | 236 |
| Permanent | Anthony Toner | 243 |
| Ballad of the Café Capri | Niall McGrath | 248 |
| Contributors | | 258 |

# INTRODUCTION

For years I have taught the Armagh Writers Group that the five elements of a story are: character, place, object, strange event or happening, and twist. That is like saying a motorcar is made up of metal, plastic and rubber. Every author included in this anthology has taken those five basic elements of a story and turned them into something magical and uniquely theirs.

Katherine Martin is an American living permanently in Belfast with her 'Dan.' When she is in Ireland she is homesick for America and when she is in America she can't wait to get back home to Ireland. Her language, her patois, is a wonderful blend of Irish-American.

Don't try to read Howard Wright's entries the way you would a normal story, lie back and let the words sink into you. Gary Allen, another good Ballymena man like myself, does the same. Reading Gerald Kinsella is like reading Robert Frost, but with a delicious intensity, and Kevin Gormley swears his story was not written the week his wife, Marion, was in bed with the flu. She says he wouldn't dare.

Niall McGrath writes with sure hand, leading you to a peak then dropping you into an ending you should have seen coming, but didn't, and Rosemary Jenkinson, in a few short pages, turns a selfish, self-centred character into someone you can admire.

Marie O'Nolan's stories linger with you long after you have finished reading them, and Gordon Williams has a wonderfully warped view on every day living. Csilla Toldy writes with an delicious intensity and AF McKenna has a unique style.

Three years of Irish classes at school taught me only a love for the cadences of the Irish language itself. Daití Ó Muirí's music of the soul has been beautifully counterpointed by Frank Sewell's delicate translation.

Jim Meredith leads you, with a gentle master's hand, into a surreal world well grounded in fact, where shiver builds on shiver. Beyond Stephen McMurray's world of implied horror, there lies hope, whereas Brian Kennedy's stories are based firmly on family life where anything can and does happen, and Sam Millar's story has an extraordinary compassion for our fellow men. Claire Dagger's story makes you look at children and think 'Life couldn't be like that for them?' Unfortunately....

Brian McNulty is such a delicious writer your eyes just eat up the pages, and Anthony Toner, being a typical newspaper reporter, only arrived with his story when the presses were already running.

On a practical note. Authors write in almost as many different ways as the things they write about. I have changed fonts and formats to bring some sort of visual cohesion to this collection but, other than to correct obvious typographical errors, I have left most works unchanged as to punctuation and grammar. My voice is not that of the author and even a comma in the wrong place could change the whole tone of the piece.

I would like to thank the Arts Council of Northern Ireland for their funding which made this anthology of new North Irish writing possible. And especially to John Brown, and Niall McGrath of the Black Mountain Press, for their vision, which inspired it in the first place. I would like also to thank Niall for guiding me through the technical intricacies involved in bringing out an anthology, and for allowing me some creative accounting in the number of authors I could use. The initial concept of a platform for eleven local writers kept getting expanded upwards as I found more and more stories that I couldn't bear to leave out.

Finally a word of thanks and appreciation to my wife, Patricia, who matched me story for story and gave me a reader's insight into the submissions.

John McAllister

Armagh – September 2002

# TAKING STOCK
## John McAllister

Along the river there were only farm dogs and evasive answers. They were the least of Sergeant Barlow's problems for the rain wasn't taking time to come down and the Dunlops were playing their usual Orange card. For most of the year it was merely a case of injuries sustained while resisting arrest but at the beginning of July, with the marching season in full swing and them good Orangemen and Barlow a Catholic, a *Roman* Catholic, then it was police brutality.

A sheepdog shot out of an old shed and barked. Barlow kicked at it with his foot and the bicycle wobbled under him. He kicked again and turned into the lane leading to the Widow Todd's house. Across from the entrance to the lane was the farm belonging to the Chairman of the Police Authority. Not that he lived there of course, not grand enough for the wife. District Inspector Harvey would personally visit the chairman at his town house, drink a whisky and record a pack of lies. 'My dear, Harvey, me plant a crop of beet?'

'Lying git,' said Barlow into the rain and dumped the bike against the farmhouse wall. The half-door leading into a small porch was open. The porch was dry because the rain was driving away from it. He banged the upper door. When the widow appeared he held up a ledger wrapped in oilcloth. 'Census, missis.'

She nodded, it was a nervous habit she had, of her body agreeing with her mind before she said or did anything. 'Come in.' There was no warmth in her voice. She led the way into the kitchen and put the kettle on the range.

He stood uncertain, his cape already forming puddles on the flagged floor. 'Your crops, the acreage... the usual.'

She pushed a chair away from the table. 'Another year.'

'And a bad one too, missis.' The deal table was scrubbed white; his hat made a dark stain of damp. He took it off again. 'But it's near the twelfth and they say God's an Orangeman.'

Barlow hung his hat and cape out in the porch then he unwrapped the ledger and put the oilcloth on the floor. He was relieved to see that the damp stain on the table was already fading.

He worked ponderously through the ledger. He could have answered the questions himself because the widow cycled the same crops: wheat, root and fallow year by year. Only the bog meadow along the wandering river remained forever in grass. He kept his eye on the page because each answer, whether yes or no, was accompanied by a nod and he found that confusing.

A mug of tea sweetened with two spoonfuls of sugar appeared in front of him. He drained it and it was promptly refilled. In between times she stirred a pot of stew for her tea and an even bigger one of porridge for the pigs in the morning. Barlow was so hungry he could have eaten the porridge but there was no offer.

The widow interrupted his questions. 'There must be more to life than your ledger.'

He looked up, startled, and saw an angry pain on her face. He said, 'Sometimes I wonder myself, missis.'

He wasn't sure what else was expected of him so he drank his tea. The widow nodded vigorously and turned back to her stirring. Once the ledger was filled Barlow swung the cape over his shoulders and left.

'Funny woman,' he said to himself as the bike creaked down the lane. It was always the same with her, never welcoming but never unfriendly. A kind soul, people said, with her only son dead in the war and her husband before that. With fifty acres she could have got another husband but every approach had been met with a steady rebuff.

At the bottom of the lane the dog came at him again. He was ready for it this time and his boot nearly connected. The dog gave a yelp and disappeared into the shed. Barlow felt better as he peddled the long miles back to the station.

District Inspector Harvey and the Chairman of the Police Authority were waiting for Barlow. Barlow didn't mind his clothes dripping onto Harvey's carpet.

Harvey sat at his desk. The Chairman stood to the right of the Queen's picture: upright, firm, hands behind back. Harvey said that he and the Chairman had been talking, the local twelfth parade needed careful handling. It wasn't just a question of no triumphalism while marching through the Catholic area of the town to the railway station; there was also the point that he, Barlow, led the parade. 'No harm in that,' said Harvey, and hastily added he was sure that Barlow's loyalty was to his uniform and his fellow officers.

Barlow nodded. If he had a 'political' opinion it had to do with Chairmen who were never out of the station.

The Chairman said, 'We are particularly concerned this year because of the complaints lodged against you by a member of the Dunlop family.' He looked annoyed, something he did anytime the Dunlops were mentioned; the lorry load of drink stolen from his brewery at Christmas still rankled. 'The Dunlops, as you well know, are stalwarts of the lodge; they carry the banner. So it would be unseemly if...' He looked over at Harvey. 'Laurence, you explain.'

The explanation was simple. Harvey had deployed his forces to make sure there would be no trouble. A ring of policemen would accompany the parade to the railway station.

Barlow said, 'Last year there was only me and a constable bringing up the rear.'

Harvey flushed. 'Are you questioning my judgment?'

The Chairman's words boomed in the room, he had that sort of voice. 'Barlow, I have nothing against you leading the parade. But what you do at the Catholic Church, really!'

Barlow looked at the Queen and wondered what her opinion was. 'It's like this, sir. A lot of the Orangemen are old soldiers like me.' His eyes drifted to where Harvey would have worn his medal ribbons if he had any. 'They like a bit of swank so I call the time. And when you're on parade you have to salute somebody.'

Harvey was outraged. 'An *eyes right* at the Catholic Church?' The Chairman coughed and Harvey controlled his temper. He was determined, he said, that it wouldn't happen again. And anyway Barlow had a more important job to do this year. There had been a lot of cattle stealing in the area recently and the Chairman was concerned that somebody would try to steal his prize Herefords, particularly on the twelfth when he and his men were away with the lodge. Harvey's instructions were detailed and took nearly five minutes to deliver.

Finally, he asked, 'Any questions?'

Barlow finished writing into his notebook, *from eight at night to six in the morning and all day the twelfth*. He put his pencil away, he put his notebook away.

He stood in thought. 'Sir, seeing you brought the subject up. Why does the parade go past the Catholic Church when the train station is at the other end of town?'

The shed was open-sided. The dog lay in the only dry corner and was wary of Barlow. The Herefords were in the field across the way, or rather Barlow hoped they were. When the light went they were sheltering against the far hedge and he had no intention of going looking for them. He was wet already, from his feet to well above the hang of his cape and from the collar down. The two damps met at the seat of his pants.

A car came crawling along the road, its lights picking out the shafts of rain angling into Barlow's face. He muttered to himself and stepped out when the car stopped beside him. The dog barked, Barlow told it to shut up.

It was Harvey checking up on him. 'Nothing to report, sir,' he said.

'Stay alert, I might be back later.'

Barlow watched Harvey drive off. He looked at the dog, it was back in its bed. 'You could have piddled on its wheels.'

The widow appeared. She was wearing a man's old coat thrown over her clothes. 'Come up to the house.'

He was glad to follow her, summer or not there were blocks of ice where his feet should have been. The kitchen was warm and she had supper on the table: the remains of the stew and homemade wheaten bread; the kettle was already singing on the stove. She pushed a chair out for him and he dared loosen his jacket by a button.

She nodded, 'Take it off.' He did and she hung it before the range; it started to steam in the heat. She nodded again. 'Boots too.'

He gulped his mouthful of food down, he begrudged wasting the taste and the heat. 'I'm supposed to be on guard duty, missis.'

'The dog will bark if anyone comes.'

She had been cleaning the family silver. One picture in a silver frame was of her and her husband on their wedding day; she standing taller than him, he always was a weed of a man, and her looking out of place in white.

He said, 'You were a fine looking woman.'

She said 'Were.' The photograph was wiped and put away. 'All these years and nothing to show for it but hard work.' She fussed with the kettle at the stove, nodding all the while. 'I come from a big family, I never slept on my own until I was a widow.'

Barlow ate slowly rather than commit himself with words. She put his drink down before him, a hot whisky with cloves, a strong one. She joined him with her own whisky and they drank them in silence.

'Smoke, I know you do,' she said. He lit a Woodbine and puffed slowly while she cleared away. He offered her one and she said, 'No.' He kept the pack held out. She hesitated, nodded and took one, nodded again and drew the smoke into her lungs. She let it out with a sigh of pleasure.

When it was finished she stood over him. 'I'll go up.' She pointed to the ceiling above his head. 'Keep the window open and you'll hear the dog.'

He had another Woodbine and watched its swirls of smoke along the ceiling and listened to her footsteps as she got ready for bed. When the house was silent again he stripped off his clothes and hung them before the range to dry; his combinations last of all, and those with a bit of thought. He went up the stairs to the bedroom above the kitchen.

He thought it might be her room. It was delicate, all little fancies and full of smells. He was sure when he got into the double bed, it had a hot water bottle already going cold. The widow was there as well. She was naked and waiting.

The singing of the birds woke Barlow; the early daylight glaring in the open window had made him restless. He looked at the widow. She was lying with her hands behind her head staring at the ceiling.

'It's the twelfth,' she said.

'Of course it is, missis, isn't the sun shining?'

Barlow was nearly glad of it after three nights with little sleep. He looked at her, hoping. The widow liked to make the first move.

She kept staring at the ceiling. 'I'm due another call about pulling the Ragweed.'

'You are that.' He risked a hand on her leg.

She rose over him, the blankets falling away from her breasts; they sagged on her bony frame. 'When the time comes, Mr Barlow, would you send another constable?'

'Now why would I be doing that?' He turned her under him.

The dog barked, he tried to ignore it. It barked again.

He got out of bed and looked out the window, afraid it was Harvey making an early morning check. He could see some sort of vehicle parked near the bottom of the lane. 'I'll be back.'

She nodded her head then she made it shake. 'It must stop here, Mr Barlow. My neighbours wouldn't like it, not with a Catholic.'

'Nor my wife.' He said deliberately.

Her nod was slow and thoughtful. 'I was aware of that too.' There were tears in her eyes as she held out her hand.

He nearly spat before they shook as if settling a deal. He dressed quickly and left the house.

Barlow was nearly at the end of the lane before the echoing thud of cattle hooves on wood seeped through his abstraction. 'Begod,' he said, and drew his truncheon.

The dog came out to meet him. 'Git,' he said. The dog ignored the order and stayed quietly at his heels as he peeked out the lane. A lorry was backed into the gateway of the Chairman's field and he could see the shapes of three men driving cattle into it with sticks and whispered shouts. Two animals were already in the lorry. He tiptoed down the road, keeping the bulk of the lorry between himself and the men. They were busy loading a third animal.

One of the men said, 'What's the difference between Sergeant Barlow and one of these cows?'

Barlow smiled. 'Begod, it's the Dunlops.'

The man answered his own question. 'The cow's eyes are wider apart.'

There was a roar of laughter.

Barlow stepped around the side of the lorry. He swung his truncheon and caught the comedian a crack on the point of the shoulder. The second man was still laughing when Barlow sideswiped his elbow. The third one saw him coming and had the advantage of being at the top of the loading ramp. He swung his boot at Barlow's head. Barlow caught the man's knee with the truncheon and he fell in among the cattle. It was three to one against so Barlow went over the Dunlops twice more: elbow, knee and shoulder, to make sure they were properly subdued. Then he prodded them with the truncheon and the dog nipped at their ankles until they were in the lorry.

Barlow swung the ramp up and secured it, leaving them among the cattle. He tried to pat the dog, it snarled at him so he swung his boot. It seemed happier as it retreated into the shed.

District Inspector Harvey was all bustle and fuss. The parade had started from the Orange hall late because they had waited for their banner men to turn up. Finally the Chairman had dammed the Dunlops to hell and given the order to march.

Harvey had gone ahead to the Catholic Church. Edward the tramp was there; his old greatcoat had been brushed down and he was wearing an ancient suit and tie. He nodded politely to Harvey. Other than Harvey and Edward the whole area was deserted except for some children swinging off the railings and two policemen for each child. Harvey began to think he could have used less security to push the parade through.

He tensed as the off-notes played by the Kirktown Silver Band died away and the morning air was filled with the sound of a single kettledrum and the tramp of marching feet. He checked again for trouble as the lodge and its banner swung into view round the corner.

An old lorry came spluttering along the road. A policeman stepped out and held up his hand. It drove on and he had to jump clear as its wheels threatened to nip his toes. It stopped at the Catholic Church and Barlow got out. He stretched and yawned.

Harvey came storming up. 'Barlow, what are you doing here?'

'Bringing your banner men, sir.'

Barlow went round to the back of the lorry and let down the ramp. The Dunlops hobbled out, they were covered in muck. The cattle tried to follow them, Barlow drove the animals back with a roar.

The three men huddled together as the policemen closed in on them. There was a lot of laughter and the holding of noses. Nobody went too close or got too funny, the Dunlops were always dangerous and had long memories.

Harvey quickly questioned Barlow about the attempted theft of the cattle. He ordered the Dunlops to be led away to the cells. Their bruised muscles had stiffened and they could only move slowly.

Harvey was outraged. 'These men are injured.'

Edward said, 'Three against one, a prima facie case of police brutality.'

A shout of laughter went up from the watching policemen.

The Orange parade was almost on top of them; Harvey wanted the lorry moved. The engine churned but would not kick into life. He rushed off to try it himself.

Barlow looked in disgust at the marchers who could see something going on at the lorry. As old soldiers they knew to keep looking ahead but they had lost their concentration and the rhythm of their stride was beginning to break up. The Chairman was at the front of the parade carrying the silver sword. His face turned beetroot red when he recognised the Dunlops and his cattle.

Barlow began to call the time. 'Left... Left...' The marchers stride picked up, their arms swung that bit higher.

When they drew level with the Catholic Church, Barlow roared. 'Parade. Eyes... right!'

# NEVER EVER
## James Meredith

I stood up. I was OK. I looked around the room and saw them. They were sleeping, Adam on the settee, James on a chair.

I felt my legs where they hurt. My tights were ripped and both my knees were skinned. My fingers came away bloody. The crotch of my tights hung torn between my legs where I hurt most. I was going to be OK.

The bastards! I couldn't believe they had done this to me.

The fuckin' bastards! I couldn't believe this had happened to me.

"I'm Adam," he'd said. "Pleased to meet you."

I was standing at the bar in Benedicts waiting to be served. I'd been waiting nearly ten minutes. It was Friday night and the place was jam-packed, two deep at the bar. I was sure the bar staff were deliberately ignoring me. Every time I tried to get their attention, their eyes passed over me and found someone else to serve.

"Hello?" I shouted, trying to be heard above the pounding music and the incessant chatter. "Can I get some service here?"

Nothing.

I was about to give up and move on to another pub when a barmaid suddenly moved toward me. I leaned over to speak when she asked the fella standing next to me what his order was. Fuck this, I thought. Then the fella turned toward me and shouted above the din, "What are you drinking? You're not having much luck getting served."

"Just a pint of Tennants," I shouted back. I was about to say thanks but he had already turned back to the bar and added my order to his.

I'd been drinking since four that afternoon. I'd woken up at twelve that morning with a stinking hangover. I got up, washed myself and brushed my teeth, gagging a little when I tried to reach the back ones. I threw on some clothes, brushed my hair and walked down the road to a café. I ate some soup and wheaten bread, washed down with a cup of black coffee, and smoked my first fag of the day. I began to feel a little better.

I spent the afternoon browsing in the charity shops along Botanic Avenue. I bought a cheap metal bracelet and a paperback book, then decided to go to Laverys for a drink. I bought a pint, settled at a corner table in the back bar and began to read.

Laverys is my local, my favourite pub in Belfast. It's the sort of place where you can go for a pint on your own and people don't think you're sad, or strange, or desperate. Plus the fellas aren't constantly trying to chat you up and get off with you. Not unless you wanted them to. And I didn't. I didn't want to get involved with anyone. Not anymore. Not since Joe.

The fella handed me the pint of Tennants. "Thanks," I shouted. I tried to give him the fiver but was jostled by some big lanky ganch pushing his way through the crowd. The fella collected his change and lifted two pints of Guinness from the bar. He leaned toward me and shouted, "Me and my mate have a table over here. C'mon over." He moved away, I followed.

"Hey, Karen, how's it goin'?" I looked up from my book and saw Malcolm towering over me. Malcolm was a born-again Christian and reformed piss-head who couldn't get over his habit of going to the pub every day. Instead of beer he drank pints of lemonade and tried to talk Jesus to the other customers. Most ignored him or told him to go fuck himself and Jesus too. I liked him.

"Hello, Malcolm. Pull up a pew." I stuck a beer mat in the page I was reading and closed the book.

"I'm not disturbin' you, am I?" Malcolm asked.

"No, not at all. Crap book anyhow."

Malcolm sat down, reached over and lifted the novel. "I would never have figured you for the Mills and Boon type somehow," he said.

"A girl's got to have some romance in her life," I replied.

"The only love you need is Jesus' love, Karen. And all He asks of you is for you to love Him back." Malcolm raised his pint and swallowed half the lemonade in one gulp.

"Give it a rest, Malcolm. I'm not in the mood for a sermon."

"I'm Adam," he said. "Pleased to meet you." He handed one of the pints he was carrying to the fella sitting at the table we'd stopped beside. "This is my mate, James."

"Hello," I said. "Listen, here's the money for the drink."

"No, keep it. It's on me."

"It's Ok. I can buy my own drinks."

"Listen... sorry, I don't know your name."

"Karen."

"Listen, Karen. I'd like to pay for the drink. I just got a new job and I'm celebrating. Please take it." He smiled.

"OK. Thanks." I raised my pint. " Congratulations on the new job." We drank together.

"Are you here on your own, Karen?"

"I'm meetin' someone here," I lied. Just in case.

"Why don't you join us while you're waiting," he said, sitting down next to James.

I studied them both. Adam was tall and thin, his fair hair cut short. James was darker and more filled out. They both seemed young, twenty-one trying to pass for twenty-five.

I didn't really want to stand on my own in a busy pub. I always feel awkward and uncomfortable. It's only for one drink, I told myself. I sat down. Adam smiled. He seemed OK.

"So," Adam said. I waited for the conversation to begin, for the questions that are always asked when strangers meet: What do you do? Where do you live? What are you into?

"You're very individual looking, Karen, if you don't mind me saying." Adam lifted his pint and drank.

"Am I?" I was a little taken aback. He was very direct. There was an air of self-confidence about him. His smile stayed just the right side of mocking. His smile was a challenge.

"Yeah, all the girls who drink in here look the same. Just look around you." He gestured with his drink. James leaned forward, joining in the conversation.

"Aye, look at them all. Like Steptoe wives," he smirked.

Adam laughed. "Stepford wives, you plank."

"Oh... right."

"Why don't you go and get another round in and leave the jokes to me," Adam told James. "Will you have another one, Karen? How about a wee short?"

I still held the crumpled fiver in my hand. "This is all the money I have," I said.

"Put your money away. We're celebrating, remember. What are you drinking?"

I thought about saying no, I really did. I thought about finishing my pint and going home. But I didn't want to. I didn't want to go back to my empty flat. I didn't want to be alone, not tonight. I asked for a whiskey and diet coke.

Malcolm was at the bar ordering another pint of lemonade and a Tennants for me when Joe walked in with Ruth. It was after eight o'clock. I was a bit pissed but felt like I could drink all night.

Malcolm had stayed with me, drinking a pint of lemonade for every one of my beers. He didn't seem to mind other people drinking even though he said he used to have an awful drink problem. That was before he was born-again, though.

Every now and then an old friend of mine and Joes would drift into the back bar and come over to say hello. They'd ask how I was getting on since Joe moved out. I'd smile and tell them I was grand; I was getting on with things. They'd stay for a few minutes then move on when they began to feel awkward. I had nothing to say to them anymore.

Malcolm didn't mention Joe at all. He talked about his past, the things he'd been involved in before he found Jesus, or Jesus had found him. He showed me the tattoos on his arms that he kept hidden beneath his long sleeve shirts. The tattoos he'd had done in prison. Some of the things Malcolm talked about, some of the things that Malcolm had done, scared the life out of me. But he never once mentioned Joe.

Adam lifted two fags from his pack and offered one to me. I took it and let him light it for me.

"What was I saying? Oh, yes, all the other girls in here. I mean, they all look like they buy their clothes in the same shop, go to the same hairdressers, use the same trowel to put on their make-up." He smiled again.

"Maybe you should drink somewhere else then, get to know other girls," I said.

I couldn't believe it. I was flirting with this guy. I wasn't sure if it was because I was a tiny bit drunk or because I agreed with what he was saying. I hated the women in this place too. I hated their confidence, their poise. They all seemed happy in their skins.

Or maybe it was his smile. I wouldn't have looked twice at him if he'd walked into Laverys earlier. He wore the same basic blue jeans and leather jacket so many fellas did in Belfast: Low maintenance, no effort.

Adam was speaking again. "Girls like you? I'd like to, if they were as pretty as you. Sorry if I sound forward." He blushed.

The lights were dim but I was sure I saw his cheeks colour. One minute he was confident, the next he was blushing like a boy.

Strange fella.

"Do you do this all the time then, Adam? Approach strange girls and give them compliments?"

"No, not really," he said. "I didn't mean to give you a compliment." He blushed again.

"You didn't mean what you said, then?"

"I meant what I said alright. I just don't want you to think I'm chatting you up."

"Pity." I stubbed my cigarette out, lifted my pint to my lips and drank. Adam leaned back in his chair, smoking.

I reached into my coat pocket and pulled out my fags and lighter.

"You smoke a lot, don't you?"

"Only when I'm drinkin'," I replied, lighting the fag with my Zippo.

I like the taste of petrol on the first drag. I like it so much that one time I dipped a whole cigarette in petrol and tried to smoke it. The fag had gone up in flames and I'd singed my eyebrows and burnt half my fringe off. I was drunk at the time. I hadn't thought it through. That's my problem, never thinking things through.

"Are you OK, Karen?" Malcolm asked when he returned from the bar.

"In what way?"

"You look a bit… is it because Joe's here with Ruth?"

"Is he? I hadn't noticed." I reached for the pint and drank, trying to hide my face behind the glass.

I swallowed gulp after gulp of beer. I didn't want to stop drinking. I didn't want to talk to Malcolm about Joe and I didn't want anyone to see the tears that had welled up suddenly in my eyes.

I wished the pint was like the porridge pot that I had read about in a story when I was a little girl. It was a magic porridge pot that was somehow never empty. The more you took from it, the more it had in it to give. I couldn't remember why the pot was magic, or who had owned it. I could only remember that it was magic and that at the end of the story it overflowed and filled the world with porridge and all the people on earth were drowned.

I drank until my glass was empty. I looked at Malcolm's face, distorted through the thick glass at the bottom of the pint. He looked like a giant.

"C'mon, Karen. You don't need to do that."

I set the glass down, burped and felt the beer threaten to rise. I scrambled for my fags and lighter and coat.

"I've got to go, Malcolm. Thanks for keeping me company."

As I stood I felt my stomach contract and acid rise in my throat. I clamped my hand over my mouth and rushed toward the back exit, knocking over a chair as Malcolm stood to take hold of me. I pushed him away and stumbled through the door into the back alley. I heaved and heaved. The vomit splashed off the cobblestones and splattered my boots and tights. A cold sweat broke out on my brow and I laughed amid the retching, thinking that now I had become the magic porridge pot and would puke and puke until the whole world was drowned. I heard the door open behind me and felt a hand begin gently rubbing my back. A voice was telling me it was alright, I was Ok.

I hoped otherwise, but knew it was Malcolm.

James returned from the bar carrying all three drinks in his meaty paws. As he set them on the table some Guinness sloshed over the side of the pints and into my whiskey and diet coke.

Adam had been telling me about his new job, as a camera assistant for some production company in town. I vaguely remembered their name from one of the 'Troubles' dramas Joe and I had watched on TV a few months before. Something about an ex-prisoner trying to win back his wife after years inside. James worked for the same company, as something called a boom operator. I nodded along as if I knew what that was.

What Adam really wanted to do was direct movies, and we talked for a while about films. He was a Tarantino and Guy Ritchie fan, hated Ken Loach and Mike Leigh, and dreamt of making the ultimate crime caper movie, featuring DeNiro and Gary Oldman as ex-IRA terrorists planning a daring heist in the heart of London. Adam reckoned they could both handle the accents.

I was starting to feel tired. The whiskey and coke tasted sour with the dash of Guinness in it, and the heat of the crowded pub was making my eyes heavy. I tuned out of the conversation, which centred on whether Uma Thurman or Madonna would make the better love interest in Adams planned movie, and watched the boys as they talked.

Adam moved his hands around as he spoke, punctuating his speech with sweeps of his arms and a raising and lowering of his eyebrows. James sat still, listening with hooded eyes, his chin tucked in, revealing a little fat around his neck.

My thoughts drifted to what had happened a few hours before. I'd made a fool of myself. I'd made a fool of myself in front of Joe. He'd never want me back now. He probably thought I was mad.

Malcolm held the door for me as I stepped from the alleyway back into the bar. I looked to see if Joe was watching and just caught his eye as he turned and said something to Ruth.

"Why don't you go through to the bathroom and clean yourself up," Malcolm suggested. I could feel the splashes of vomit turning cold on my legs and my stomach knotted tight each time I breathed. "I'll get you a coffee," Malcolm said. "It'll help you sober up."

I managed a wave of acknowledgement and walked as quickly as I could to the toilets.

I washed my legs and boots down with a swathe of toilet roll soaked in water and rinsed my face and hands in the sink. I looked at myself in the aluminium sheeting, which served as a full-length mirror. I looked at the short, dumpy girl staring back at me. Did I really believe that Joe would be happy to stay with me? There were so many beautiful women in the world. Tall women. Tall women with long shapely legs. Legs that weren't like mine.

Joe used to joke about my legs, especially my ankles. He said you could tell I was from the country when you looked at my ankles. He said they were made for working the fields in a strong wind. He said they were like the trunks of small trees, thick and sturdy.

That's why I started wearing Doc Marten boots. They hid my ankles.

I moved closer to the mirror and looked at my face. My eyes were red and strained with the effort of boking. My face looked pale and tired. I was so ugly. I looked like a troll.

Ruth wasn't ugly. There was no doubting her beauty. Her long hair was black and shiny, unlike my short dyed crop. She had large eyes with a cat green slant, a nose which tilted at just the right angle, and lips that would never need to go near collagen. And she was tall. Tall and shapely, in proportion. I looked myself over again, the short, dumpy girl whose tits were too small and whose arse was too big. It was like looking in a fairground mirror. No, Ruth was not like me, not like me at all.

I remembered when Joe first met her. We were at a party. Ruth arrived on her own. From the moment she walked into the living room, Joe couldn't take his eyes off her. She was wearing a short black dress with black tights, and her legs seemed to go on forever.

I tried to get Joe to dance with me, but he said he wasn't in the mood. He wandered off to the kitchen to get another drink.

I danced on my own.

The next time I saw Joe he was talking to her. They were standing together in the hall. Ruth was laughing at something he'd just said. I stood in the doorway of the living room, watching them. They looked good together. An All Saints song was playing on the stereo and I remember thinking that if I didn't get Joe away from her I might never see him again.

I ended up getting very drunk that night. When we finally got home, I remember Joe helping me undress and putting a basin at my side of the bed in case I needed to throw up. Although he climbed into bed beside me, I could sense that his thoughts were elsewhere, and for the first time in a long time we slept with a distance between us.

After that night Joe and I began to argue more than ever. It was as if he was trying to provoke me. Suddenly, everything I did was wrong. He said I embarrassed him when we went out. I drank too much and made a fool of myself. He said he never enjoyed himself anymore, that he was too busy worrying about what I'd do next.

Then one day he came home from work and told me he was moving out. He told me that he couldn't live with my mood swings and possessiveness anymore.

I tried to reason with him. I told him that I was sorry, that I'd change. I told him I could make him happy again, that it could be as good as when we first started going out together. He said that he had to go.

I got angry. I accused him of seeing someone else behind my back. I did all the things I'd seen in second-rate TV dramas and laughed at before. I told him he couldn't go. I stood in front of the door, watching as he packed, telling him he'd have to hit me before I'd let him leave. He stood in front of me silently, waiting.

"I'm sorry," he said. I knew it was no use. I moved away from the door and flung myself onto the settee, burying my face in the musty cushions. I didn't watch him leave.

The next time I saw him he was with Ruth. I was walking down the Dublin Road one evening and saw them go into one of the fancy new restaurants that had started to spring up all around the town.

I hadn't seen him in Laverys since we'd broken up, not until tonight. Why did he have to come back here, to my pub, and show off his shiny new girlfriend to everyone?

Well, I wasn't going to let him get away with it. I wasn't going to take that from him. He'd hurt me enough. I wasn't going to let him take the one place I liked to be, the one place where I felt I belonged, away from me.

We were in a taxi on the way to a party. James sat in the passenger seat talking with the driver. I was slumped in the backseat with my head against the cold windowpane, watching the streaked neon lights of Shaftsbury Square blur past in the rain.

Adam sat beside me, his hand in mine, his thumb making warm circles on my palm. We had stayed in Benedicts until just after midnight. James had gone off to talk to someone he knew at the bar, and Adam sat and talked to me.

We had a good time. The more whiskey I drank the more the memory of Joe faded. I let Adam keep buying the drinks. I told him about my childhood in the country. I told him about how I was bullied at school, and how the only friends I felt I had were the chickens and the lambs. Adam didn't tell me much about himself, other than him wanting to get out of Northern Ireland. He hated the place, couldn't wait to get away. Mostly though, he seemed content to sit and listen as my mind danced from story to story. At one point he asked if I had a boyfriend. I told him no.

James returned just as I was telling Adam about my time at Queens. He told us that the fellas he was talking to were moving on to a party in the Holylands. He asked if we wanted to come along.

"What do you think, Karen, are you in the mood for a party?" Adam asked.

"Why not?" I replied. "The night's still young."

James suggested we leave before the pubs kicked out. Trying to get a Taxi would be a nightmare if we waited.

"C'mon then, Karen. Hurry up." James told me. I downed my drink in one.

We moved toward the front door, squeezing past the people crowded around the bar. The stench of aftershave and perfume and sweat made me feel dizzy and I stumbled against Adam. He took hold of my arm to steady me. His hand moved down and enveloped mine. I let it stay there.

Outside a light rain was falling. A fleet of taxis stood waiting outside Laverys. We staggered across the road, dodging moving cars, and jumped into the first cab in the queue. As the car pulled away from the kerb I saw Malcolm walking along by McDonalds, his head bowed against the rain.

I walked into the back bar of Laverys and saw Malcolm talking to Joe and Ruth at the end of the bar. I squeezed past two skinheads playing the fruit machine and walked right up to them.

"Why the hell are you here, Joe? Why can't you just leave me in peace," I shouted. I noticed Ruth turn her head away.

"Karen, I got you a coffee. Let's go sit over here." Malcolm gripped my shoulders and tried to turn me away.

"Fuck off, Malcolm. It's none of your business," I spat, shrugging him off.

"Why don't you just go home, Karen?" Joe said, quietly.

"Home?" I cried. "Where's home, Joe? Is that the flat where we lived together for nearly a year? Is home the place where we used to make love? The place where you held me and told me how perfect I was for you. Is that home, Joe? Well, is it?"

Joe just looked at me. He didn't have an answer.

"I can't go home, Joe. That place doesn't exist anymore."

I started to cry. I ran my hand along the drinks on the counter and swept them to the floor. I kicked out at the broken glass. I kicked out at the pain I felt. I wanted to throw myself to the floor, wanted Joe to see my freshly spilt blood.

A bouncer ran in from the front bar and grabbed me.

"Right, you. You're barred. Out."

I was rushed through the bar and out into the street before I knew what was happening. The last thing I saw before I was bundled away was Joe turning to Ruth and taking her in his arms. I stood in the street, feeling lost and alone. I needed a drink.

The taxi stopped outside a house on a street I didn't know. James paid the driver and we got out of the car. Adam pulled some keys from his trouser pocket and unlocked the front door.

"Thought we were going to a party," I said. The lights in the house were off and I didn't hear any music.

"We are," Adam reassured me. "We have to pick up some booze first. This is our flat."

He stepped into the hall still holding my hand. James followed us.

We moved into the living room and Adam switched on the lights, adjusting the dimmer switch until there was a low glow.

James switched the stereo on and fiddled with the radio dial until he found a dance music station.

"I'll get the drinks. They're in the kitchen." He disappeared back out into the hall.

"Grab a seat," Adam told me. I collapsed onto the settee.

"Are you OK?" He asked.

"I'm fine," I laughed. "Just a tiny big pissed."

"Still want to go to the party?"

"Oh, yes."

Adam sat down beside me on the settee. He reached for my hand.

"You know I really like you, don't you Karen?" I nodded. "I think you're beautiful," he said. I laughed at him. "I do. Really." He leaned towards me and kissed me lightly on the lips. I remember thinking that my breath would stink of stale vomit.

He kissed me again, with just a little more force.

I gave myself up to him. I wanted to be held and kissed. I wanted to be told I was beautiful and made to feel as if I was beautiful. I wanted to be loved.

Adam was kissing my neck. I moved my arms around his waist, pulling him closer to me.

I opened my eyes and saw James standing over us. He was smiling at me.

"Room for one more?" He asked.

"What? What's goin' on? Adam?" Adam sat up and looked at me.

"You don't mind, do you Karen? Me and James are best buddies. We share everything."

I pushed Adam off me and tried to stand. Adam took hold of my arm. He squeezed tight.

"I want to go," I said.

"What about the party? Don't you want to go?" Adam asked.

"No... no, you go on. I'll just go."

"You don't need to do that. We can have our own party here."

"Please," I begged.

James moved towards us. Adam smiled.

I stood up. I was OK. I looked around the room and saw them. They were sleeping, Adam on the settee, James on a chair.

30

The bastards! I couldn't believe they had done this to me. The fuckin' bastards! I couldn't believe this had happened to me.

I felt a sudden pain inside of me. A sour acid taste rose in my throat. I needed to get out of there. I moved silently across the room and out into the darkened hall. Another cramp hit me and I almost bent double with the pain. I needed to go to the bathroom. I needed to go so bad.

I turned and crept my way along the corridor. At the end of the hall were two doors, one facing me, one to my right. I tried the first door and hit lucky.

I stumbled toward the toilet and just managed to reach it before my bowels emptied. I almost screamed with the pain.

I sat slumped there for I don't know how long. I remember thinking of Malcolm. I wanted to find him. I wanted to find him and ask him why people hurt each other in so many different ways. I wanted to ask his God to explain it to me.

I must have passed out. When I came to I was lying on the bathroom floor.

I picked myself up and moved to the sink. I washed my hands and looked in the bathroom mirror. My reflection didn't look like me anymore. My lipstick was smudged across my face and my mascara had traced the ghost of my tears down my cheeks.

It was my right eye, though. It was my right eye that made me gag and retch and retch again but nothing came up. I was empty.

My eye was swollen half-closed and the brown of my iris looked like a scab floating in a sea of blood.

James had done that bit of damage to me. He punched me because I wouldn't suck him. He punched me twice, then grabbed me by the hair and forced my mouth around him. I tried hard not to think about it.

I had to get out of there. I'd no idea how long I'd been passed out on the bathroom floor. I had to get out before they woke up.

I turned to leave. Adam was standing in the doorway. I saw the hate and the fear in his eyes. He moved toward me and I knew it was never going to be Ok ever again.

# MYSTERY SHOPPER
## Brian McNulty

Myrtle Montgomery became a mystery shopper. It was the ad in the paper started it. Tucked away in the corner of a page full of other advertisements seeking everything from car painters to kitchen assistants.

CASUAL WORK
GET PAID TO SHOP
ARE YOU OBSERVANT? DISCREET? RELIABLE?

Myrtle thought she was all of these. She reckoned the ad had been placed in it's discreet position on purpose to weed out people who lacked her powers of observation.

MYSTERY SHOPPERS REQUIRED
VISIT LOCAL OUTLETS
OBSERVE STAFF AND SERVICE
REPORT RESULTS BACK TO US.

Myrtle thought of the number of times she'd been given the wrong change. The way girls nowadays seemed to talk out of the corner of their mouths and chew gum like big galumphs. Not like the trim, polite shop assistants of her day. Mystery shopper. The more she thought about it the more she liked it. The idea of being able to pass judgement on all that bad service.

She wondered how mystery shopping worked. Would she be issued with identification? A badge like a detective's. A gold shield she could whip from her handbag and push under the nose of some hapless assistant.

'Alright nobody move! This is a mystery shopper enquiry, somebody get me the manager!" Like something on the television.

Four days after posting off for details Myrtle received a typed letter in reply. Her name scrawled in blue biro after the 'Dear'.

Dear Myrtle

Thank you for your enquiry regarding the Mystery Shopper scheme. We at LEXICON CUSTOMER SERVICES LTD. are engaged by major retailers across the country to monitor the level of consumer satisfaction enjoyed by their customers. To achieve this we employ the people who are always right, YOU, THE CUSTOMER!

Should your application be successful you will join the ranks of those charged with improving the level of customer service to us all. You will be providing a service to the community as well as earning useful cash in your spare time. Fill in the enclosed application form and return it today.

Yours sincerely
Philip Dobson
Marketing Manager

A separate sheet was attached with a column of boxes in which to print her personal details in block capitals. Myrtle fetched a pen and filled it in immediately.

NAME.... MYRTLE MONTGOMERY

MARITAL STATUS...Myrtle sucked the end of her pen for a moment then wrote SINGLE, supposing that when called for interview she could tell them about Samuel. AGE.... 62 PREVIOUS EMPLOYMENT... HOUSEWIFE

Housewife, she supposed, was an ideal qualification for being a mystery shopper. There was no job like it. Rearing three children and seeing them all out into the world on Samuel's wages from the Post Office had taught her all there was to know about getting a bargain. Making a silk purse out of a sow's ear he'd called it.

She glanced instinctively at the picture of the girls on the mantle piece. Taken when they were teenagers. Standing in a row outside the church at Samuel's sisters eldest ones wedding in all their finery. Hair freshly done pageboy style in the fashion of the day. Strange how it was always Samuel rather than the girls she thought of when he looked at the photograph. The way he'd lined them all up, telling Joanne to square her shoulders and ordering them to say gorgonzola the way he did every single time he took a picture. He had worn his grey suit that day. As he had at every funeral and wedding for years before and after. Samuel had been one of those men for whom buying a new suit was a transaction almost as drastic as buying a car. Something to be weighed up and considered carefully before making a decision.

'Sure the one I have 'll do rightly" he would say and in truth he was right.

Samuel had little use for a suit, fashionable or otherwise. His circle of family and friends were the type who frowned upon change of any kind. The wearing of the same suit for a dozen years was a sign of dependability. A reassuring nod that all was as it should be.

A week passed during which Myrtle's life hummed along much as it had every week in the nine years since Samuel was taken. She did her crosswords, read the papers, watched TV in the evenings and went to the Leisure Centre for her weekly swim. She went to the cinema twice. Once to watch a new French film she'd read about in the newspaper and once to see a movie starring Maggie Smith and Judi Dench about an old English country house in the twenties. Myrtle loved films like these. Liked to imagine herself mistress of some grand estate teeming with servants. Watching from an upstairs window as visitors arrived for shooting weekends or opulent dinner parties. Their long lean cars crunching to a halt on the sweeping gravel drive.

She waited for the post every morning. Most of her mail these days seemed to be from the book club or shiny brochures advising her to mortgage the house again and live off the proceeds until she died. Funny how the people pushing this idea all seemed to be so young. Had they any idea how long it had taken Samuel and her to pay off the loan on the house. In their day being in debt, even for a home, was such a terrible burden. A crime almost.

Nowadays it seemed there was something wrong with you if you didn't need a big loan from one of these companies to pay off all the little ones.

Finally it arrived. Recognising her own handwriting on the stamp addressed envelope she ripped it open greedily.

Dear Myrtle
We have great pleasure...

She had made it! No need for an interview. She must have fitted the bill perfectly well without one.

The letter went on to instruct her in the art of mystery shopping. All commonsense things Myrtle would have known anyway without being told. Her assignments would arrive by post. The first four mentioned in the letter were to be completed within one week starting tomorrow. Confidentiality was vital it said. Important not to let people know who you were or what you were doing. LISTEN and WATCH was printed in bold red capitals across the bottom of the page several times. There was no identification.

'It is vital never to reveal your identity as a mystery shopper. This safeguards you against any negative reaction from staff and ensures that you can visit the same outlets on more than one occasion'. Myrtle hadn't thought of this but it made perfect sense. She would be anonymous then. Moving unnoticed through the crowds on a secret mission. The thought of this gave her a little thrill of excitement. She was now a bona fide mystery shopper.

Next day Myrtle rose at a quarter past seven and had her usual breakfast of tea and a single slice of plain white bread toasted lightly on one side and spread thinly with marmalade. She watched the BBC news, marvelling at how those reporters stuck in the Middle East coped with being away from home so much. She wondered how their families made do, or if they had families at all. The lives some people lead, she thought, flitting about all over the place. Samuel had never been one for going away much. His hours at the Post Office had been as regular as the bus he travelled on to work every day. Weekends were for the garden and the television and in the later years waiting for the children to visit when they had time.

When the news was over it was time for either Kilroy or that coloured girl Trish on the other channel. Myrtle was often torn between these two and even though she wanted to be off couldn't resist waiting to see what problems they were going to solve between them this morning. Kilroy, who she thought too impossibly good looking to be any good at all, came on.

'MY DAUGHTER HATES ME!' was today's topic. Myrtle watched the first few people speak, harassed looking women with hard set faces who probably deserved fine rightly to be hated. Tiring quickly of their whining discontented voices she flicked over to the other side.

Trish had already started but as with Kilroy there was a helpful little caption so you knew right away what it was about.

' LESBIANS MAKE BETTER MOMMIES!'

'Oh dear", murmured Myrtle, watching as a fat girl with her hair in rats tails and a ring through her nose mumbled into the microphone about 'loving her little babbie to bits' even though she'd conceived it with a glass tube like some sort of Frankenstein experiment.

"Desperate" she said to herself, stabbing at the remote and turning the TV off. "Shocking altogether ". Then, with Samuel's last photograph, the one taken on the beach in Tenerife where they'd went for their twenty fifth, staring owlishly at her from inside it's dark brown frame on top of the television, she set off for her first day as a mystery shopper.

Myrtle parked her car in the shopping centre car park and thought it a pity her new job didn't extend to this part of the experience. If it had she'd have complained bitterly about having to walk so far to the door. The entrance to the place seemed miles away, just about visible over a sea of car roofs. Huge capital letters stuck on the end of metal poles rose at intervals from the shimmering metal reminding her not to forget the one nearest her. One day she'd spent ages wandering breathlessly along the rows searching frantically for her car until eventually coming across it almost by accident.

Inside the place seemed bigger than ever. A hall as big as a cathedral opening on all sides into acres of shop floor covered in all manner of things. On her right the rightly lit food hall. To the left a miniature forest of clothes extending to the horizon. A sign as big as a bungalow hanging from the roof pointed straight ahead. EVERYTHING FOR THE HOME AND GARDEN! In the distance Myra glimpsed giant shelves stacked with huge cardboard boxes rising into the dimness of the ceiling.

As she watched a yellow forklift truck rumbled down one of the aisles. Weaving it's way through shoppers pushing trolleys laden with more boxes bearing foreign writing. Myrtle squared her shoulders and felt very small. She felt like a secret agent in fact. Preparing to pit her wits against impossible odds.

Today's mission was the furniture department of Masons store, an English company with branches in most large shopping centres.

YOU'VE TRIED THE REST NOW TRY THE BEST! screamed the ads on TV with that girl who used to be in 'Coronation Street' throwing herself down on one of their sofas like a big child bouncing on a trampoline.

Myrtle sneaked a last look at her letter.

'Approach staff as a normal customer would, ask plenty of questions and note interaction of staff with customer'.

Right, here goes, she thought, refolding the letter carefully and putting it back in her handbag.

At first Myrtle had difficulty locating a salesperson. She wandered through a maze of brightly coloured suites of furniture marvelling at the price of things.

'SALE STOCK PRICES SLASHED'

Even with prices 'slashed' most of the suites cost well over a thousand pounds. Some of them were almost two thousand. The monthly payments alone were more than her weekly pension.

Myrtle thought of her and Samuel buying furniture from Big Norm's warehouse on the Newtownards Road not long after they were married. She smiled to herself as she remembered how Samuel had dickered over the price. Slyly showing the notes in his wallet to the slick haired young man with the suit who'd tried to make a sale by offering them easy terms. Thinking as they weren't long married they'd be an easy touch.

"Cash on the nail son" Samuel had said "What's the best you'll do for readies?"

That was Samuel all over.

"Can I help you madam?"

Myrtle started. No one had called her madam for a long time. At first she thought the salesman who'd appeared at her elbow could read her mind, his voice sounded just like the boy Samuel had finally bought the suite from all those years ago.

"Er... yes. I'm looking for a new suite please."

As soon as the words left her mouth Myrtle felt foolish. What else would she be here for? There were suites in every direction almost as far as she could see. There were so many suites that the people moving among them looked as if they were wading slowly through a gaily coloured ocean of fabric.

The salesman seemed not to notice.

"Certainly madam, and what type did you have in mind?" He wore a smart suit and looked about nineteen. There was a tiny nick on his cheek where he'd cut himself shaving that morning and a gold stud in his left ear. He smelled strongly of talcum powder.

"Umm.. I'm not sure.. er.. Type?"

"Well we have threes and twos or twos and ones or two doubles with..."

"Just an ordinary three piece suite" interrupted Myrtle.

"Well what price range did you have in mind?"

If Myrtle had really wanted a three-piece suite the last place she'd have come would have been here. Even if she did ever lose her senses and mortgage her house to live out her days in luxury she could never imagine spending this much money on anything. Her car, parked near C or was it D outside had only cost half of what they were asking for most of these suites.

"I'm not quite sure yet... er... My house is just being decorated... and.. umm.."

"Tell you what dear" he soothed, demoting Myrtle instantly from madam to dear as he glanced over her shoulder at a young couple gazing at a lemon coloured settee priced at £1499, "Why don't you have a look around and if anything takes your fancy just give me a shout eh?"

"Oh thank you," said Myrtle breathlessly, feeling a little dizzy at the pace of the conversation.

After he had gone Myrtle tried to remember what she was supposed to remember for the mystery shopper report form she had to fill in after every encounter.

She realised miserably she couldn't even remember the young man's name.

He'd had a plastic badge on his suit. Richard... Robert... something like that. She was supposed to give him problems to solve. She was supposed to ask about warranties, money back guarantees, delivery times. She was supposed to pretend to be rude and see what he did. She was supposed to ask for the manager and see how long it took for him to come. Mystery shopping was proving more difficult than She'd thought. She would have to work at it.

Myrtle's second assignment the next day was a little less intimidating. A place too small to drive a forklift truck around in. Andersons Babywear had just the one store but one big enough nonetheless to be a client of LEXICON CUSTOMER SERVICES. Myrtle reckoned there were at least seven or eight assistants stationed among the rows of little jump suits and miniature fancy dress costumes babies seemed to wear nowadays. She wandered aimlessly through the racks for a while, fingering the tiny woollen clothes and wondering how her three had managed without all this. Samuel's mother had knitted all the children's baby clothes. She remembered how uneasy it had made her feel at first. How she thought she should really put a stop to it but never seemed to have the energy. Easier just to smile and say thank you every time Samuel set another parcel on the kitchen table.

'Excuse me Miss"

Myrtle's target was one of the older assistants, a faded looking girl in her mid thirties who Myrtle thought, for no reason she could put her finger on, was only working here part time. There were dark stains under her eyes and her smart blue skirt was straining at the hips with that hard to shift pregnancy weight Myrtle remembered from after her first.

'Yes' the girl said brightly, although Myrtle could tell from the washed out look of her she'd rather be at home getting a good sleep than standing here with her feet killing her in those high heels.

'I'm looking for something for my wee granddaughter, do you have this in blue?'

Myrtle handed her a bright orange toddler's playsuit covered in pictures of the Teletubbies. Myrtle knew the names of the Teletubbies from her morning viewing. Was fascinated by the oohing and aahing noises they made that was some smart person's idea of baby language.

'She's dying about them" she explained, as the assistant, who had 'Sheryl McCormick' printed on her nametag, took the tiny garment from her and examined the label carefully.

"Umm, just let me check in the back, won't be long"

Sheryl was nice decided Myrtle. She wondered if she had a husband at home. Where he worked. Who was minding the baby? He mustn't have much of a job if his wife had to stand in this place three mornings a week. Maybe he didn't work. Maybe he lay at home and watched Kilroy while the baby squalled and kicked in the cot his wife had bought here with a staff discount. Maybe they weren't even married. Maybe he wasn't her husband but a partner. A significant other. She'd heard this term one night on the TV and wondered why people these days didn't seem to get married as much as they used to. In the papers she read about people who even reared families between them and stayed together for years without ever getting married.

"Sorry, we only have it in yellow" said Sheryl regretfully, returning and replacing the orange suit on the rail. "I wouldn't even show it to you', she said, ' it's even brighter than this one"

"It is a bit loud, " agreed Myrtle, noting how Sheryl hadn't tried to convince her the orange suit wasn't that bad or spin her a yarn about how her wee one loved the Teletubbies too and maybe there was something else she'd like to look at instead. She took a step backwards as if to allow Myrtle room to breath."

How old is your granddaughter? " she asked politely.

"Twelve months," lied Myrtle. The untruth springing easily to her lips. She realised suddenly she could have produced an entire life story for the pretend granddaughter if required. Embellished it with funny little anecdotes so no one would ever guess she was made up. But Sheryl didn't want any stories. She just ran her fingers through her limp blonde hair and tried bravely not to look tired.

"Have you any yourself dear," enquired Myrtle, keen to test her theory.

"Just the one wee girl"
"How old?"
"Seven months"
"Is she sleeping right through yet? "
"Divil the bit "
'Never worry, it's only a stage, soon passes"
Sheryl looked doubtful.

"Believe me, I know, I reared five of them and not a one let me have a full night's sleep the first year" said Myrtle, getting into her stride and inventing two extra children of her own to go with the imaginary granddaughter.

Sheryl looked at her watch with one eye and took another step backwards.

"Think the one I have is more than enough", she laughed, though Myrtle detected an edge to it. A hint of something buried just beneath the surface. Child was a mistake she thought. An accident. Maybe she's not even married, or doesn't know who the daddy is. Maybe she should be on Kilroy.

MY CHILD WILL NEVER KNOW IT'S FATHER!

"Well thank you for your help dear" said Myrtle, "All the best... bye now"

As she left the shop Myrtle thought she might score Sheryl a bit higher than she deserved. Maybe the management would give her a rise. Perhaps the bit of extra money would be just what was needed to help her out of whatever mess she was in. 'Sheryl McCormick provided the mystery shopper (they never used their own names in their reports) with helpful assistance. She was polite and anxious to please' She would leave out the bit about her not pushing for a sale. Maybe the shop wouldn't like it. It was all very well assistants being polite but they had to actually sell something.

As she left Andersons Myrtle came over all depressed and teary. A feeling that just hit her sometimes. There seemed no reason for it. No warning. It just seemed to sneak up and jump into her chest when she least expected it. She went to the butchers to buy a little chicken for her tea as a treat. The young man behind the counter bright and cheery as ever.

"Mornin' missis, what can I do you for?"

Butchers always seemed happy. It was a pity they weren't in the mystery shopper scheme. Myrtle would have given him top marks. They seemed to have a special relationship with old ladies. Calling them 'my darlin' and 'love' in a way few took exception to. They belonged to that exclusive group of people who could talk to old people that way without making it sound as if they were talking down to them, treating you like some sort of wrinkled handicapped child.

As she left the butcher's Myrtle dropped her purse. The big sensible leather one Samuel had given her for her birthday. There was enough space in it for a little notebook she had bought to jot down remarks after each mystery shopper encounter. As she bent down to pick it up a surge of dizziness washed over her. She lifted her hand to her forehead and waited for it to pass as usual. As she knelt her gaze fell on a point across the street. On a space between two parked cars and a view of a small section of the red brick wall of the Haymakers Arms Hotel, a windowsill and a portion of the window itself. She blinked for a second and waited for her vision to clear and when it did, felt another surge, this time of a lightness in her chest she hadn't felt for years yet which was as recognisable to her as a childhood toy for there, sitting behind the glass sipping his usual half pint shandy, head clearly visible between the letters A and Y of the etching on the window and looking exactly as he'd done the day he'd left, sat Samuel.

Later that evening Myrtle sat in her armchair and tried to watch Coronation Street. A cup of tea and a chocolate biscuit balanced precariously by her side. The completed mystery shopper form on the kitchen table where she'd left it. She thought of how Samuel had looked when he'd left the Haymakers and plodded off down the street. Trailing behind that woman like a little dog. After her initial shock she realised he had changed after all. He was thinner. The cords on his neck straining from the weight of the shopping bag pulling down on his arm. He seemed to have more hair although maybe it was just the way he'd arranged it over his head that made it look that way. He'd bought new glasses as well although she supposed that after nine years that wasn't entirely unexpected. His clothes seemed younger. In all the years she'd known him Samuel had never worn jeans and there seemed something faintly ridiculous about a man in his late sixties, especially Samuel, wearing them now. The way they drooped around his backside and hung off him as if his behind had withered away from a wasting illness.

Myrtle had tailed them for a little while, popping quickly into a shop every time they stopped or went into one themselves. She would dawdle inside near the door, lifting things without seeing them and keeping her eye on the door of whatever place they had gone into. Every time they came out she waited until she was sure they were continuing on their way before starting to follow them again, keeping a close eye in case they turned in her direction. The woman was about her age, perhaps a little younger. She wore a tweed skirt and sensible flat shoes with brown stockings. And one of those green shooting jacket things people from the country wear to walk Labradors in and drive Range Rovers to the shops. Myrtle had known he'd fallen in with someone else but never who. She hadn't liked to ask at the time.

She followed them as far as the top of the High street then let them go. Watching he bald top of Samuel's head finally disappear among the crowds of shoppers. Feeling faint and weak from all the walking she sat down on a bench in the square to get her breath back and stayed there for half an hour. Watching the people going about their business as if there was no tomorrow and thinking how much she'd enjoy a cup of tea to revive her before finally, the chill seeping into the backs of her legs, she took herself off home.

Over the next few weeks Myrtle threw herself into her mystery shopping with a determination she hadn't felt for anything in a long time. With every form she filled in and posted off she received six pounds fifty. LEXICON usually sent her three or four together and soon she had a little sheaf of cheques pushed behind the toaster on the kitchen worktop. She got better at it. Every time she filled in a report she grew in confidence. She learned what to look for, how to judge people. She began to enjoy talking to the assistants and learning about their lives. Some, she recognised, were just passing through. In the same way she was not a real shopper they were not real assistants. They were doctors or engineers in the making. Students working to pay the rent. There were the no hopers as well of course. Those doomed to struggle from one poorly paid job to the other while the years passed and their chances faded and their feet grew sore from standing all day talking to old women like her checking to see if they were doing their job properly. She often found it hard to write something bad about a person who was rude or patronising or didn't pay attention to whatever little drama Myrtle invented to test them but it had to be done. LEXICON wanted the truth and would soon learn to ignore her reports if they all sounded the same.

'The manageress appeared slightly impatient when I said the insurance warranty on the CD player seemed very expensive.

Myrtle learned things like this about the retail trade. Learned to spot the hidden costs behind a bargain. What they said they were knocking off the price would invariably reappear as an extra payment for a guarantee or warranty. If the item was so great a buy why on earth would it suffer some catastrophic failure in the first year? There was even insurance you could take out if a certain part of the machine went wrong.

She spotted Samuel three more times over the next month and became adept at following him and the woman in the flat shoes without being seen. She memorised the number of their car, a four-year-old Landrover Discovery with a dog in the back behind a wire mesh grill. Not the Labrador she'd imagined but a scrawny looking red setter. She wondered where he'd been all these years and what had brought him back to the same town she'd moved to after he left. She wondered did he even remember she'd spent her own childhood here before moving away when her father got his big job with the Council. Maybe Samuel had been here all along. Their paths destined never to cross in the same way fate had decided thirty five years ago that Samuel would smooth his Brylcreem slick hair down with one hand and with the other motion her to dance in the smoky upstairs lounge of the Brown Derby Social Club.

Maybe they had almost bumped into each another and just didn't know it. The thought of this made Myrtle cringe. What would she have said? What would he have said for that matter, or the women with the green jacket who looked as if she would never be stuck for an answer? Especially to anything Myrtle might ask her.

Myrtle sat on the edge of her bed and stared at herself in the dressing table mirror. It was the first time she had examined herself carefully for a long time. Usually if she was going out she would just take a quick look to check her face was on straight. Dabbing at some imaginary blemish more out of habit than anything else. Her hair, still gold in places was glossy and healthy. She stared into her eyes and tried to see herself as others saw her. A straight-backed, firm jawed old woman with no particular feature more outstanding than the rest. She had long ago decided she was ordinary. Indistinguishable. Moving through her life with as little fuss and commotion as possible. Anonymous. Ideal for mystery shopping but ill equipped for much else beyond watching Kilroy and making cups of tea.

Normally Myrtle had no difficulty sleeping. Went over a few moments after a chapter of whatever book she was reading but that night, for the first time in years, she tossed and turned restlessly for hours.

Next morning Myrtle stuffed her notebook in her purse and set off for the shops as usual. She stopped at the bank and cashed the cheques, which had been piling up behind the toaster. She rarely bought anything on her mystery shopping trips. Usually she took the transaction to a certain point then pulled back. Old people were always doing this anyway and were notoriously slow to part with their money. Often an assistant who'd been doing quite well would let slip some little remark with a hint of irritation and cost himself a few black marks in Myrtle's report.

"You're the boss madam but you'll not get better value anywhere else believe me"

Myrtle tried on a pair of dark blue shoes in the first shop. They were expensive and stylish and flattered her ankles nicely. There was more of a heel on them than she was used to.

"Don't bother wrapping them dear, I'll wear them to break them in".

The assistant smiled indulgently and went off to fetch a carrier bag for her old ones.

'Miss Young in Watson's footwear was very impressive, she was polite and courteous at all times and is a credit to her employer' she wrote in her notebook outside the shop.

Next stop was Harrison's. Long before multi national companies started building clothes outlets the size of football pitches on the outskirts of every big town in the country Harrison's was doing a quiet public service by providing women between fifty and seventy with somewhere to shop that didn't deafen you with music or force you to try on clothes in a room full of teenagers with smooth flat bellies and legs like racehorses.

Myrtle could have written the report before she went in.

'Harrison's staff were extremely helpful to the mystery shopper. Nothing was too much trouble. A cup of tea was even provided'.

The girl in the shop did herself a power of good when she said the jacket and skirt Myrtle chose made her look ten years younger. She was right though. Myrtle turned herself sideways in front of the mirror, smoothing the material with her palms and admiring the way it's clean simple lines clung to her hips.

In the hairdressers she looked at herself in a mirror again as a girl called Maureen tussled with her hair and asked her about her holidays. Myrtle lied and made up a story about Gran Canaria and a bus trip round the island, watching as the girl scooped and shaped her hair into a style Myrtle thought reminded her of Elizabeth Taylor when she played Cleopatra in that film with Richard Burton.

"Whatever you think," she'd told her. "What would you do if it was yours and you were my age?" The recklessness of it excited her. When Maureen lifted the dryer away she hardly recognised herself.

Afterwards, self conscious in her new clothes and hair, she had a cup of tea in her usual café. Watching the world, or at least those inhabitants of it in the High Street that morning flit across the window.

She'd chosen her seat with care. It was far enough into the shop to make her invisible to passers by yet close enough to the window to allow her a view of the street. People, she'd learned, were creatures of habit. The assistants she dealt with every day usually approached every customer in much the same way. She'd watched them. Sometimes after one of her mystery shopper approaches Myrtle would dally a few minutes in the shop to observe them dealing with the next customer. Some of them said exactly the same thing every time they spoke. Good morning/afternoon/evening, can I help you at all? Or 'Are you OK there? Anyone looking after you?

She wondered if they knew they were doing it. If after a certain time doing something your mind went into a sort of autopilot and made you speak to a person with one part of you while the rest of you sat back and listened or thought of more important things.

" Everything alright for you there? "

It was one of the waitresses checking if she wanted another pastry or cup of tea.

"Yes thank you," smiled Myrtle,

At that moment Samuel walked past the window. For a dizzy second Myrtle thought he was alone but then the woman in the green jacket strode into view, four or five steps behind and trying to catch up after looking at something in another window. This was the closest she'd been to the pair since she'd first saw them almost four weeks ago. Their nearness, even through the window, gave Myrtle a light-headed, breathless feeling as if she was having another one of her turns.

She paid for her tea and fiddled with her handbag in the doorway, delaying opening the door to allow them enough time to travel further up the street. Her legs felt as if they didn't belong to her as she watched her hand reach out and grasp the handle, the noise of the cars in the street and the hum of the people talking in snatches hitting her in the face as she pulled the door open towards her. On the pavement she turned to her left and felt herself lift her face into the breeze. She was aware of the split second she would have before she would look down the street and narrowed her eyes a little to get used to being outside before opening them fully.

There was another second before the jumble of people walking in all directions rearranged themselves into an order and she scanned the pavement ahead. Even then it took a while and she had a moment of panic thinking she'd mistimed her exit. She imagined the horror if she discovered Samuel and the woman in the green jacket were looking at her instead.

She saw them. Further down the street than she thought. Fifty yards at least. Walking side by side without touching. The woman carrying a blue plastic carrier bag Myrtle recognised as having come from Jamison's hardware store. Something small inside. Perhaps a bag of nails or screws.

Samuel had both hands stuffed in the pockets of a yellow nylon jacket. Myrtle thought it made him look like an American tourist. The sort of thing old men wear in the mistaken belief it makes them look fashionable.

She shadowed them for a while, vaguely aware of people looming into view then passing on behind her, their faces pale and contorted, chattering to each other in an unintelligible rush.

Every time Samuel and the woman paused to look in a window Myrtle slowed her pace slightly but didn't stop. Once she thought they might be about to turn around and she felt her legs flex and her eyes flicker sideways to see what shop she could duck into in but the moment passed and when Myrtle walked past where they'd been saw they d only stopped to look at the photographs in the estate agents window.

The risk in being this close made Myrtle's breath come in quick little gasps. She was no more than fifteen or twenty yards behind them now. Surely they would see her. She was breathing so fast she thought they must be able to hear the sound of her heart thumping in her chest.

There was only ten yards now. Myrtle could see the wrinkles in the back of Samuel's jacket, the way his dirty grey hair curled in a little loop behind his ears. A burst of sun suddenly bathed the street, the light filtering through his hair where it sprang up from his forehead. All that remained from the Elvis quiff of his youth She saw the way he still walked on the instep of his right shoe. The slight limp from his bad knee.

She thought she might still have time to pull away. Turn off into a shop and disappear.

She glanced into the inviting doorway of Coburn's outfitters and thought how sensible it would be to step over the welcome mat and push the revolving door and lose herself among the racks of skirts and jackets and underwear.

Instead she could only watch as her hand reached out and tugged, quite deliberately and with more force than she'd intended, on the sleeve of Samuel's silly yellow jacket. The material was slippery and odd to the touch.

Cheap dirt she thought, as Samuel's head swivelled ever so slowly around in her direction. He paused, the stiffness in his shoulders not allowing him to turn around faster. The woman hadn't noticed her yet. Out of the corner of her eye Myrtle saw her take two more steps while Samuel's head turned slowly towards her.

Up close his face was sunburned as if from a recent holiday.

Myrtle let go of his jacket and stopped. Feeling the world drop away from around her and the tightness in her chest squeezing like a vice, as she looked him full in the face. She felt the heat in her cheeks and the blood pounding in her ears as the words she'd rehearsed for weeks every night in the bedroom mirror formed in her throat and pushed themselves up into her mouth.

Her lips were dry as paper and she licked them once, tasting the lipstick sweet on her tongue, then, before she could change her mind she lifted her chin, looked him full in the face and spoke to Samuel for the first time in over nine years.

"Come back," she said.

# THE SKY PAINTER
## Brian Kennedy

Every time I walked my granny home from Mass and there was a streak of red in the evening sky she would say, 'look Eamon, son, there's Seamus sending us love.' On other days if there was a patch of blue like a rip amongst the Grey she would stop mopping the tiles at her front door and proclaim to the sad crowd of clouds. 'SEAMUS, you missed a bit.' And then cackle with laughter.

Granda used to hum a never-ending melody to himself, even when he was eating. He would call me into the scullery and cut a doorstep of bread and then plaster it in thick butter and marmalade. He'd hand it to me like communion and whisper, 'don't tell your granny.' I would automatically go into the back yard and devour it as quickly as possible before heading back into the sitting room with the hiccups.

We got let out of school early one day and instead of going home I went straight to granny and granda's without even thinking. The door was open as always but the curtains were still drawn and I thought about how granny used to do this to her budgie when she wanted to pretend it was night time. There she was with her head in her hands and my own mother was just staring straight ahead at the clock that granda would let me wind up with an enormous key.

I heard a clatter from the kitchen and so I ran past the dividing curtains expecting to see him but I stopped the minute I saw Auntie Noreen's frame bent over the sink starting to do some dishes. My sandals slapped the vinyl floor as I rushed past her into the yard looking for granda. No sign of him, just tin after tin of paint stacked to the top of the four walls and a speckled rusty ladder. He must be at the bookies I thought to myself but I started to shiver even though it was hot outside.

Auntie Noreen didn't talk like my ma even though they were sisters. When she said my name it sounded like she had come to the end of a prayer I turned around to see her wiping the foam from her hands along her waistline. When I met her gaze it was only then that I realized she was crying. She held out her arms to catch me as I bolted towards her but I kept going on past until I got to the stairs I took them three at a time until I reached the landing.

There were two rooms and .I sometimes slept in the smaller one on Saturday nights if Ma and Da were going out. Granda would make up a story about me and him sailing to the moon to look for sweetie mines and building a hut made entirely out of chocolate and crisps We would make a fire and the smoke from the chimney turned into a never ending supply of candyfloss when it hit the air.

Then in the morning he would let me roll papers for the real fire and strike the matches while granny had a lie in. I heard my mother's voice calling from downstairs just as I reached for the door handle of my grandparent's room. It was almost too dark to see at first, but there was a tiny crack being blown in the closed curtains, that meant the top window, was open. I went towards it to pull them apart when I realized someone else was in the room. I spun round to see the silent figure of my grandfather stretched out on the perfectly made bed. I found myself starting to say, 'sorry granda I didn't know you wanted to sleep,' when my mother reached the doorway and said quietly, 'Eamon love come here.' She grabbed me too tightly when I reached her and we sat down at the top of the stairs crying for ages.

The priest came and granda was laid out in his coffin in front of the empty fireplace. The first thing I noticed was the silence. The great big mantle clock had shut up and my sister Mary was making sandwiches in the kitchen for the relatives I'd never met before. Granda's brother Noel looked so much like him I nearly asked him to make me marmalade special. People kept coming up to me and ruffling my hair and saying they were sorry I had managed to saved a bit of chocolate in silver paper so I went over to granda's coffin and slipped it into the pocket of his Sunday trousers even though it was only Thursday. He still looked asleep to me and I kept wishing he would just start yawning and stretching and sit up blinking at all these people in his living room. It was his dead room now.

An old woman with shiny rings on each finger and thumb started singing words to the tune that granda always-hummed saying that it was his favourite from when they were kids. His hands were locked in prayer and threaded with mammy's rosary beads I touched his fingers but they felt so cold and hard that I knew he was gone. His lips were the same colour as his face now and his hair was parted in the middle just like one of the old photographs on the wall. The rest of his body was hidden under cards with holy pictures on the front. That night some men came and took him to the church at the top of the road.

The next day I was kept off school but I still had to wear my uniform. We walked from the chapel to the graveyard in awful rain. Loads of men took it in turn to carry the coffin on their shoulders the whole way up the main road. Some of them wore overalls like granda's covered in speckles of multi-coloured paint and caps with a single cigarette tucked into the side. I marched silently behind the long black car with my Da and granda's brother Noel. We helped put the coffin into the car at the gates of the cemetery. There was a huge hole dug out of the muck where my mother and her sister were holding on to granny. The priest threw holy water on top of the already drenched coffin and the men tried to hold their balance as they lowered granda into the ground.

For once in my life I wished I was back at school. The rain continued the whole way home and we had to put all our clothes as well as our coats in front of the fire to dry. Da gave us scalding oxtail soup in cups and toast. Mary and I went to bed early and I don't remember falling asleep. I just woke up disappointed that I hadn't dreamt about granda. The house was so quiet now that all the people had gone. I lay there wondering if he was watching me. The priest in confession said that god saw everything. How much could granda see stuck in a box under all that muck?

I went back to school and the teacher offered up a prayer in assembly for granda and someone else's sister who'd been hit by a car.

I went round to see granny most days helping her with the shopping and carrying in the coal from the yard I was even allowed to sleep over during the week if she wanted me to. The tins of paint just stared as I made repeated trips to the shed for more coal and sticks. Some months later we were sitting in the yard after the last of them had been cleared by some of granda's work mates the day before, to make room for a kennel and a Kerry Blue pup that mammy had bought for her as a surprise to keep her company as the days were getting shorter again. The rain had finally stopped and the first of the sun's rays had appeared, bringing with it the most beautiful rainbow.

Granny took one look at it and tutted to herself before looking at me and said, 'look Eamon, do you see that? God must be a very patient man I mean how long has my Seamus been up there and he still hasn't decided what colour to paint the sky!"

# COGADH / WAR
## Daithí Ó Muirí

Bhí sé sa tairngreacht go mbeadh cogadh sa tír agus go ndéanfaí ionsaí ar an gceantar seo. Údar magaidh a bhí ann ar feadh na mblianta go dtí gur thosaigh scéalta ag teacht ó oirthear na tíre go raibh gach ceantar i mbun oibríochtaí móra chun iad féin a chosaint. Ní hamháin sin ach bhí airm fhaobhair á ndéanamh acu, gléasanna móra cogaidh á dtógáil, trúpaí á dtraenáil. Bhí an-amhras orainn. An raibh sé i gceist acu muid a ionsaí? Chun an scéal a phlé reáchtáladh cruinnithe poiblí, bhí freastal maith orthu agus tuigeadh gan mórán achair go raibh údar imní i ndáiríre ann. Labhair na seanóirí faoin tairngreacht, tugadh cluas dóibh agus corraíodh na daoine leis an gcaint faoi dhoirteadh fola. Socraíodh sa deireadh go dtógfadh muid balla mór cosanta timpeall ar an gceantar.

Na clocha ar ceapadh i gcónaí go raibh a bhfairsinge ina mallacht orainn chonacthas anois gur mhaoin fhíorluachmhar a bhí iontu. Tosaíodh ar iad a iompar as gach áit go himeall an cheantair. Ní hamháin gur soláthraíodh dóthain cloch le balla thar a bheith ard, thar a bheith tiubh a thógáil ach chuir baint na gcloch le feabhas na talún. Ba ghearr go raibh barr maith le feiceáil i ngarraithe nár cuireadh síol riamh cheana iontu. Cuireadh caoi ar bhóithre agus tógadh bóithre nua. Shaothraigh siúinéirí go crua chun carranna móra láidre a dhéanamh. Bhí an-éileamh ar na hasail arís, ainmhí iompair agus tarraingthe a raibh dímheas air le blianta anuas agus capaill mhóra á gceannach isteach ó cheantair eile. D'oibrigh na sluaite, fir, mná agus gasúir ó dhubh go dubh ag líonadh agus ag folmhú carranna, ag iompar na gcloch ó áit go háit, ag tochailt agus ag tógáil. De réir a chéile bhí an balla ag dul in airde.

Bhí de dhea-thoradh ar an obair seo ar fad gur tarraingíodh na daoine le chéile. D'oibrigh siad as lámh a chéile agus bhí rath ar na bailte dá bharr. Chothaigh an obair mhór spraoi mór agus reáchtáladh féilte ag na crosbhóithre. Cumadh amhráin nua, athbheodh seanamhráin agus insíodh na seanscéalta arís. Bhí muid bródúil as ár sinsir. Bhí tóir ar sheanchas na seanóirí. Ainmníodh geataí sa bhalla i ndiaidh seanlaochra. Níorbh fhéidir é a shéanadh, bhí misneach as an ngnáth le mothú.

Bhí siad ann, cinnte, a dúirt gur obair amú a bhí i dtógáil an bhalla. Ach chuaigh a líon i laghad de réir mar a mhéadaigh líon na n-oibrithe. Daoine a raibh sé de mhisneach acu a rá nach raibh siad go hiomlán taobh thiar den obair caitheadh anuas orthu nó rinneadh magadh fúthu. Ach ansin thosaigh ráflaí. Go raibh na hoibríochtaí sna ceantair eile tite as a chéile, go raibh meirg tagtha ar na hairm, na gléasanna cogaidh ag lobhadh faoin tsíon, na trúpaí scaipthe. Labhair seanóir amháin faoin ionsaí a bhí le teacht agus tugadh aird go forleathan air. Dúirt sé go raibh tuiscint róshaolta againn ar an tairngreacht. Dúirt sé nach ar ár gcolainneacha a dhéanfaí an t-ionsaí seo. Nach sáfaí le sleánna muid, nach ndícheannófaí le claimhte muid, nach ndófaí le lasracha muid. Ach go ndéanfaí ionsaí ar ár spiorad. Rinne na daoine machnamh ar a ndúirt sé. Ach cén chaoi, a d'fhiafraigh siad, a ndéanfaí ionsaí ar spiorad an duine? Ní raibh a fhios ag duine ar bith. Cén chosaint, a d'fhiafraigh siad dá chéile, a bheadh ar an ionsaí seo? Ní raibh a fhios. Ach bhí a fhios nach ndéanfadh balla, cuma cé chomh hard, cé chomh tiubh, cosaint ar ionsaí dá leithéid.

Tá an obair tréigthe againn anois. Cúis náire dúinn an balla leath-thógtha. Tá na gasúir imithe ó smacht, iad le feiceáil ag rásaíocht ar asail suas is anuas na bóithre ó mhaidin go hoíche. Cloistear na mná óga ag canadh amhrán ó cheantair anoir. Suíonn na fir thart díomhaoin, ag ól agus ag achrann, leathshúil ar an airdeall ag fanacht leis an ionsaí ar ár spiorad.

# COGADH / WAR
## Dathi O'Murhi
*Trans by Frank Sewell*

It was prophesied that the country would be at war and that this area would be attacked. There was a lot of joking around about it for years, until stories started coming in from the east that all areas had begun on mass efforts to defend themselves. Not only that, but they had sharp weapons, were building up armouries, and training troops. We were very suspicious. Did they want to attack us? Public meetings were organised to debate the matter. They were well attended, and it was soon realised that we had good reason to be worried. Elders talked of the prophesy; people listened to them and were fired up by the talk of bloodshed. Finally, it was decided that a great defensive wall should be built all around the area.

Huge stones whose size and width had always seemed a curse to us, now seemed like a godsend. Work commenced on moving them from everywhere inside the area to the outskirts. Not only were there enough stones for an extremely high, thick wall, but removing them actually improved the land as well. Soon there was good growth in gardens that had never been sown before. Roads were improved, and new roads built. Craftsmen worked hard to produce big strong transport vehicles. Donkeys were in great demand again (those beasts of burden who could haul and carry but had been looked down on for years now), and work-horses were bought in from other areas. Crowds of people, men, women, young boys, worked round the clock, filling and emptying vehicles, shifting the stones, digging and building. Gradually, the wall was rising.

The positive outcome of all this work was that the people were united. They worked together in unison, and the townlands benefited as a result. The great work created a great atmosphere, and there were parties at the crossroads. New songs were composed, old ones revived, and the old stories were told once again. We were proud of our ancestors. The elders were asked for their stories and remembrances. Gates in the wall were named after olden heroes. There was no avoiding it, an extraordinary spirit was in the air.

Sure, there were some who said that building the wall was a waste of time. But their numbers decreased as the number of workers increased. Anybody brave enough to say that they weren't fully in favour of the work, was put down or made a laughing stock. But then certain rumours started. That in other areas the work efforts had collapsed into disarray, that the weapons were rusting, the armaments rotting in the open, the troops scattered. One elder spoke of the coming attack, and his words were widely heeded. He said that we had taken the prophesy too literally. That this attack would not be a physical one on our bodies. That we wouldn't be hacked by spears, beheaded by swords, or burnt in flames. Rather, it was our spirit that would be attacked.

The people thought over what he had said. How, they asked, could the human spirit be attacked? No-one knew. What defence, they asked each other, could there be against this attack? No idea. But they knew rightly that no wall, no matter how high or wide, could defend them against that kind of attack.

We have given up the work now. The half-built wall has become an embarrassment. The young lads have gone wild, racing donkeys up and down the roads morning to night for all to see. From an area east of here, we can hear young women singing songs. The men sit around with nothing to do, drinking and fighting, half-watching out for the attack on our spirit.

# MOBILES
## Gerard Kinsella

Where the hell is she? She said she wouldn't be long. I hope nothing's happened. I don't know if I like the people she works with. 'Specially that fool who thinks he's Casanova. Why she even gives him the time of day I'll never know. Women are so blind to these pricks. I suppose it's flattering when some handsome guy flirts with you. He's not even that good looking. What am I talking about? Forget it, she's not that shallow, is she? What if they're all drunk and he has a rare moment of actually being funny? A chance glance across the smoky bar. A smile even.

What time is it? Twelve thirty, Jesus it's not that late. But she definitely said not later than twelve. She has to work tomorrow. Fuck it, go to bed. Forget it, you're just tired. I'll make some tea, smoke a fag and go to bed. Be sensible, get a grip. Alright, two fags then.

Late night tele is such a load of old balls. Come to think of it, television in general is bollocks. It's so patronising. I'm sure everyone was really excited when it first came out. Thinking of the possibilities, only for it to be blanded out beyond bland. I remember my Grandfather coming to visit every Saturday especially to watch the wrestling. He didn't have a T.V. and was like a big fat kid with a new toy. They said tele would educate people, open up a whole new world to the masses. I even think he didn't realise each fight was choreographed.

I'll read my book. Fuck it, one more fag. I can't concentrate. I'll give her a ring, that's what mobiles are for, right? But I don't want to hurry her, ruin her night. She's probably having a great time. I wonder if she talks about me when she's out. Or does she forget about me? Shit, when I'm out I don't think about her. So what? You can't think about someone all of the time. It's not healthy. You have to trust her. I do trust her, don't I? She's not that kind of girl.

That's what I used to say about Alison. God, the way I defended that bitch. Two years down the toilet. How can people be so dishonest? Hold on a wee sec. It's not like you're a saint yourself. These things happen, what with drink and drugs and the right/wrong situation. I never went out with the intention. But it does happen. She could be with someone right now. He offered her a lift home. They get chatting. I'll ring her. It's not possible to connect your call. Please try later.

What the fuck does that mean? She's switched her phone off. Why would she do that? Maybe she lost it? But it would still ring, right? Why would she switch if off? They're in the pub, it's not like it's business or anything.

I really wish I hadn't done that. I should have went to bed. Jesus Christ, I feel sick. What if something's happened, something's gone wrong? Why doesn't she phone me? One call doesn't take long. Fuck it. Calm down. Chill out. Relax, everything is fine. She probably switched it off by accident. Bumped into someone or something, hit the off button. Yeah, right. I fucking hate mobiles. That's what Jenny used to say. But then she was permanently stuck in the '80s. Haven't thought of her in a while, wonder where she is now. She was sweet, really sweet. My God that was six years ago. I remember that time on the bus when we had just started going out.

The sun blurring through the windows making me sweat. Jenny smiling and saying she was happy for the first time in ages, wishing we could just sit there side by side and never get off. Come to think of it, she was a bit of a romantic idiot. Whatever happened to us? We were happy for months. We had some good times her and I. Wonder what she's up to? She mightn't even be in the country. She was always talking of Australia and all that sun. If I met her now would there be any spark left? Would we get on well? Give knowing glances. Or would she be a complete stranger? It's funny to think you can be so together with someone, so one with them. Then after some time be distant, apart. Even when you know it's not going to last forever, you still can't imagine life without her. And when you're not with a girl anymore you can't remember what it was like when you were with her. Maybe it's just me, maybe it's a memory thing. I drink too much, I know that.

Or maybe we are never really one with our partners. We just soft of meet half way, or three quarters of the way with that half overlapping.

Perhaps the whole thing is just a distraction, a mist over the truth of the matter. That we are all together in being alone. One drink and a fag and then to bed. I have to work tomorrow for fucks sake. A wee night cap, calm me down. Am I in any way closer to Karen than I was with my ex's? Well at this moment in time obviously. But if you take away the time difference, is there a difference?

I was terribly attached to Rebecca, obsessed even. I was convinced she was the one, completely convinced. And after four years I end up running away from her in the street. She recognised my red jeans disappearing 'round the corner. Phoning me the next day, telling me to keep on running.

Maybe it is me. She wanted to have children and I just shat myself. I was twenty three and truly felt that was something adults did. I was waiting for that golden day when the world would make sense, I wanted to be one hundred per cent sure before I went anywhere near that kind of responsibility. One hundred per cent sure. What the hell does that mean? I've never been one hundred per cent sure of anything, especially women.

One more whiskey. If she's not back by one thirty I'm going to bed. She would never have done this in the beginning, no chance. She's starting to take me for granted. I know she is. Of course she is, that's the best part of a relationship. Just assuming you love each other. Not worrying about stupid girl boy bullshit.

Hold on a second. Just assuming you love each other? Maybe she doesn't love me anymore. I really have to give up the cigarettes. She has been acting kind of strange lately. At David's house warming she was a complete nightmare. She was flirting outrageously. Alright, so was I, but that's what you do at parties. It wasn't the flirting, it was something else. What was it?

Everyone was talking and no-one was listening. I was going 'round everyone at the party, talking more and more, working myself up into a frenzy, words overlapping. Then meeting Karen on the stairs and for a moment not recognising her. Everyone felt like a stranger. Karen was a stranger.

Maybe I don't love her anymore.

If she was shagging someone right at this moment what would I do? I would feel very nauseas indeed. But that's just a natural reaction. Is it this nausea I am shying away from? That's no reason to stay with someone. I'd kick her out into the street the stupid bitch. She would you know, she could. She's stupid enough to throw away everything we have. I know she is. What do we have? Oh my God it is me. I don't love her anymore. I haven't loved her for months. I've been putting it off. Jesus I really have. That night after David's house warming, I remember now. Sitting in the back seat of the taxi staring out at the heavy rain, Karen asleep with her head on my knee. Oh my God, maybe it wasn't just the booze. I remember now, looking out into the night and feeling completely, absolutely alone. The sheer joy of feeling that isolated, that free. The adrenaline rush at the moment of clarity. The beauty as the street lamps lit up the rain drops n the window. It was then I decided to leave her. I've always had this ridiculous fear of being alone. Running around like a headless chicken craving distractions. But sooner or later you have to face the facts.

You get what you settle for, at the expense of the real thing. Trying to make things work. Slowly but surely you end up doing things you don't want to do. Then you don't notice anymore and after some time you don't know what you want. But she seems to have a good idea so let's go along with that until…How could I be so stupid? I promised myself after the last one, no more. No more bullshit, no more self-deception, no more lies. Jesus, it's so easy to keep going through the motions. You don't die when you lie, when you deceive. You keep up the pretence of living. You can live your whole life having never lived at all.

"You still up?"

"Oh, ah, yeah. I mmm…"

A hug and a kiss on the neck.

"Have you smoked all these fags?"

"Ah, yeah. I was reading my book. I phoned you earlier but your phone was switched off."

"I know. It was Johnny Johnson. He made a real prick of himself tonight."

"Oh?"

"He got completely wasted to the point where we got him a taxi.

The stupid twat kept ringing me telling me he loved me."

"Oh, yeah."

"Then he started phoning Mary, then Denise. He's going to be very embarrassed tomorrow, that's if he makes it in at all."

"Oh, so you had a good night?"

"It was alright. I'm glad you're still up. I missed you tonight."

"Really?"

"Don't look so surprised. I do love you, ya know. Come to bed."

"Ok."

## AS QUIET AS THE GRAVE
### Kevin Gormley

I killed my wife today.

I served my beloved breakfast in bed and while she was bemoaning the fact that the toast was burnt again – here I have to admit that I've taken a childish delight over the years in burning her toast or putting too much sugar in her tea or over-cooking her egg – I jabbed a knitting needle into her eye, pushing it home until it would go no further. I jiggled it about a bit, too, though not to be cruel. I just wanted to be sure. Women like my Hilda are hard to kill. Unfortunately, I made a bit of a mess. My wife's eye leaked all down her cheek. If she'd still been able to speak at that stage I'm sure she would have told me that, as usual, I couldn't even get the simplest things right.

Not to worry, though. At least I'd achieved my objective and that was the main thing. My darling Hilda, wife and companion for over forty years, sat dead in her bed, a needle in one eye, a look of utter surprise in the other and a piece of toast grasped in her fist. Not very dignified, I agree, and probably not even very fair, but neither of these things mattered. What was important was that, after a lifetime of listening to her complaints and doing her bidding, Hilda was finally quiet. No longer would she be able to criticise everything I did. No more would I shudder at the sound of her braying laughter or cringe at the incessant whine in her voice. I was free. I could look forward to enjoying silence; the one commodity married life had consistently deprived me of.

Silence!

How long had I savoured that word? Too long, I would say. Most of my life, in fact.

But all that was at an end. There was no more Hilda to disrupt the calm, no more constant demands on my time, my energy, and my patience. I would no longer be a slave to someone else's routine. The possibilities before me were endless.

'I should've done it years ago,' I remarked, instinctively bracing myself for the inevitable rebuff, for the sarcasm that had been Hilda's idea of convivial conversation. When none came, I regarded my ex fondly. 'You're going to keep your own counsel on that one, are you? Can't say as I blame you.'

The look of surprise in her remaining orb could also be interpreted as a glare, if you tilted your head the right way and used your imagination. I scowled back, refusing to be intimidated. She didn't drop her gaze, though, and I hated her for that. Even in death, she was able to stare me down.

'But that's all you can do,' I said, grinning at her. 'Isn't it, you bitch?' Calling her a bitch made me feel so good that I did it again. Then I experimented with a few other expletives I'd felt like using over the years. I had quite a repertoire and Hilda's tea had gone stone cold by the time I was done. She'd taken a couple of sips, put the cup on the bedside table and reached for the toast. Just like she always did. I'd allowed her a bite and a final complaint before springing my little surprise. No one could ever accuse me of being insensitive to her needs.

Even now, I commiserated with her. 'You've let your tea go cold. Would you like me to make you another cup?' The old Hilda would have said that she did want another cup and don't put so much milk, or sugar, in it this time. The new Hilda was neither demanding nor reproachful. She had an introverted air about her, like she had something on her mind.

'Maybe I should just clear these things away,' I offered, and then thought better of it. I didn't have to tidy away her breakfast if I didn't want to. 'Or perhaps I'll leave it until later. What do you think, dear?'

She didn't think anything, apparently, and so I decided to leave it. Nor did I take the piece of toast from her fist. It said everything you needed to know about my Hilda; she was a grasping old hag, right to the bitter end.

'And don't try to deny it,' I challenged her.

My sweetheart, naturally, did no such thing.

'And don't sulk, you know I hate it when you sulk.'

I didn't, actually. I loved it when she gave me the silent treatment.

'And don't think you're going to sit there all day and have me attend you hand and foot. Those days are over. You'll have to pull your own weight from now on.'

And quite a weight it was, too. Twenty stone, at least.

'So maybe a diet is in order,' I concluded, no longer sure if I was laughing or crying, only aware that I had to get a grip on myself. It occurred to me that a drop of brandy might help. It would serve to calm me down and I could celebrate my liberation at the same time. It would also be one in the eye for Hilda; she hated me drinking as a general rule but a tipple at such an early hour would have appalled her.

I headed downstairs, poured myself a generous measure and sat at the kitchen table. Normally, I would be washing up the breakfast dishes by now and listening to Hilda cackling at the portable TV we kept in the bedroom. Instead, I savoured my drink and gazed out the window at the back garden. The sun was burning away the last of the early morning mist and birds flitted and sang from the hedges. I promised myself a few lazy hours on the lawn this afternoon, reading or dozing or perhaps enjoying a beverage or two. I could do such things now. I could eat when I wanted, belch and fart whenever and wherever I pleased and do countless other things that hadn't even occurred to me yet. Freedom, I realised, would take some thought.

I judged that another brandy would aid the cognitive process and help with the mellow mood I was acquiring. I was relishing this second libation when I heard the floorboards creak in the upstairs bathroom. Hilda was on the move. Some days she was too weak to get out of bed without assistance but on other occasions she could be quite lively. She was even known to make her ponderous way downstairs so that she could sit on the couch and supervise my activities. It would just be my luck that this was one of those times and here I was with neither a plate washed nor a pot scrubbed. Worse! I was idling *and* I was half-lit.

I wasn't about to be caught so easily, though. In a matter of seconds I'd drained my glass and dropped it into the sink alongside my own breakfast dishes. I ran the water, added washing-up liquid and was up to my elbows in suds before I realised what I was doing. I was trying to mollify a dead woman. My imagination had crept up behind me, shouted *boo* and I'd jumped out of my skin. It was pathetic. It was laughable, too, and as relief flooded my system I allowed myself a small chuckle at my own expense. There's no fool like an old fool, I mused as I dried my hands. But fool or not, I still reckoned I was ahead of the game. Another tot of brandy would confirm that view very nicely. This time I took it straight from the bottle.

The floorboards creaked again.

They didn't. I knew they didn't and yet my body convulsed with panic, sending me into a coughing fit that brought tears to my eyes and made my chest feel like it was about to burst. It took a couple of minutes to get the spluttering and wheezing under control and by that stage I was as mad as hell at Hilda for getting me into such a state. I couldn't allow this to continue. I hadn't killed the old biddy just so she could rule my life from beyond the grave.

I went back to the bedroom and, sure enough, she was exactly where I'd left her. I gave myself a bit of a scare when, just for a moment, I thought that the body had moved slightly, but on closer inspection I realised I was wrong. She *had* been sitting up as straight as that and her head *had* been inclined towards the TV. As for the smirk on her face, that had always been there. It was her habitual expression. I was so used to seeing it that I barely noticed it anymore.

'You're dead,' I informed my late though scarcely lamented spouse, 'deceased, departed, defunct, D.E.A.D. *dead*. And don't you forget it.' To further prove the point, I reached out and touched the cold flesh of her face and stared into the unblinking emptiness of her remaining orb. I pinched her, too, just to be on the safe side. Handling her made my skin crawl but that was hardly a new experience for me. Neither was her lack of response. Hilda was as frosty in death as she had been in life.

Probably just as well, I reflected as I lifted her breakfast tray and carted it back to the kitchen. A warm Hilda, a *feeling* Hilda might have been much more difficult to dispose of. The bitch in the bed had ceased to mean anything to me years ago.

We had been close at one time, back at the start of our marriage when we shared so much in common. Hilda had been quite pretty and, I must say, I was no slouch in the looks department myself. We were a popular couple, going to parties and throwing the occasional shindig ourselves.

The onset of Hilda's illness didn't stop us socialising. Rather, it made us twice as determined to be part of things and added a new dimension to our activities. We saw how fortunate we had been and how selfish we'd become, so much so that we decided to make recompense. The parties we threw after that weren't just for our friends and neighbours, they included the less fortunate among us as well. My wife developed a particular fondness for the waifs and strays of the world, allowing them to stay in our home and to treat it as their own. Dear Hilda. She had been quite the saint in her time.

The memories had me almost reduced to tears as I trudged about the kitchen, washing and drying cups and saucers, cleaning work surfaces until they sparkled and taking the occasional nip of brandy for comfort's sake. By the time I was done I was a bit wobbly on my pegs and I decided to have a lie down. The couch in the living room beckoned and for the first time ever I had a mid-morning nap, even though there was a voice inside me that insisted I had a lot more housework to do. Old habits die hard but I didn't have to give way to them. I forced myself to relax, to sleep. Any tasks I had to perform – like finding a new resting place for my wife – could wait until later.

I awoke about an hour afterwards with a foul taste in my mouth and a head that felt at least twice its normal size. Worse, I'd dreamed that Hilda had crept downstairs while I slept, seen all the chores left undone and her prone husband, and had decided that such behaviour would not do. When she said that things *would not do*, it usually meant trouble for someone. No guesses as to who was in the shit this time.

'Not so,' I reminded myself, 'the dead can't dictate terms to the living.' I eased off the couch, feeling very much like an old man, and smoothed my rumpled clothing. I'd put on a fresh white shirt earlier but now I noticed that the front of the garment was stained with buttery fingerprints. I stared at the marks for a full half minute before I realised what they meant.

Someone had grabbed me while I slept.

Someone who thought that mid-morning naps *would not do*.

'No,' I whispered, disbelief and dread turning the brandy in my stomach to acid. I put my fingers on the blemishes, hoping to find that I'd caused the stains myself, but I already knew that they'd been made by stubby, vicious little digits and not by my own slender, artistic ones. The marks were wet, too. As if someone had been clutching a piece of toast just prior to handling me.

'No,' I insisted, but the brandy in my guts paid no heed to my denials. It came charging up my gullet in a scalding torrent and jetted across the living room as if trying to exit the premises before something *really* weird happened. *It's not the only spirit on the move today*, I thought, aware of the hysteria that was waiting in the wings but seemingly powerless to prevent it from making its grand entrance.

My stomach contracted again but there was nothing left to throw up. That didn't stop my body from trying, though, and I spent the next few minutes retching and coughing and generally wishing that I were dead. By the time the episode passed, I was on my knees with tears streaming down my face and my arms wrapped around my ribs. My eyes felt like they were out on stalks but, ironically, all of this discomfort had chased hysteria away from the wings and back into the dressing room where it belonged. I was calm and in control when I got to my feet. I was also determined that I was taking no more crap from her upstairs. It was way past time to finish what I'd started.

Easier said than done, though. I might have dreamed of killing my wife for years but the actual deed itself was a spur of the moment kind of thing. I hadn't planned to stick her in the eye with a knitting needle and I *definitely* hadn't given any consideration as to how I intended to conceal what I'd done. It occurred to me that I didn't have to hide anything, that I could fess up, plead temporary insanity and throw myself on the mercy of the court. Given my age plus the fact that I'd been caring for an invalid for years, I could probably expect leniency. Maybe even sympathy. For a few seconds it was a very tempting scenario.

But not possible, alas. If I went that route, there would be cops crawling all over the house and, regardless of how careful I'd been in the past, they were bound to find signs of those waifs and strays I mentioned earlier. Quite a number came to our parties and stayed over, but not all of them left. No one ever came looking for them at the time but I couldn't take the chance that someone somewhere missed them. In this instance I preferred to let sleeping dogs lie.

No police, then. And no simple solutions either, it seemed. Hilda was going to be a burden to me for a little while yet.

'I hope you're satisfied,' I said, glancing out the window to see if the garden offered any possibilities. It was well tended and bordered by high hedges to allow for privacy, but it was uncomfortably close to a number of neighbouring properties. Any attempts at burial or cremation would be spotted from upper storey windows, giving rise to yet more awkward questions. Anyway, the prospect of digging a hole – or constructing a pyre – and then delivering Hilda on-site was too much to bear. She wasn't exactly diminutive and I was neither as young nor as strong as I used to be.

Damn.

Turning away from the window, I ambled through the downstairs rooms in the hope of finding inspiration. Only the kitchen, and in particular the knife rack, gave me any ideas and as I repeatedly returned there I realised what I had to do. I also understood that I'd been avoiding the inevitable, allowing my mind to play tricks on me instead of facing up to the obvious solution to my problem. When the TV in the bedroom came on I ignored it. When my wife's familiar cackle joined the din upstairs, I ignored that too. They were figments of my imagination, delaying tactics I'd used on myself. Killing was easy for me but I'd never faced the gruesome task of getting rid of a body before. That had been Hilda's department.

'My responsibility now,' I murmured, choosing the largest knife on the stand. My stomach rolled as I hefted the blade and the racket above stepped up a notch, but I allowed neither of these things to distract me. Instead, I concentrated on adopting an optimistic attitude. Like not having to worry about buying meat for months.

Just like Hilda, I had a huge appetite for life.

# THE PRICE OF KNOWLEDGE
Marie O'Nolan

The bookshop was crowded when I saw him do it again. The routine was always the same: he would slip a small volume from the philosophy section into a side pocket of his knapsack, then walk to the popular fiction counter where he chose a cheap paperback, apparently at random, then he would go to the desk and pay for that. He would even have a few friendly words with the assistant before leaving without undue haste by the main door. The first time I had seen him do it I had been torn between reactions of shock, indignation and pity. I almost rushed to the desk to report him but something held me back. Perhaps it was his youth and good looks or a certain air of vulnerability about him or perhaps something untapped in myself; I still don't know. Anyway for whatever reason this particular day, when he left the shop I decided to follow him and my life has never been the same since...

My husband and I, an early middle-aged couple lived in a small house in a quiet suburban terrace on Dublin's south side. I usually went into the city on Thursdays. It was my day off from my part-time job. After I had tidied the house, cleared up after the breakfast and prepared a casserole for our evening meal, I took a train about eleven o'clock. I did some shopping, had a light lunch either with a friend or on my own, then spend the afternoon in a cinema, a gallery or a museum. By arrangement I would turn up at my husband's office for a lift home at about five o'clock. We would arrive at our front door to be assailed by the appetizing aroma from the kitchen oven from my timed casserole a little after six. It was a weekly routine I enjoyed and had no reason to break, that is until after I saw what happened in the bookshop. Perhaps in some strange way it was for me the end of a kind of innocence.

One of my stops on a Thursday was a busy bookshop in the city centre. I would usually browse there for at least half an hour before buying something to read on the train on my next visit. I often bought a poetry collection about which I had read a review in the weekend papers. I seldom read poetry except on the train. There was something about the motion of the wheels, the climactic breaks of speeding and slowing down that made poetry the proper kind of reading for train travel, for me. It was not that I was a particularly bookish person, my husband not at all. I suppose it could be said that Jack and I, by some people's standards, lived uneventful and unimaginative lives. Even our holidays were spent always in the same way, touring in West Cork or Donegal every year, even staying in the same guesthouses. We had only once been abroad in Spain but we chose the wrong overcrowded resort and had no wish to repeat the experience. All of this makes it more out of character for me to have decided to follow a strange young man from a bookshop.

I found it hard to keep up with him. It was not that he walked particularly fast but he was tall and took long strides. Once I drew level with him as we waited at a crossing for the lights to change but I was afraid to scrutinize him too closely in case he would realize I was keeping him in sight. However I judged him to be not more than twenty. When the lights changed he moved off in the general direction of Trinity College. That tallied. He did look like a student as much by his air as his appearance. That ruled out one of my first suspicions that he was a serious dealer in stolen books. When we got to College Green I expected him to turn in through the gates of the college but he didn't; instead he went on up Grafton Street. I followed, trying to keep a discreet distance between us. He stopped outside a bookshop half way up but did not go in, just looked briefly at the display in the window of the latest best seller. As I passed I heard him give a sniff of what sounded like contempt at what he saw then he crossed the narrow street and turned into Bewley's Cafe. It was a little early for my own lunch but I decided to do the same.

The cafe was fairly crowded and there were a few customers between him and me at the self-service counter but I could see that he chose a mug of espresso and a plain bread roll without butter. I chose my usual cappuccino and mixed salad sandwich. At the table I joined, two women who were discussing a third, a mutual friend or enemy; it was hard to say from the mood swings of their conversation. However I paid little heed to them; I was more concerned with keeping my quarry in view. He was already seated alone at a table nearby. He took up two chairs, using one to accommodate his knapsack. After a mouthful of coffee he produced it out of his bag, the stolen book, not furtively or guiltily but, I can only say, reverently. He handled it as one would something precious and valuable. It was slim with no dust cover, dark blue with gold lettering, like one of a special series. From where I sat I could just make out the title, Essays *of Michel Eyquem de Montaigne*. Before he even touched his roll he replaced the book of essays carefully in his bag. As he ate and drank he read the paperback he had bought, bending its spine back careless with one hand while he held his mug or his roll alternately with the other. I noticed that as he read his eyes and mouth formed an expression of amused contempt. On leaving he left the paperback behind on the table. I inferred instinctively that it was not an oversight on his part but a deliberate action and I was duly intrigued by the irony of it. It appeared that he chose to steal what he thought of as gold and to pay for what he believed was dross. I simply had to find out why so I got up quickly and followed him out, taking the paperback with me. When I caught up with him I would pretend that I thought he had left the book behind by mistake but I was held up on the way out by the sudden influx of the lunchtime crowd. By the time I reached the street he had disappeared. I walked three times around the leafy elegance of St Stephen's Green on chance but he was nowhere to be seen. I finally threw the paperback into a refuse basket near the old bandstand.

On the following Thursday I browsed for over an hour in the city bookshop in the hope of seeing him but my young thief did not appear and I was the one who felt cheated. When I finally left the shop it was starting to drizzle so I decided to take a bus to Merrion Square and have lunch in the restaurant of the National Gallery after which I might wander among the pictures for the rest of the afternoon and keep dry. After I had eaten I set out with no particular viewing plan. It was when I found myself in front of a Murillo that I realized there was someone standing beside me. I glanced around and found my excitement rising when I saw my young thief of the bookshop. He had a catalogue in his hand and I could not help wondering if he had paid for it or did they, in fact, give them out free at the desk? I smiled briefly as one would to a stranger encountered in a shared isolated place or incident and he casually returned my greeting. My eyes returned to the painting. I noted its name. *The Prodigal Son receiving his Portion,* but it was not the figure of the prodigal son, depicted only in profile, that I noted (the painter may have intended this) but that of the wronged brother who stood behind his father, his hands poised in front of him, one above the other in silent judgement. At close quarters I realised that my companion looked a little like the older brother in the picture, despite the seventeenth century clothing. There was the same look of puzzled discontent on his face. The silence of the afternoon hung heavily between us, ranging, as it were, over the centuries. I sensed a certain shyness on his part to start a conversation with a woman almost old enough to be his mother. I felt it was up to me.

'Do you think the painter is already making his own judgement?' I asked.

'Perhaps. The judgements of art are cleaner.'

'What does that mean?'

He shrugged.

'One should not have to pay for the things worth having.'

'Like good books and the like, you mean?' I remarked pointedly.

His eyes flickered with sudden suspicion, which he was not quick enough to disguise. I decided to play him along a little.

'Why do you do it?' I asked after a pause.

He had recovered enough to prevaricate.

'Do what?'

'You know right well. I saw you do it.'

'Saw me do what?'

'Take books in Eason's you didn't pay for.'

His face flushed with what could have been either anger or guilt but he still kept up a front.

'Look, Mrs – whatever your name is. You must be mistaking me for someone else. I've never seen you before in my life.'

'Well I've seen you and I could name one of the books you've taken.'

'What book?' he challenged.

When I named it his whole subterfuge collapsed so completely that I felt almost sorry for him.

'I... Do you work in Eason's?'

'No. I'm just a private citizen that goes there every Thursday.'

'Why Thursday?'

I briefly explained my simple routine.

His lip curled sardonically. It cleared categorized me as 'one of those.'

I bridled.

'There's no need to sneer at my habits just because they are less, shall we say, adventurous than your own.'

'I apologise.' His contrition seemed genuine enough although there was the suggestion of derisive glint lingering in his eye.

'Well, what have you got to say for yourself?' I asked, facing him, I suppose, a bit like a mother.

'Like I said: one should not have to pay - '

'"For the things worth having,"' I finished for him. 'From where I stand that could be a recipe for chaos.'

'Now who is making moral judgements?'

'I've made no such judgement. If I had I would have reported you at the time.'

'Why didn't you?'

I looked at him in the frail afternoon light of the gallery and could not find an answer I could put into words.

'Perhaps I lacked courage or that I considered there might be extenuating circumstances.'

I knew it sounded lame and I was not surprised when he laughed outright.

'It was a book for Christ's sake, not a loaf of bread to feed a starving family in the nineteenth century. You can do better than that surely.'

'Watch it,' I threatened. 'I could still report you.'

He held his palms in the air in a somewhat theatrical gesture of surrender.

'What can I say..?'

'Convince me why knowledge should be free,' I challenged.

He thought for a moment, his eyes on the high windows of the gallery. The light in them was a little wild, I thought. It made me feel slightly dizzy.

'That which can be bought is already corrupt.' It had the trite ring of a quotation.

'Is that why you threw away the book you paid for?'

He looked at me in frank astonishment this time.

'Jesus! Are you some sort of clairvoyant? How..?'

'I followed you into Bewley's last Thursday.'

'Look, I give up. I'll do anything you say. Do you want me to return the book?'

'Books,' I corrected.

'Books. Do you want me to return them?'

'Have you read them?'

'Of course. Why else would I have taken them?'

'Then couldn't you just slip them back with the same sleight of hand?'

'On second thoughts, no. Books worth reading are worth keeping.'

'Even if you had the money to pay for them?'

'That's the size of it.'

'You mean if you pay for them they are already tainted in some way?'

'Something like that.'

'But most things have to be paid for one way or another.'

'We live in a tainted word.'

'But you yourself or the state – I take it you're a student – has to pay for your education – for knowledge. Does that not already taint it?'

' Not if it's paid back in kind.'

'Meaning that you repay for knowledge with your acquired knowledge? It goes back into the pool?'

' He looked at me with what seemed like approval.

'You're a very bright lady.'

I didn't feel bright. On the contrary this strange young man and his even stranger philosophy had given me a headache. I needed a cup of tea. I prepared to leave.

'Well..?' he said holding out his wrists as if for handcuffs. 'Are you

75

going to make private citizen's arrest or not?'

'I don't think so,' I replied wearily pushing his hands aside. 'Not today anyway. Oh, go away.'

He took me at my word.

'See you round,' he called back over his shoulder.

I looked after him striding away with the beginnings of something more than regret. I turned back to the picture. Our conversation had given a new uneasy meaning to the prodigal son counting out his portion while his elder brother looked on accusingly. In fact it had given a new uneasy meaning to everything.

I was later than usual meeting Jack that evening.

'Had a good day?' he asked as he always did.

'It was OK.' I returned noncommittally.

I decided not to tell him of my encounter with the philosophic young thief. I knew what his moral judgement would be and I had no wish to hear it. Later when we were eating our Thursday casserole the subject of holidays came up and I found myself suggesting that we might venture abroad that year instead of going on our usual vacation in Ireland. He said he would think about it.

When my young friend had said he would see me around it was not just an idle phrase. I should have guessed that that would not be the end of it. Michael (as I discovered was his name) began to turn up on my Thursday visits in various places in the city. I encountered him once in Stephen's Green sitting reading on a free seat near the blind people's scented garden. For almost an hour in the full redolence of lavender we discussed books, not the stealing of them but rather the reading and enjoyment of them. Although he had read far more widely than I, he professed to be intrigued by my predilection for reading poetry on the train. On another occasion he sat down beside me at the cinema and we enjoyed a foreign language film together (I could never get Jack to go to one because of the sub-titles.) Meeting me in a sudden downpour in Grafton Street without an umbrella, one afternoon he took me to shelter in his bed-sitter, which turned out to be in a nearby back street over a bicycle repair shop. He gave me instant coffee in a chipped mug and supplied me with a worn, faded but clean towel to dry my hair. He made no attempt to hide his collection of slim, blue and gold books, the special series, which now appeared to be almost, complete. They had been given pride of place on some rough, unplaned deal shelves within reach of his bed. I made no comment and we talked of other things. When I was leaving, he kissed my cheek. On my way to meet Jack, my face burned with a new pleasure and my lips with and old privation. That was not the only time he took me to his room but we never discussed again the possibility that I might inform on his thieving. Of course I knew what he was up to but I got such pleasure from his company I didn't care. The suspicion that he was merely seeking my company so as to ward off betrayal did not seem to matter. He was opening up so many doors for me I was prepared to pay the price. However, a few months after our first meeting he devised a way of freeing himself from my moral bondage.

In late September when Jack and I had just returned from a successful holiday on one of the Greek islands I found a parcel waiting for me. It contained a collection of the poems of the Chilean poet, *Pablo Neruda*, whom Michael knew I admired. It was a slim volume with no dust cover, dark red with gold lettering, obviously part of another special series. I had to pretend to Jack that I had ordered it. I handled it with both reverence and doubt. Stolen? I had no way of knowing for sure. If I accepted it would I become his willing accomplice and lose him? If I did not would I be making sure that I would go on seeing my knowing young thief for as long as I wished? The choice was mine...

# HEAT
## Stephen McMurray

The rising sun bled into the sea and dyed the blue sky red. It was going to be a scorcher.

Kevin Mace lifted his head from the water and gulped. He had showered already but that hadn't worked. Now he was trying a bath. He would have put some ice cubes into it but the electricity was dead. Either there had been a power cut or Mike had forgot to pay the bill.

He appreciated Mike's offer to lend him the summerhouse and a car but it irritated the hell out of him that he'd left no supplies. All he had found were some old clothes, an identity bracelet of sorts with Mike Vance's name on it, a few grimy towels, some old pots and pans, a couple of magazines and an old locked, wooden chest. He'd phone him later and see if he would drive by and bring some food with him.

He ducked his head under and took a mouthful of water. He spat it out. It was salty. The plumbing must have gone as well.

Leaning back, he looked up at the ceiling. A five-bladed fan hung motionless. For some bizarre reason it reminded him of a dead starfish. As if he was floating above it and it was lifeless on the bleached white sand.

God it was warm. He reached out and grabbed his watch. Ten-thirty. He closed his eyes and tried to relax.

The sea came to him. He could hear it, shattering against the rocks and hissing over the burning sand. He could feel it washing against him, surrounding him, submerging him. Then the taste of salt again. He was falling; down and down and down. Into the cold. Into the darkness.

Perhaps he could find shelter here from that terrible, blazing sun. A blood-red eye that sought him out wherever he went.

As he fell he thought he could see something move on the seabed. It was dark, its shape indistinct. But as he drifted closer he could make it out. It was a fish. A dead fish, floating on its back, its belly distended. It was enormous. It was completely still apart from the ripples under its skin.

Down and down floated Kevin until he was just above the piscine corpse. Then, as he watched bemused, its abdomen split apart. From the gaping wound came an explosion of bones. Human bones. Arms, legs, feet and hands. They swirled passed him, the skeletal fingers pointing at him as they were washed away by the tides.

He awoke gasping. He had fallen asleep again. The heat always made him do that.

A noise from the other room startled him. Coughing and spluttering, he clambered out of the bath. He crossed the floor, opened the door and peered out into the room beyond. There was nothing apart from a trail of sand that led to the hall. He thought he had swept all that up last night when he arrived. But then he didn't remember much about last night. It had been a long drive, he had been exhausted, and it was already dark when he got here.

He was up now so he may as well phone Mike. He swept the sand from the floor and dumped it into the bin. Then he got dressed. By the time he got his clothes on he was warm again.

Reaching into his pocket, he fished out a hankie to wipe the perspiration from his forehead. As he lifted it out something fell from it. It was a small silver key. God knows where that came from. He picked it up and put it back into his pocket.

Kevin lifted his mobile phone and dialled Mike's number. A woman's voice said he had reached some hospital or other. Wrong number obviously. He hung up and tried again. This time it was engaged. He would phone later.

As he walked to the living room the sun reflected of the silver roof of his car outside. It blinded him momentarily. He shielded his eyes. Images of the flash burned across his retinas for a few seconds. He then made his way out of the living room.

Maybe he could drive up and get some supplies himself. He reached into his jacket and removed his wallet. Flipping it open, he looked inside. The letters L.K. were emblazoned on the leather.

"What the hell. Whose wallet is this and where the hell is mine?"

He didn't know where he had picked it up from and he had absolutely no idea what happed to his own but he certainly couldn't go around spending other people's money. He had no choice but to wait until Mike dropped by.

He looked at his watch. Eleven o'clock.

The sun was rising higher. As it rose so, too, did the temperature. He felt as if his brain was being cooked in his skull. His head began to throb.

He went and collapsed on the sofa. He felt the crumpling of paper as he sat down. He reached behind him and brought out a newspaper. It was the usual headline stuff, some murder or other. It all seemed familiar to him somehow. He looked at the date. No wonder. It was June 1st 2001. It was a year old. He checked his watch again. A year to the day in fact. He tossed it aside.

He was sweating again and his head hurt like hell. He rubbed at it but it had little effect.

There was that noise again. It sounded like someone walking over bare floorboards. He got up and made his way cautiously into the bedroom. The trail of sand was back and this time a trail of wet footprints accompanied them.

They led to the bathroom.

Sneaking his way over to the door, he thrust it open. Just for a second, through the gap, he could have sworn he saw a shape slipping out of the open window. Rushing over, he stuck his head out. But there was nothing, just the scorching sun glaring down at him. He brought his head back inside.

The bathroom smelled odd, like the sea had washed through it, leaving its scent behind. What the hell was going on?

He was about to leave when he noticed the bath. It was full of water. He had emptied it when he had finished. He knew he had. What's more something was floating in it.

Kneeling down, he reached in and scooped it out. Seaweed. There was bloody seaweed in it. He reached in again to retrieve some more. It was knotted and tangled. Leaning over further, he grabbed it with both hands. He hauled it out. It was then that he realised why it was so heavy. It was entwined around a severed human head. Its dead eyes gazed at him.

"Jesus Christ!"

The head was that of an elderly man, slightly bald. Limpets had attached themselves to its face. Tiny crabs scuttled across its pale-blue lips.

As Kevin stared at it the lips opened. A gush of water came from its mouth and, with it, the remains of a decayed fish. The pungent stench almost made Kevin sick. Then after disgorging its contents those dead lips spoke. They said only one word, "Why?"

Kevin dropped the head into the bath and threw up on the floor. Staggering back to his feet, he leaned against the wall. He looked back at the bath. It was empty.

What in God's name was happening to him? He must have passed out with the heat and had some really weird dream. Either that or he was hallucinating.

Drenching his face with water, he stumbled out and into the living room. Maybe if he just sat down for a while he would be all right. He didn't want to sleep, though. God knows what nightmares he would have.

There was a radio somewhere. In the cabinet by the door. He had no idea how he knew that but when he looked, sure enough, there it was. He took it out. It was covered in dust and looked as if it hadn't been used for a while. He turned it on, put it on the coffee table and sat down.

He was sweating profusely now. The heat was burning his skull, frying his brain. His skin felt as if it was on fire.

The news came on. A newsreader, with suitably refined voice, spoke.

"Police are searching for Dr Larry Kelvin who disappeared in mysterious circumstances last night from Mt Romario hospital. His silver BMW is also missing. The chief suspect in this abduction case is Mike Vance..."

The newsreader read on but Kevin was no longer listening. What the hell was going on? Was the world going crazy today or was it just him? Had Mike actually kidnapped this guy or what?

Kevin had had enough. He was getting out of here. Grabbing the car keys from the table, he rushed out of the door. The heat of the sun was almost instantly unbearable.

He walked towards the car. The sunlight glinted of its bodywork.

The coruscations hit him in the face like bullets of light. They made the throbbing in his temples worse and disoriented him. By the time he got to the car he felt weak and nauseous. He leaned against the car to steady himself. The silver paint gleamed in the sunlight, apart for a spot just below the lock of the boot. That was discoloured by a circle of red.

Puzzled, Kevin took the keys from his pocket. Slowly, he opened the lock and raised the boot.

"My God, Mike, what have you done?"

Crumpled on the floor was a body of a middle-aged man dressed in a suit. He was covered in blood.

Overhead a gull screeched. Kevin jumped up, startled by the sudden noise. His heart raced. His head pounded. He slammed the boot closed.

There was no way he was getting in the car. The house was his only option. He would go back and try to find a weapon with which to protect himself. Maybe he would use the mobile to phone the police. Or maybe not. Maybe they would think he was involved. Either way, he had to go back to the house. He couldn't stay out here in this heat.

Staggering back to the house, the sun burned his neck and back. Sweat dripped from him. His breath was laboured. Every exhalation hurt him, his throat being dry and raw.

He made it back along the path. The nameplate of the beach house that hung above the door, swung on one rusted chain, the other having broken. "Sunrise Dreams," it said.

Kevin climbed on to the veranda. He stumbled against the wall, dropping his keys. He bent down to pick them up. As he touched them a hand thrust itself through the gaps in the wooden slats on the floor. It gripped him by the wrist. It was wet and cold. Bits of flesh were peeling back to reveal bare bone. Its fingernails had gone, leaving blackened skin beneath.

Kevin yelped and pulled himself free. The hand vanished below the floor. Kevin watched as its owner skulked off, slithering under the floor of the house.

Opening the door, he ran into the hall. The second he crossed the threshold the door slammed behind him. He span around. He couldn't believe what he was seeing.

Tendrils of some sort were sprouting from between the walls and tying themselves around the door handle. Others were pushing through the gaps between the door and the frame. Then he realised his feet were wet. He looked at the floor. He was standing in a foot of water. Bits of flotsam washed past.

Running from the hall, he headed for the living room. When he entered the smell of the sea was overpowering. Damp patches had formed on the walls and ceiling. Algae grew there, rapidly spreading in circles of green. It was forming patterns.

Something crunched under his foot. He looked down. It was a seashell. He scanned the floor and realised it was littered with them. But they weren't scattered randomly. They formed shapes. They spelled out words. They asked the question, "Why did you do it?" He looked back at the walls. The algae patterns queried him likewise, "Why did you do it?"

Kevin ran into the bedroom. The trail of sand had mutated into a mound. A cross of driftwood protruded from it. There were words etched into it. It said, "Karen R.I.P." Something moved beneath it.

Kevin turned and ran back out. The bathroom. There was a window there. He could escape from there.

He opened the door. He regretted it instantly. The floor was littered with the corpses of various sea creatures. Something with tentacles. A half formed jellyfish. The skeletal remains of fish.

The bath was full again too. And something was rising from it. As the water was shed from its form, Kevin could see what it was. The severed head had found a body. It was an amalgam of molluscs, anemones and clams. Its serpentine limbs were half flesh half seaweed. Kevin ran out and locked the door behind him.

The trunk. There might be a weapon in there. On a haunch, he took the small key from his pocket and ran over to it. He placed it in the lock and turned it.

Behind him he heard the combined thumping on the bathroom and bedroom doors.

The chest lid opened. He rummaged inside. To his dismay there was nothing there but some old photograph in a dusty frame. He tossed it aside, breaking the glass.

Suddenly there was the snapping of wood. Spinning around, he saw the mollusc man standing before him. His seaweed arms flailed the air.

Then the bedroom door shattered. Through it came a woman. At least something that used to be a woman. It looked female because it wore a dress. But the mimicry soon ended when the dress burst open. Where her breasts should have been there were two mounds of squirming maggots. Now unclothed, the writhing mass spilled on to the floor. The facade over, it stood there a naked skeleton.

"What the hell do you want with me?" screamed Kevin, tears now welling up in his eyes.

"Why did you do it?" asked the mollusc man.

"Why?" said the skeleton woman.

"It wasn't me. Whatever it was, it wasn't me. I don't know what you're talking about." Sobbed Kevin, backing away.

He turned to run but slipped on something. It was a fish, still alive and flapping. By the time Kevin had got up he had been grabbed. The man held him by the hair, the woman by the neck.

That was it, thought Kevin. They had him and now they were going to kill him. Bizarrely, however, the mollusc man was holding up the old newspaper with his other hand.

"Why?" he said, and thrust it up in front of Kevin's face.

Kevin had no choice but to look at what was in front of him. The Story read:

"The bodies of Mr Brian Vance and his wife, Karen, were discovered today outside their beach house. Mr Vance had been decapitated, his head thrown into the sea. Mrs Vance had been buried alive on the beach. Their son, Mike, has been arrested.

Doctor Larry Kelvin who has been examining him said he was suffering from multiple personality disorder, probably exacerbated by extreme heat."

"My God Mike killed his own parents. He murdered them.

"Why?" persisted the female, and lifted a photo to Kevin's face. It was the one he had broken earlier.

It was a photo of a middle-aged man and woman and a male of

about twenty.

The skeletal hand turned it over.

An inscription on the back read, "Mum and dad with Mike."

"Why?" hissed the woman.

Kevin looked again at the photo. Mollusc man and skeletal woman; they were Mike's dead parents.

"Jesus, I don't know why he killed you. I hardly know him."

The thing that had once been Mr Vance growled and grabbed his hair more tightly. He dragged him over to the wall. There was a mirror hanging there. He twisted Kevin's head and made him look into it.

For a second, Kevin struggled but Mr Vance's grip was strong. He had no choice but to look. Meanwhile, Mrs Vance had thrust the photo back up to his face.

Then it hit him. He looked at his reflection. He looked at the photo. Reflection. Photo. Reflection. Photo. Kevin Mace. Mike Vance. His whole identity suddenly shattered like a million glass fragments. He wasn't Kevin Mace. Kevin Mace didn't exist. He was Mike Vance.

With revelation came the memories. That summer's day a year ago. A blazing sun. The heat. The ever-increasing heat.

They had asked him to fix the sign on the veranda. One of the chains had snapped. He had snapped with it.

He saw it all now. His father screaming as he brought the axe down upon his neck. His mother's eyes, blue and tear-filled, the image of a burning sun reflecting in them as he kicked the last of the sand over her head.

The tears came and he reached out.

"It was the heat, mum. Dad, it was the heat."

The next day the city awoke to the usual assortment of disaster and mayhem. Radios everywhere told the same, old news. A well-spoken newscaster told the latest.

"The body of Dr Larry Kelvin was discovered in the boot of his car. The car, a silver BMW, was found outside the beach house of one of his escaped patients Mr Mike Vance. The body of Mr Vance, chief suspect in the case, was found inside. Sand was found in the mouth of his severed head and covering his torso suggesting he was buried alive before his head was removed with an axe. There are no suspects, at present, in the case of Mr Vance's murder.

"And now the weather. Yesterday's heat wave seems to be over. Today will be dull and cloudy with no forecast of sunshine at all."

# OBJECTS
## Gary Allen

He wakened with a jump, could feel her warm beside him. After a few moments, he heaved himself over and lay on his back. She was sitting with a pillow propped behind her, reading a thick paperback novel that she held in one hand. She didn't look at him. Her eyes quickly read to the bottom of the page, then she set the book in her lap and reached over to the bedside cabinet for her tobacco and matches. The box dropped from her fingers to the floor, and she had to stretch out of bed to reach them. As she flung herself back, one heavy breast fell out of the baggy shirt she was wearing. With one hand she put it back, then she rolled a cigarette – the smoke leaving him nauseated – and took up her book again.

He jumped up and swung his legs out of bed, then he sat for a while until his head stopped swimming. Behind him he could sense her huffily rearranging the bedclothes back around her legs. He walked over to the chair where his clothes lay in a pile, and quickly dressed. She was still reading, the book now lying in her lap, her head bent and the dyed hair hanging over her face. He pulled aside the curtains covering the large bay window, looked out upon the late morning.

It was dull. A day heavy with massed clouds and the promise of rain. In the garden below, the hippies, who occupied the room beneath them, were playing with a saucer object. It rose in the air, then fell back to the outstretched hands. Beyond the garden lay what he knew to be the sea, now a dark reflection of the clouds. The appearance and reappearance of the bright coloured objects from the garden irritated him, so he let the curtain fall closed again.

He hadn't particularly wanted to come, and things were only made worse by the claustrophobic seaside-resort with its out-of-season people, its sand, its ring of mountains, and dreary weather.

Picking up his coat, he put it on. Without looking at her he mumbled, 'I'm going out for some cigarettes.'

Surlily, and without looking up from her book, she said, 'There's roll-ups here.'

'I know,' he sighed, 'but I'm going out for a real packet of fags, alright?' and without waiting for a reply he opened the door and went out, down the stairs and past the hippies who were only larking about half-heartedly now.

He walked along the street, passing the hotel that had been bombed several seasons before – the walls still standing, the windows empty and rimmed with black – then along the seafront. The rain began to fall heavy and steady, so the first shop he came to he went in and bought a packet of cigarettes, his eyes avoiding the cartoon-postcards, buckets and spades, plastic swords and water-rings.

He took out a cigarette and smoked it as he hurried back along the seafront, passing old men rushing towards the hotels and nursing homes with their morning papers.

When he reached the house the rain had eased. The hippies had gone inside, but had left the object in the garden. He took it, crossed the road and narrow strip of pebbles, threw it into the sea.

Neither of them spoke much, and when they did it was just terse commands for a cigarette, the time, or a drink of milk. He was slouched on the seat, his hands pushed deep into the pockets of his coat, his chin tucked into the collar, resting on his chest, as though he were trying to hide. She sat up straight on the bench, a little distance from him, staring in front of her smoking a rolled cigarette: he sighed, hunched farther into his coat.

They had been sitting in the shelter like this for almost an hour. When he had got back to the house, she was already up and dressed. For breakfast she had bought a small loaf, some cheese and milk, and brought it to the shelter where she took from her cord-bag a kitchen-knife and a tub of margarine, and made sandwiches.

'Let's get something hot to drink,' she said as she put the objects back into her bag.

He followed her out the shelter, towards the town.

The café stood overlooking the sea. She pushed open the door and went in, and he quietly followed. A few couples of various ages were in the enclosures along a wall that was almost completely glass and faced the sea. A few old people sat in the middle of the room sipping their coffees, staring over the rims of the cups. They walked to a table near the door and sat down. As they waited to be served she set her bag on the table and fumbled inside for her tobacco and matches.

The proprietor came over, her notebook and shortened pencil at the ready. She was a middle-aged woman with dark, shaggy hair and Spanish-looking features. He couldn't understand why he was staring at her until suddenly he realized that the one side of her face had a subtle deformity – the eye and corner of the mouth slightly crooked.

'I'll have a cup of coffee.' He heard Jean say.

Looking away form the proprietor's face he mumbled that he would have coffee as well. When she had written down their order and walked away he offered Jean one of his cigarettes and then asked if she had noticed the woman's face?

'It wasn't that bad,' she answered, then she began to tell him about a friend of hers who had been kicked by a horse, the right side of her face completely shattered: he wasn't listening, watching the woman busy behind the glass-counter.

When the coffee was brought he turned his head away and looked at the sea until she was gone. It was lukewarm, and although Jean complained to him, he didn't want to make a fuss, so they drank the distasteful stuff in silence.

He glanced around the café at the other couples who were talking and eating, an except one middle-aged couple who sat silently, she staring through her butterfly-rimmed glasses at the sea, he at his hands resting on the table, as though he were reading them. They had always talked patronizingly about couples who sat in pubs or cafes, or other public places, without speaking to one another – and then he realized that Jean had stopped talking.

He looked at her as she stood, took her bag and walked towards the door. He got up too, irritated by her behaviour, by the cups of half-drunk coffee. The man he had been watching lifted his eyes from his hands and looked at them as they left.

The rain had stopped. They walked across the damp sand down to the edge of the sea. She walked a little distance in front of him, her head bent in the wind, her eyes scanning the sand. Now and then she would lift her head and look around her.

She had stopped and was standing with her hands in her pockets, slightly stooped over, looking at something. When he came close he saw that it was a seagull. He thought at first that it was dead, but then it began to jerk and convulse, to vomit onto the sand.

'It must have swallowed something,' she whined, 'What will we do?' and she looked around the deserted beach, then she glared fiercely at him and shouted, 'Well, do something.'

He stood watching the dying bird, trying to control his anger.

'We'll have to end its suffering somehow,' she mumbled, more to herself, as she searched about her until she found a piece of driftwood, then she raised it and brought it down upon the bird's head.

He lunged forward and caught her arm just as she was about to strike again. She looked at him with astonishment. He wrenched the wood from her grip and threw it far behind him. She stumbled back, then stormed off in the direction of the town.

The gull was barely alive. He looked down at it and the whole world turned in his stomach. He lifted it, and with ease and expertise, wrung it neck, then he flung its body as far into the green waves as he could.

It was an old pub, built at the end of the last century. He had been there for some time, aware of the darkness that had crept down from the mountains lying beyond the frosted glass. He couldn't remember how many glasses of whiskey he had drank, but he knew that he had had enough.

Outside, he tried to sober-up a bit in the chilly night air. He thought of Jean lying in bed, reading her paperback novel, rolling cigarettes – and he felt no regret. He smoked a cigarette, and softly whistled an old tune as he waited for the last bus home.

# CORPORATE BONDING
## Niall McGrath

This was it – paradise! Dolores had definitely arrived, she confirmed to her grinning reflection in the mirror as she surveyed her luxurious hotel room from the balcony doorway. The plane delay and flight had been stifling, boring, stressful, but worth it, well worth *this*.

A warm breeze from the shore troubled Dolores' long fair hair as horns honked and the wail of traffic and chatter of night-lifers ebbed up from the avenues. The click-clicking of cicadas reverberated from exotic gardens, the scent of palm and fern wafted intoxicatingly. There was a buzz about Monaco that was already intoxicating.

In the vase on the table beside her, a single bird of paradise flower stood proudly, its orange beak and stiff green plumage giving the room a surreal touch. Dolores lifted the bottle from the cooler bucket with a scrunch of melting ice and hugged the soaking, freezing glass when she deciphered the italic script: *champagne*.

Dolores removed a tissue from around a tall, slender glass and winced as she uncorked the bottle. The muted pop didn't prevent a gush of bubbles from cascading from the neck. She poured herself some of the frothing champagne and took a long, cool sip.

Dolores threw herself on the huge bed and dialled home. Jim was in.

"We got here late," she told him.

"What's it like?"

"Brilliant! Oh, Jim, you should see the room! These exquisite little lamps, the smoothness of the furniture, and this magnificent view! I can't wait to see it in daylight tomorrow. I can make out the palace, the Casino's all lit up, and there's the silhouette of the rock..."

"Great. I'd some craic today." He was off, rattling on about work. Dolores held the receiver to her ear as she sipped the champagne. At last, he paused.

"Well, sure you can tell me more when I get back. We've got a meeting now."

"At this time of night?"

"Well, we are late. And it's about tomorrow's agenda. I love ya, bye."

Dolores had worried about leaving Jim for the first time in six years. But then the stories some of the managers at work had told, of them leaving their sticks in the clubhouse lockers back home, not even taking them with them on their 'golfing' trips to Portugal, made her think men liked a wee break from their partners, too. But what did they do? she wondered. Drink and talk – talk about *what*? Football, cars?

There was a knock at the door. Dolores rushed to open it. It was the boss, Hilary, in a fresh frock. Her eyes glinted gaily behind her pebble specs; the mouth spread across her face, framed as it was by that business-like, pudding bowl hairstyle, into Hilary's recognisable, cheeky grin.

"Well, Dolores, do you believe it now?"

"It's still not quite sunk in yet," she replied with an excited waver in her voice.

"The good life *does* exist," Hilary assured Dolores. "This is it, here. And it's ours to enjoy. Come on downstairs with the others. Let's have some fun!" Hilary urged in that gritty Northern accent.

Dolores glided down the wide, curving marble-railed staircase from the first floor to the entrance foyer with a sense of excitement so palpable it was like a second skin she'd spontaneously grown. Dolores and Hilary met the others in the bar. That quiet, dishy young bloke Jared was passing around glasses of champagne. He knew how to dress trendily, Dolores noted.

"Ladies and gentlemen, just one quick formal word." Hilary raised her glass with her voice. "Continental breakfast is available from six till nine. We meet nine thirty in the Grimaldi Suite for the team building exercises."

A shared groan.

"Don't worry, it'll be fun! That's all the announcements – except – congratulations on your outstanding performance this year, and enjoy your well-earned stay here. You're all 'Simply the Best'!"

"Imagine Jared getting here," said Naomi.

"Why do you say that?" Dolores asked, sidling from the group with her dumpy, ginger-mopped compatriot.

"He's so *new*. Only been in eight months."

"But he got the sales. He's got a flair for it."

"Those lot are off to the Casino. Let's join them."

The Casino Royale was much vaster than Dolores had imagined, basing her ideas on movie clips. And much noisier. Everywhere chips clacked, a gallery of one-armed bandits punctuated the air with electronic blips, bell-rings and gargles, while the cacophony of punters' conversations created an aural pandemonium.

Her workmates all got chips and headed for the roulette wheel. Someone handed Dolores a glass of Martini. It tasted bittersweet, but she persevered with it as they placed their bets on the first spin.

Black nine! In an instant, a croupier was sliding additional chips Dolores' way! She must be on a winning streak, she thought – first this trip, then success in the Casino. They all placed bets again. Red fourteen – her number came up again!

"Whoa! This lady's something else!" purred a tuxedoed dude beside her. When he smiled, his blue eyes sparkled like gems.

Dolores felt Naomi tugging her skirt. "That's Sonny Lehman, the Formula One racing driver!"

Now Dolores recognised the former World Champion. Of course, he lived here in tax exile. He was with a scraggly haired, moustachioed, bald-headed man who also seemed vaguely familiar.

"This is my pal Errol!" Lehman introduced them.

"Gan-gyah! Gan-gyah!" the weirdo greeted, offering a spliff, which she refused.

As they watched the roulette wheel intently, Dolores felt Errol's clammy huge paw resting casually on her shoulder. She extricated herself from his grasp.

"He's the lead singer of that rap group that was big a few years ago," Naomi whispered, seeing that Dolores was mystified.

Black thirteen – no one won.

"Aw, poor blondie!" Sonny commiserated with her. "Another drink?"

They offered their chips to the altar of fortune a few more times.

Their newfound friends chattered away about their Ferraris, yachts and holes-in-one. Dolores and Naomi nodded from time to time, expressed interest half-heartedly, sipping at their drinks as the roulette wheel ignored their prayers.

"Oh, hi, girls!" Errol chirped.

Two leggy young women, with figures that insisted they could only be models and wearing flimsily cut evening dresses were prancing towards the bourbon swigging stars. Watching the two men cavort with the models brought home to Dolores just how drunk they were. They were slurring their speech, and even Sonny's eyes were veined red.

"Come on, let's slip away while they're distracted," Dolores tugged at Naomi's arm.

Naomi followed, but then asked, "Why go? They're interesting fellows."

"How many have you had?"

"Less than you."

"I've only had one vodka!" Dolores objected as they reached the front steps.

"Jared got you one, or was that a Martini? And Sonny definitely got you one..."

"Bloody hell, it's nearly one!"

"Here's a taxi!" Naomi screeched ear-splittingly.

The ride back to the hotel was a blur amid the darkness of the neon-lit streets. Dolores noticed chubby-faced young lads stepping gingerly along the pavements, while beautiful girls swayed in couples or in gangs - how innocent they seemed; and suddenly she felt... *mature*.

When Naomi said goodnight at the elevator and Dolores made her way to her room alone, suddenly the silence engulfed her. Slightly dizzy, she lay with the light on for a long time, sweaty, wanting to sleep she was so exhausted, but unable to do so. She tried a cold shower and drinking water, but still the night's humidity disturbed her.

She flicked on the TV without any sound and stared at a B movie for a while, changed channels from sport to CNN to comedy classic repeat, back to the movie. She wondered should she phone Jim, but it was three am, four am, five thirty, he had to work in the morning, she couldn't really be bothered. At last, Dolores dozed off for a few hours.

She took a long bubble bath and made it in time for an unwelcome breakfast as her stomach churned.

At the breakfast table Naomi was chirpy, despite her previous night's session. Dolores felt reassured by the grogginess of several of the others, though tried to hide her inner malaise as much as possible.

"All ready for the team-building?" Hilary intoned affirmatively.

Dolores just wanted to go and lie in bed, but knew if she did so she would feel just as uncomfortable as she did now. I'll have a wee rest at lunchtime, she comforted herself.

The conference room swept round in an oval shape. The furniture was sheer, shiny top quality mahogany. Dolores poured herself glass after glass of orange juice and water from the jugs before them, sipping incessantly.

Following Hilary's preamble, their first task was introduced to them. They were split into teams and given a box of Lego each. Their task was to construct a bridge of a certain span in a set time. Dolores groaned as her team-mates gathered around the table to work frantically against the clock. She couldn't even sit down, though her legs felt weak. Jared suggested some clever features and their team soon proudly displayed a craftily built bridge.

Once the bridges were built the torture wasn't over. They had to reduce the number of bricks they had used and calculate a bidding price for the contract, specifying time and penalties for additional bricks they might use or time they might take.

So they laboured. Naomi and Dolores were trying to do the calculations. Her head was numb, Dolores could hardly concentrate, but she was sober enough to know Naomi was talking bull.

"*This* is they way we do it," Dolores snapped.

"I'm only trying to help," Naomi defended herself.

"That's it, take charge," Hilary jested as she circled the room.

"Everyone's contributing splendidly," Jared tried to ease the atmosphere between them.

Their next assignment was 'The Indivisible Load'. A convoy of wagons would have to transport huge power station components from the port to the power station. There were railway lines, with train times, to negotiate, and bridges. Which route and which size of wagons would be best? More calculations! Dolores excused herself and headed off to the ladies.

She discovered her rumbling tummy had decided to explode. Someone banged the door of the cubicle beside her. How embarrassing! But they were soon making the same awful noises. Dolores took a fit of giggling. She tried to stifle it at first, but then she heard the other person giggling, too.

"Is that Dolores?"

"Jenni?"

"I recognised your laugh! Have you got the heebie-jeebies, too?"

They tittered conspiratorially.

When they returned to their teams, the comments flew. "Were you two spying on each others' solutions? It's corporate espionage!"

"I can't get my head round that stuff at all!" Jenni confessed to the amused group.

"Back in time for a coffee break," Jared teased them.

Dolores determined to make an effort in their third and final exercise. This time, they were assigned to a team leader who gave them a task: to construct a Mars landing vehicle on their table from certain pieces of equipment. Dolores suggested various connections. Her team leader, Martin, abrasively dismissed her ideas. As they were completing the task, Dolores was giving the responsibility of naming the vehicle.

"Mars Rover?" she ha-hummed.

"Too bland," Martin dismissed.

"Red Rocket," John chipped in.

"No. Anyway, it's Dolores' task. Come on," he snapped at her like a fierce school master, "we're running out of time."

"I can't think of anything," she moaned.

"This isn't good enough."

Indignantly, she told Martin, "I've got it. The Mars-raker. As in

Moon-raker."

"Pathetic. We'll have to call it Martin's Martian Explorer."

"You cheeky bastard!" Dolores exploded at him. "You ungrateful, pig-headed…"

The group were roaring with laughter. Dolores didn't care, she was livid. "I don't know what you lot are amused by, he's been a brute to this team!"

"It's all an act," Hilary soothed.

"No, he's always like this, especially to me."

"I am the authoritarian type of manager," Martin tried to explain. "And Sally was the democratic one, involving his team. And Jared was the laisse-faire type."

"But there's more to it than that," Dolores went on, unconvinced though the penny was dropping. Suddenly, she was fighting to recover her dignity.

"Watch out, Martin," Jared took the heat off Dolores, "or we'll have the union onto you."

Lunchtime at last! They filed into the dining room.

Seafood platters, even oysters, salads, quiches, an exquisite array of the finest Mediterranean cuisine. Dolores had a little carrot and coriander broth and French bread – which helped to smother the raging volcano within her belly.

Hilary explained the choice of sightseeing trips on offer. Although she was tired, Dolores wanted to see as much as she could, decided she could rest later. She raced to her room to get the francs for the coach trip she was interested in. But her purse was less abundant than she had imagined. Did she really waste that much in the Casino last night? She found her credit card, safely tucked away for emergencies, but noticed the expiry date was last month. Of course, a new one had been sent, she'd put it away in the drawer, had forgotten to check which one to bring!

Naomi arrived at her door.

"I'm not going," Dolores announced. "I'll lie on the beach and read my book."

Dolores grabbed her beach bag and met the others downstairs. She went with Hilary, Nadine, Terry, Frank and Emma. Dolores noticed Naomi, Jared and others boarding their coach. She pursed her lip regretfully, wishing she were going with them. But the sun was high in the late summer sky, the clouds were small and wispy; the afternoon heat embraced them all with unconditional favour. As soon as she reached the beach, Dolores' good spirits revived.

At the beach was a mix of European nationalities. Two lithe German girls near them, who were sunbathing topless, peeled off their bikini briefs, right there in front of everyone, and slipped on a new pair, so they could trot into the ocean and splash about. Within a few moments, they were back at their loungers, peeling off the wet briefs, drying themselves with their towels and putting on the dry briefs so they could sunbathe again.

Terry and Frank shared mischievous, knowing nods with Dolores on seeing the athletic girls' antics. The two blokes went for a swim themselves in the gently lapping sea. Their whoops of delight amused Dolores, Hilary, Nadine and Emma as they relaxed on their sun beds. Dolores smoothed cream on her exposed arms, legs and torso. She lay on her back, dropping her shades over her eyes. Soon, her mind vortexed into sleep.

She turned over onto her stomach for a moment, waiting for her skin to warm before reaching for the lotion. The next thing she knew, Dolores was shivering. A bank of cloud had appeared over the coastline and hidden the sun. She asked Emma to rub cream onto her back for her as the sun reappeared. Settling down for a little longer, Dolores' head swam once more.

"Come on, lazybones, time for dinner!" Nadine woke her some time later.

After another steamy bath in her room, Dolores realised that she felt better. The tiredness that had dogged her earlier had gone. She extracted her formal dress from its protective suit-cover and slithered into it. She applied make-up and lipstick at the mirror by the bed – that huge, empty, tempting bed that made her thoughts stray.

She was back at work, reliving the meeting they had gone to. Hilary had brought the head of human resources over from head office for a debate on staff's future expectations. Dolores had pen and notebook at the ready.

"Martin, do you think this is a fun company to work for?"

"Well, sure, there should be banter to an extent. But you've got to draw the line somewhere, business has to be professionally conducted."

"Do you think it'll be fun doing team-building exercises in Monte Carlo? Because you are all 'Simply the Best', this year's star performers and that's where you're going next month on an all-expenses paid trip!"

Dolores sat dumbfounded as they all began to clap. Hilary's ruse had worked.

"May I just say," Jared piped up cheekily, "what a *wonderful* company this is to work for!"

Dolores had noticed him looking across the open plan floor space at her from time to time, or sitting at a table in the canteen with his team. It was shortly after the surprise prize win announcement that Jared had spoken to her for the first time. At the coffee machine. It was late afternoon. She was dumping a plastic cup in the recycling bin. He was waiting for a cup of tea to descend from the machine. Yawning.

"It's alright for some," he had said to her. Instantly, she was aware that a ripple of anticipation had undulated through her whole body, hoped to God he couldn't notice.

"I'm off out now," she had responded, inwardly fearing she had sounded too abrupt. To the cinema, with Jim, actually. As usual.

Blinking hard, inspecting her lipstick in the hotel room mirror, Dolores sighed. What will be will be, she tried to reassure herself, as she got up to go to dinner.

It was a formal gala dinner, all the guys were wearing tuxes, the ladies were immaculate in their new gowns. Dolores deliberately avoided over-indulging, only sipped one glass of wine with her meal.

"So," Hilary wound up the dinner, "enjoy the bar and I hope you all return home refreshed, convinced it's fun to work for this company!"

It was as she was getting up that Dolores noticed the backs of her knees were sore.

"Your back's all red," Jared announced.

"Ohh!" Dolores moaned.

"I noticed a late-night pharmacy up the road, they'll have some cream. Come on," Jared came to the rescue.

Dolores went out into the thronging streets with him.

"Is it sore to walk?" he asked.

"Not too bad," she hissed as her limbs ached.

They found the pharmacy, which was just closing, and Dolores struggled with the local language to explain what she wanted. On the way back, Dolores found herself chatting with Jared as if they had known each other forever. At the hotel, they went towards the elevator.

"I can't reach my back myself."

They went up in the lift in silence.

At her door, as Dolores swiped the keycard, Jared examined the tube of cream.

"They've given you the wrong stuff! This is anti-sunburn shampoo! Naomi might have some cream, she was using it earlier. I'll just nip down and see."

Dolores went into her room and sat on the edge of the bed. She stared at the phone on the table for a long time. Shadows were dancing around the walls like butterflies, cast by the glints of traffic headlights below. Dolores caught a glimpse of her intense expression in the mirror. There was a rap on the door.

Dolores walked slowly across the deep-pile carpet. When she opened the door, she was surprised to find Naomi grinning at her. Jared was at her shoulder.

"Need some relief?" Naomi sang, waving a half-squeezed tube.

Dolores was enraged – she hadn't time just now for this bubbly woman. Still, Dolores submitted herself on the bed to Naomi's gentle hands. As the lotion cooled and soothed her raw flesh, Dolores' mood relaxed also.

"That's great, Naomi, really lovely!"

"How was the beach, anyway? Apart from this!"

Dolores told them how Frank's and Terry's eyes had nearly popped out of their heads when they'd seen the German girls swimming routine.

"What about you, Jared?" Naomi asked. "Aren't you tempted by the fleshpots of Monte Carlo?"

Jared was on the big bed, leaning against the headboard. "Well," his cheeks reddened, "Sure, any guy would be tempted by such things. But right now?" he shook his head. "I just think how upset my fiancée would be."

Dolores started – a roughness in the linen had pricked her tender skin.

"What if she didn't know?" Naomi pressed him.

Jared shook his head. "*I'd* know."

"That's what they all say," Dolores muttered sleepily.

"I think you're ready for the sack," Naomi said.

Jared hopped off the bed. "I definitely am. See you in the morning!"

Naomi added her goodnights and they both left.

Dolores lay on her stomach for a while, before sitting up to switch on the kettle. As she waited for the water to boil, she caught a glimpse of herself in the mirror once more – and was surprised by the unwrinkled brow.

She seized the phone and dialled home. Jim, Jim! Her mind was chiming impatiently, wholeheartedly. The tone rang and rang. The answer machine clicked and Dolores heard that neutral voice delivering its spiel.

# THE BED BUGS BITE
## James Meredith

They were in the woods somewhere, hunting him. He mustn't get caught. If he was they'd push his face into the nettles again. That's what the Japs used to do to their prisoners during the war. So Willy said anyways.

But he was a Commando and he wouldn't let himself be caught, not this time. Commandos were brave, they were the good guys. He could never understand why Willy and Tonto always wanted to be the Japs. Everybody knew that they'd got beat in the war. The Americans dropped a big bomb on them, and then they gave up. The Japs were evil too. Tonto's Uncle Jamesy was in the war and got captured by them. They made him build this bridge out in the jungle somewhere – he'd seen a film about it – and didn't give him anything to eat except spiders and insects and other creepy crawlies. He'd nearly died.

Geordie kept still and listened. He was hiding behind a chestnut tree near the clearing where the big fellas went every night to drink cider. He could see the burnt grass where they lit their fires and in the branches above his head a blue plastic bag fluttered like a flag in the wind.

He could hear Willy and Tonto nearby, on the path that led from the ruins of the old Curran house through the glen down to the main road. They were singing. Singing a song about him.

"Geordie Moore, you can't run far, you wear frilly knickers and a lacy bra." It was supposed to be a song about Geordie Best, but they'd changed it and sung it about him. It wasn't funny, but they still sang it.

Anyways his Da told him Geordie Best never wore women's clothes. He'd been called after Besty. His Da said he was the best footballer in the world ever and he used to play for the Man United who were the best team in the world ever. Tonto said Man United were rubbish and they couldn't be the best 'cause they were in the second division and Liverpool, who Tonto and his Da supported, were in the first. Geordie didn't know about that, all he knew was his Da loved Man United and so did he.

Geordie peered out from behind the tree, trying not to make any noise. The dry brown leaves beneath his gutties crackled like an empty crisp packet scrunched up and thrown in the bin. He held his breath.

He could see Willy and Tonto on the path. They were both carrying sticks like rifles, the way the soldiers did in town, like they were cradling babies. Willy was walking in front, still singing, with Tonto behind him walking backwards and checking the bushes for movement. They were moving towards the clearing and Geordie knew if he stayed where he was they'd find him.

He had to move. He thought about heading across to the river on the other side of the clearing and creeping along its bank until he got to the bridge. He could hide underneath it. But if they caught him there they'd throw bricks down into the water and soak his clothes. They'd done that one time before and his Ma had given him a real hiding for getting all wet and muddy.

The only other way he could go was past the red tree and on down to the main road. He didn't want to go that way either. The red tree was haunted. A girl who used to live in the Curran house had been murdered there one night years ago. She was stabbed hundreds of times and then her head had been chopped off and stuck on one of the branches and her ghost was supposed to haunt the place looking for her head and the bark of the tree had turned red with all the blood that had soaked into it when she was killed. Geordie didn't believe the story when Tonto had first told him it but his Ma said that it was true. It had happened when she was a little girl and she said that she was never allowed to go near the glen by Geordie's Granny because of it.

It had to be the river then. He'd rather get a soaking than be chased by a ghost any day.

Geordie backed away from the tree trying hard not to make any noise. The river wasn't too far away. He could hear the cool gurgle of the running water on the other side of the clearing as it flowed down into the Lough. He turned and began creeping slowly towards the sound, moving in a crouch to avoid snagging his clothes on the overhanging branches. He stepped on a dry twig. It made a sound like gunfire. He froze. Willy stopped singing. Geordie held his breath.

Willy and Tonto were talking now. They had heard something but they weren't sure which direction the noise had come from.

Then they started moving again. He had to take a chance. If he ran they would hear and come chasing after him. He was a fast runner. His Da said he would make a good winger when he got older but he had to learn how to kick the ball with both feet.

Geordie was sure they would catch him when he got to the river. Willy and Tonto knew he was scared of the water. Even though it was shallow they knew he wouldn't dare wade across it to escape. Anyways his Ma would kill him if he got all wet again.

Then he saw the cider bottle. It was on the ground near a bush where one of the big fellas must've thrown it. Geordie reached over and picked it up. It was heavy enough. He turned and threw the bottle as far as he could in the opposite direction from where he wanted to run. It hit the side of a tree a good distance away and crashed down through its branches. He heard Willy shout at Tonto and saw them run in the direction of the noise, Tonto whooping and screaming like a Red Indian. Geordie turned and ran as fast as he could toward the river, lifting his legs high and pumping his arms at his side the way his Da had taught him.

He knew that they might hear him or see him as he ran but he didn't think of that, he just thought about getting to the river as fast as he could and heading up towards the bridge. If he could get to the bridge he could climb up onto it and then run home, up the path from the glen into the estate and then into his house. He knew that would be cheating on the game but he didn't want to be pushed into the nettles again.

He was nearly there. He was already on the other side of the clearing. He could see the bank of the river beyond the long grass. He lifted his legs higher, pumped his arms faster and tried to breath through his nose.

He made it.

Geordie looked behind him to see if Willy and Tonto were following. He couldn't see or hear anything except his own breath and a ringing in his ears. His lungs burned. He'd got away.

Then he saw the body.

It was floating near the bank, one of its legs tangled in the weeds that grew there. The dark blue denim of the body's jacket and jeans was stained black with wetness and the long hair of the head danced in the current like a large hairy spider.

Geordie stood staring, breathless. It was a man, he could tell that much. His hands were tied behind his back with blue rope and there was a hole in the sole of one of his Oxford boots.

The ringing in Geordie's ears stopped and all he could hear was the river and all he could see was the body.

Geordie moved slowly towards the bank of the river. He got down on his hands and knees and leaned over until his face was nearly touching the water. He reached out and touched the sole of the boot with the hole in it, then pulled his hand away. He stood back up and looked around him. He went to a nearby tree and snapped off a branch, then returned to the bank. He poked at the body with the stick. He poked and prodded. At last he managed to work the stick into the blue rope that bound the hands of the body. He pulled it slowly towards the bank. Geordie got down on his hands and knees again and leaned over. He took a deep breath and held it. He reached out and took hold of the wet black collar of the denim jacket with both his hands. He pulled hard at the jacket and let out his breath. The body turned easily in the water. Geordie stared down at the white bloated face of the man and the dark hole in the centre of his forehead.

Tonto and Willy came running when they heard the scream. At first they didn't see the body. They ran up to Geordie and Tonto grabbed him and told him he was their prisoner. He didn't say anything. Then Willy noticed the wet black stain on the front of Geordie's jeans and laughed and called him pissy pants. He stopped laughing when he saw the body.

Geordie was standing alone by the bank of the river. It was starting to go dark. The streetlights up in the estate had come on and it was getting colder. He began to shiver.

Geordie wanted to go home but his legs refused to move. He wasn't sure how long he had been standing there, staring at the body and feeling cold. Willy and Tonto had run off and it was quiet now except for the soft gurgle of the black water as it flowed down into the Lough.

Then he heard voices in the clearing behind him. Geordie turned and saw Willy and Tonto, shouting with excitement, leading people toward him. An old man with a dog on a lead came and stood beside him and asked him if he was all right. Two big fellas stood at the edge of the bank, nodding their heads and talking softly, lighting up cigarettes as they stared at the body. Then Geordie saw his Ma coming across the clearing, crying out to him. Something inside him let go and then he was in her arms, burying his head in her soft bosom and crying muffled tears of relief. His Ma was crying too, calling him her wee baby, her poor child, cradling the back of his head in her strong hands. Geordie felt he was safe now.

He was back in the house. His Ma had changed him out of his wet jeans and run a bath for him. He stood naked and shivering in the bathroom watching the steam rise from the water. He didn't want to get in. He started crying.

Geordie sat on the toilet seat wrapped in a warm white towel. He was listening to the murmur of his Ma and Da talking downstairs. His Da had just come home from work. There was a knock at the front door and Geordie heard his Da going to open it and talking to someone. Then there were footsteps on the stairs and a rap on the bathroom door. It was his Da. The police were downstairs. They wanted to talk to Geordie about finding the body. He went into his room and changed into his jammies, then went downstairs into the living room and sat on the sofa. The policemen asked him about the body. He told them how he had found it. One of the policemen wrote what he said down in a small black book. They asked him if he had touched the body. He told them he hadn't. They said they might have to come back the next day and ask him some more questions.

When they were gone his Ma made him some soup and he sat in front of the TV watching the news. The old man with the dog was talking about the body and Geordie saw Tonto and Willy in the background laughing and waving at the camera.

His Ma wouldn't let him go out that night. He bet Tonto and Willy were allowed to go out. They'd probably be down in the woods telling all the big fellas about how they found the body, taking all the credit for it. They probably got to have some cider and got to stand around listening to whatever it was the big fellas talked about. He knew that night they would be talking about the body. The body was Joey Murdock who lived at the top of the estate. He was eighteen and he used to stand around the fire as well, laughing and talking about whatever it was the big fellas talked about. Geordie hoped that Tonto and Willy would drink too much cider and be sick.

He spent the evening in his room, looking out his window at the faint glow of the fire down in the blackness of the glen. His Ma came up later to make sure he said his prayers and to tuck him into bed. She kissed him goodnight, brushing the hair from his forehead and planting a soft kiss there, then whispered the same words into his ear that she said every night, "Night night, sleep tight, don't let the bed bugs bite."

Geordie lay in bed and pretended he was dead. He lay on his front and crossed his hands at the base of his back, his head pushed down into the pillow, his eyes shut tight. He imagined death as a cold and watery place where everyone floated in a cold black sea and the shore remained always just out of reach. Geordie slept and his dreams were cold and wet.

# THIS LIFE
*from a work in progress*
## John McAllister

Jimmy and Doc were brothers. They worked as a team from the moment they stood side by side in the headmaster's office wondering why they had been called and what it had to do with the lanky workman who stood in the corner, screwing his cap round and round in his hands.

The headmaster made it as easy for them as possible. Their father was dead.

The Sick was no option for a man determined to educate his sons out of the squalor of working class Belfast life. Jimmy senior had ignored his occasional bouts of breathlessness and gone to work. One moment he was in the middle of Mackies foundry shouting at his mates to heave on a length of steel girder, the next he was lying at their feet.

The headmaster nodded at the workman who stilled his hands. 'Michael Quinn here, brought the word. He also brought your father's last wage packet. They gave you the week even though it's only Wednesday.'

Something boiled up in Jimmy through the pain of his loss. Before he could make sense of his confused feelings Michael Quinn stepped forward and shook his hand. 'I'm sorry for your trouble,' he said.

Jimmy left Everton Secondary School immediately and took a job in Harland and Wolffs as a trainee welder. His mother was already failing and after a few weeks he transferred to the carding room in Ewart's mill so that he could run home at lunchtime and see to things. The neighbours were very good. They tried to help but they had their own problems and eventually everything but the most intimate attention to his mother fell on his shoulders. Mornings were a rush, the evenings filled with doing housework and helping Doc with his homework.

That winter was wet and the compact terrace house became

chronically damp and impossible to heat. Their mother's asthma flared up. Jimmy tried everything including anger to keep her alive but she died with the change of year.

The day after the funeral Jimmy took Doc by the hand and they walked the long miles across the divide and up the Falls Road to the City Cemetery. They stood over a rectangle of mud marked by a simple cross; Jimmy had his arm around Doc's shoulders. Doc muttered something.

'What?' said Jimmy.

Doc said, 'It's a line from Pasternak: Life is not a stroll across a field.'

Jimmy's grip tightened as he swore vengeance on a system that had condemned the two people he loved most to an early grave. But who or what he wasn't sure.

It was nineteen seventy and the Civil Rights Marchers were tramping all over Northern Ireland. They said they were ordinary God-fearing people demanding their civil rights; Jimmy's contacts in the police told him different. They said was the IRA inciting the Catholics into another round of violence.

Jimmy had learned a lot in the intervening years. A short stint in Mackies had ended with him taking a swipe at a line supervisor. The line supervisor was bigger and heavier and knew how to hit. That was Jimmy's first lesson: keep your hands in your pockets until you have sussed the opposition. After that he laboured wherever he could get work, mostly on building sites along Lower Library Street where they were tearing down old housing to put up flats for the Catholics.

That annoyed him: the waste, the dumping of perfectly good building materials. He started coming into work early and leaving late. He used that time to strip Bangor-blue slates off the roofs and stack them in a corner. A chippie tipped him the wink and he collected roof joists as well. When he thought he had enough to make a load he dropped a lorry driver a few bob to run it home for him. Only the wood made it, Craig, the foreman, diverted the slate for his own benefit.

'You young bucks think you know it all,' said Craig when Jimmy went storming in the next morning.

Jimmy kept his hands deep in his pockets and well out of trouble. He said, 'I did it in my own time. It was stuff you were dumping anyway.'

Craig made a point of keeping his hands in sight; they were the size of soup plates. 'That's as maybe.'

'Maybe what?' said Jimmy. He knew a deal in the offing when he saw one.

From then on he spent much of the day retrieving materials for the two of them, him and Craig, to sell on a fifty, fifty basis. He still came in early and left late, and every so often he would have a friend bring over a lorry and they'd load it up with the more valuable items, ones Craig never knew about.

Things worth retrieving kept getting broken. 'I never thought,' someone would say.

'You never thought in your life,' retorted Jimmy.

Then a lorry scattered a load of slate waiting to be collected.

The driver said, 'It shouldn't be there anyway.' He just happened to be holding a wrench in his hand at the time.

Jimmy stabbed a finger. 'I'll see you in the pub after.'

'You and which army?' said the driver. He didn't look unduly worried; he could have made two of Jimmy in any direction.

'Salvation Army,' said Jimmy and went off to think up a strategy. He had calmed down enough to realise that suicide wasn't a reasonable option.

When he got to the pub all of the men from the site were there to see the fun. Jimmy's nose wrinkled at the sour smell of bodies and stale drink. The driver and two equally large friends advanced on him 'You were saying?'

It was a Friday and payday. Jimmy put his wage packet, unopened, on the counter. 'I was saying your money's no good.'

'What's wrong with my money?'

'Give me strength,' said Craig who was there as well. He dumped the driver on a stool and told the barman. 'Give brains here a pint and chaser.'

'Drinks all round,' said Jimmy.

'Good on you, son,' said Craig, and gave Jimmy a big wink. It was all he gave. When the money ran done he excused himself and left.

Every week after that Jimmy put his wages on the bar counter and from then on there were fewer breakages and things were put aside for him to pick up later.

Evenings and weekends Jimmy traded second hand materials out of his backyard. There was always somebody fixing up a room or building a pigeon loft, and not against a bargain. Jimmy sold the wood, well matured yellow pine, at a third of the price of cut white wood from the sawmills, a quarter if the purchaser was willing to take the nails out himself. The Bangor blues had the same sort of discount and he learned to haggle over the rest.

Doc was still at school. Jimmy had everything mapped out for him. 'Sums, there's always an opening for a good clerk.'

Doc shrugged. He was into the school play and existentialism in a big way. He stayed back most evenings to practice and had a photograph of Sartre on the bedroom wall.

Craig got to hear of Jimmy's shop and came visiting the little terrace house. He walked around, mean in his silence, and did a bit of counting on his fingers. Jimmy made a show of unconcern and kept his hands jammed into his trouser pockets and out of trouble.

'I'm impressed,' said Craig, eventually.

He was entitled to be. The shop had grown out of the backyard into the kitchen, and from there into the parlour and one of the bedrooms. Even then it was difficult to get around without moving things.

Craig held his hand out. 'My cut, we must have made quite a bit.'

'You think so?' Jimmy took his hands out of his pockets.

Craig bellied forward, pushing him against a cast iron fireplace. 'Fifty fifty.'

Jimmy's heart was pounding. 'That's not the way I see it.'

'Now look, son.'

Jimmy felt along the wall for something heavy, nothing lethal, something that would take out a few teeth. 'I'm not your son. Back off.'

Craig pushed harder. 'I don't want to be unpleasant.'

A cricket ball whistled past his head. It hit the inner front door and the glass shattered. Doc hefted a second ball.

Jimmy said, 'That's my little brother. He plays cricket for the school and he only misses when he wants to.'

Doc hefted the ball again. Craig backed off. 'It's your last chance. We share or I get myself another partner.'

'I'll pick up my wages Friday,' Jimmy spoke with more bravado than he felt.

'I wouldn't waste the trip.'

Craig left. Jimmy rubbed his back while he buttoned down his despair; good jobs were hard to come by. He looked at Doc. 'You did mean to miss, didn't you?'

'Why?'

Jimmy's laugh had a shake to it. 'I think you'd better come with me on Friday.'

On Friday Jimmy gave Doc a day off school and timed his arrival at the site for three thirty, pay time. He made Doc wear his school uniform and picked every piece of fluff off the jacket before he let him out the door.

Craig was expecting them. So were the rest of the crew, they all crushed into the doorway of the site hut to see the fun. The site hut was long and thin, the wooden floor sagged in places and tools lay scattered along walls half eaten by damp. The wages clerk sat as far back in the room as he possibly could. A desk and a box of wage packets were his only defence.

Craig was in front of the table; he stood with his arms folded. 'Jimmy Terence, nothing due.'

Jimmy looked about him from the corner of his eye. He felt like a trapped rat but could see no way of backing down. 'Yes there is.'

'Fuck off, sonny, before I give you a belt.'

'Lying week and a couple of days.' He gave undue emphasis to the 'Lying.'

Craig hit him, an open-handed slap across the cheek that was more insulting than an honest blow. Jimmy went staggering back. The men held him up so that he didn't fall. One of them hissed, 'Stay on your feet. That bastard has steel-capped boots and he's quick to use them.'

Jimmy's shook his helpers off. He flexed his shoulders and bunched his fists. He couldn't understand the fool pride that stopped him from running.

Craig advanced, his boots loud on the floor. Jimmy jumped forward, ducked under a swinging fist the size of a cannon ball and hit Craig. It was like hitting concrete, his knuckles started to swell.

'Fight dirty,' shouted Doc.

Jimmy threw a right-hander. Craig blocked the blow and hit him above the heart. The world stopped for Jimmy, the follow up blows were all sensation and no sound; he couldn't hear, he couldn't breathe. Then he was lying on the ground watching a toecap draw back.

'He's only a kid,' shouted the man who had warned him earlier.

Jimmy heard that.

And Craig's reply. 'He'll not make any older.'

'For God's sake.' Doc sounded impatient.

'You try it,' said Jimmy back. At least he thought he did.

Craig went for the groin, Jimmy just managed to roll outwards and take it on the leg. He cried out in pain as his thigh bone jumped in its socket. The boot was drawn back again.

None of the men were willing to risk helping Jimmy. Doc picked up a nail bar and swung. He wasn't very tall then so he went for what he could reach. The first blow shattered a shoulder blade, the next broke an arm and drove a rib into Craig's lung. Craig went down.

'Stop it,' said Jimmy. This time he knew he hadn't spoken. He wished he had left Doc at home.

The other men grabbed Doc as he went for the head. He fought them, silent and white faced, until Jimmy got enough breath together to order him to stop. Doc still held the nail-bar, everyone backed off cautiously.

Jimmy used tools and the wall to get to his feet; his left leg wouldn't lock at the knee. He held out his hand. The clerk rushed to give him his money.

Jimmy gave the packet to one of the men. 'The drinks are on me.'

He limped out. Doc followed Jimmy and the men followed Doc, leaving the clerk to call the ambulance.

❖

The Troubles came to Belfast in August 1971. Jimmy was eighteen and doing rightly: bricks and wood, fireplaces and sinks were his capital. If you wanted it he had it, and if he hadn't he got it; either way it came cheap. Doc was still at school. In his spare time he was reading The Outsider, 'In its original French,' Jimmy told everybody with all the pride of a doting mother.

Jimmy's eyes popped open. Something had wakened him. It came again, the wail of banshees from hell. 'Bloody TV,' he murmured into the night. He knew he should go down and play the heavy brother but he was warm and comfortable and didn't want to move. He pulled the blankets over his head and went back to sleep.

He heard it again. This time he came storming awake. 'I'll kill him.'

Doc was already in the room. 'Did you hear that?'

'Would you go to your bed?'

'No, listen.'

They heard more cries; a distant light flickered against the drawn blind. Jimmy kicked himself clear of the blankets and snapped the blind up; the cord spun itself around the roller. He didn't notice because he was looking at a house burning two or three streets away. He grabbed his clothes. 'Somebody must be trapped.'

'Right, said Doc, and disappeared into his own room.

They met on the stairs, Jimmy slightly in the lead, and raced out of the house. Their neighbours were already in the street or crowding their doorways.

Jimmy met Sam Gilliland; he was swinging a crowbar in his massive hands. 'What's up?'

Sam said, 'The IRA are coming.'

In the distance a sharp crack sounded. Sam grabbed Jimmy and hustled him against a wall. 'That's a 303.'

'Three o' three, what?'

'Rifle you idiot.'

'Fuck.'

Something banged into the roof above them, a piece of slate

slithered into the gutter.

Sam's grip was tight on Jimmy's arm. 'Get your stuff and clear out, this is no place for honest men.'

'It's my home, I'll see them in hell first.'

Sam pushed him towards his house. 'And they're the men to send you there. Fall back and regroup, then we can advance and retake the position.'

Jimmy tried to make a laugh of it. 'You make it sound like war?'

'Welcome to the real world son.'

Sam went off to do his own packing. Jimmy hesitated. The glow from the burning house was showing over the roofs, and women, who normally wouldn't be seen with even a hair-grip missing, were at their doors with only a blanket held round them for decency sake. The street was crowded with people yet the greatest noise was that of the wind rushing to the flames and the crackle of burning wood.

A woman came flying over. She was carrying a bundle of things in a blanket and held two children firmly by one hand. 'Jimmy, Jimmy, Jimmy.'

'Yes missis?'

'Could you give the wanes and me a lift to Sandy Row? I've got a sister there.'

Jimmy hesitated. All he had was a flatbed Bedford truck, hardly bigger than a motorcar. It would take him several runs to get his own stuff clear: the few bits and pieces left by his mother and some job lots of china he hoped to sell for a good price. He looked down at the children, they were tear-stained and snot nosed.

He knew what his mother would have said so he did it for her. 'Get on board, missis, I'll be with you in a minute.'

He ran into the house, Doc followed.

The woman's voice followed them. 'Jimmy Terence, you're the spitting image of your mother, a decenter woman never lived.'

Jimmy shoved Doc to the stairs. 'Pack and be quick about it.' He shouted after him. 'And keep the lights off.'

He himself risked a flash of light in each room. From the living room he took a picture of his parents on their wedding day and another of himself and Doc in a silver-gilt frame. There was nothing he wanted in either the kitchen or scullery. In the bedroom he scooped all the clothes he could find onto his bed, threw in the pictures and tied everything as securely as he could in the candlewick bedspread. Next he shoved the bed back against the wardrobe, searched under a loose floorboard and pulled out a little bag that clinked. It held gold sovereigns. He stuffed it into his pocket and raced downstairs again. Doc was waiting for him in the hall with the picture of Camus under his arm.

'Is that the best you could do?'

'School's out,' said Doc.

The woman and her children were already on the lorry. Jimmy looked at another half dozen who were pushing and pulling each other on board. Jimmy said, 'Where do you lot think you're going?'

'I'm on your way,' said a wee woman with a sharp nose and even sharper tongue. She hadn't said a civil word to anybody in years.

'More like, in our way,' muttered Doc.

'God bless you, Jimmy,' said somebody among the crowd.

Over the rooftops they saw another house gout flames and sparks soar into the air. The women in the truck crouched low and held their children to them. Another family got on.

Jimmy stuffed Doc and his picture into the passenger seat and jammed him in solid with the bundle of clothes. Doc was grinning. 'You've got a warped sense of humour,' said Jimmy.

'And you only get mad when you're worried.'

'Shut up.'

The lorry started, it didn't always. It rattled and banged at the best of times, shuddered like a wild beast when it went off a cylinder and created its own smog of burnt oil wherever it went. That night it ran like an angel.

The men cheered them on their way; the noise from the back of the lorry was like the middle of a good wake. They turned the corner and the wailing increased.

Two streets on the lorry started to lurch over potholes in the road where the cobblestones had been lifted. The people they passed, mostly men, had fixed stares and no greeting. Many held broken cobblestones in their hand, others axe handles; in one or two cases the axe head was still attached. Beyond that the streetlights were out. The smell of smoke hung heavy in the air.

The lorry's lights picked out a line of men blocking the road. Jimmy pulled up smoothly so as not to startle them.

One of them opened the driver's door. 'Out.'

Jimmy said, 'We're Protestants. I'm taking these women to Sandy Row.'

'We need your lorry for the barricade.'

Jimmy looked over their heads and saw a line of cars lying on their sides across the street. He might refer to the lorry as an "old bitch" but she meant a lot to him. Sometimes he wished his mother was alive. On a good day he could have taken her into the hills to breathe pure air. Maybe even the seaside, Bangor wasn't that far away. 'Over my dead body.'

'That can be arranged,' said one of the men. They closed in on him with axe handles were hefted; somebody opened Doc's door and poked at him through the bundle of clothes.

The women came pouring off the lorry. 'You're not taking it.'

'The man's taking the wanes and me to Sandy Row.'

'You expect me to walk and me eight months gone?'

The men backed off, not a retreat exactly just a step or two that allowed Jimmy to reverse out of the street.

Once turned he stopped and waited for the women to re-board. They got on muttering:

'Flipping cheek.'

'Who does that lot think they are.?'

'We soon sorted them.'

Jimmy said to Doc. 'You were a great help.'

Doc got a hand free. The blade of a kitchen knife gleamed dully.

Jimmy was angry. 'This is no time to get stroppy.'

They drove on. The side streets were no longer safe, Jimmy turned onto the Shankill Road proper and roared down the hill. They were stopped at a police checkpoint near the junction with Peters Hill, this time it was Lee-Enfields and Stirling sub-machine guns. A torchlight glared in Jimmy's eyes, another washed over the women on the back.

They were waved on.

Jimmy leaned out the window and pointed at the Stirlings. 'You couldn't lend me one?'

'Get your own,' said the sergeant. He was only half-joking.

'I might just.' Jimmy thought he should talk to Sam Gilliland, he had the oddest contacts.

They drove down Royal Avenue. The place was bright-lit and eerie. Only the odd police car passed, there were no pedestrians. At the Castle Street junction, the bottom of the Catholic Falls Road, the lights were against him. He stopped. A car came up behind him and ran the lights. 'What the hell,' said Jimmy, and went on.

A line of men guarded the entrance into Sandy Row, some held Union Jacks nailed to sticks, others were more threatening.

Jimmy stopped well short of them and shouted at the women. 'Off quick.'

The men advanced, the women took their time. Jimmy sweated, Doc started to wheeze.

The line of men stopped. The man who had given the order to halt, came on on his own. He carried a flag on a stick. Jimmy started to whistle Colonel Bogie but there was something about the man that was more dangerous than funny and the notes died on his lips. There wasn't much difference in their respective heights because it was a small lorry and the stranger was a very tall man. He was broad and fleshy, clean-shaven in spite of the late hour, and his skin was so smooth it glistened in the near dark.

He said, 'You're Jimmy Terence.' His accent had more than a hint of Southern England in it.

'Am I?' said Jimmy.

'You are. You've done a bit of work for me.'

'No I haven't. I don't know you from Adam.'

'You have you know, you just didn't know it.'

'Well I hope you paid me.' The women were off at long last. For all their hurry to get to Sandy Row they didn't seem to know what to do once they got there. Jimmy jerked his thumb in their direction. 'What about them?'

'We've the church halls open and the kettle on. As many as you can bring we can cope with.'

Jimmy thought of the silent men lining the streets and the barricades going up. 'There's not much chance of that.'

'Tell them the Man said it was all right.'

Jimmy started to laugh, felt the steely eyes boring into him and cut it off. He tried to cover. 'It might take a bit more than that.'

The Man turned and indicated, it was the most regal wave Jimmy had ever seen outside of the Queen. Two men came forward. One of them was carrying a second flag; the other had a limping slouch of a walk. It was Jimmy's old adversary, Craig the foreman; he looked everywhere but at Jimmy. The Man took the flag off the first man and handed it in. 'Tie it to a wing mirror.'

Jimmy passed it over to Doc, who muttered, 'What do you think this is, Crackerjack?'

A lot of the loneliness Jimmy felt in the night disappeared, he was more respectful now. 'You couldn't back that up with a Sterling sub-machine gun just in case it's the other side?'

The Man spoke to Craig who held out something else for Jimmy. It was a revolver. 'Not him, the other one,' said the Man.

Craig took the gun round and it handed in. The butt slipped neatly into Doc's hand, it almost clicked into place.

On the way back home they detoured to Jimmy's 'shop', the stables of an old brewery, now defunct.

The gates swung open as they approached, a man poked his head out. The man was stubby built and not particularly bright. His name was Peter Dawes; everybody called him Peter Paws because he had one obsession, dogs, Doberman Pinchers. Two adult dogs stood close to his feet and he cradled three pups in his arms as he spoke. 'I thought it was you, the old bitch is running well tonight.'

'Don't even mention it,' said Jimmy, and drove on into the yard. Doc got out, Jimmy sat on. Beyond the lights of the lorry was darkness as far as the distant high-rise flats; one of them was on fire. The houses surrounding the yard were bricked up and derelict. Jimmy loved the place; his impossible dream was of owning it some day.

Doc had disappeared. Jimmy followed the sound of a sledgehammer on concrete and found him knocking in the rear window of the largest house. He was making hard work of it.

Jimmy settled himself against the return wall. 'What do you think you're doing?'

Doc paused briefly. 'Opening the door to our new home.'

'Aye,' said Jimmy. 'Aye.' He couldn't bear to watch a handless worker doing what came easy to himself. He took the sledge off Doc. 'This way.' Three blows and the window was in, five more and blocks, glass, wooden frame, the lot were lying in the kitchen floor. He stepped through the window and struck a match. The room was musty and there was the sour smell of mice. It was still furnished: a table and a few chairs. The match went out, Jimmy struck another one. There was an old newspaper in the hearth, he put the match to that and light flared.

Doc was waiting with the bundles of clothes. 'Aye,' said Jimmy, again and took them off him. Doc came back with twigs, Jimmy threw then on the fire and by the time they were burning Doc was back again with a half bucket of coal. 'You'd make a great wee housewife,' said Jimmy.

They collected tarpaulin and rope and went on.

The street, when they got back, was half blocked with bundles and furniture. Jimmy had to snake the lorry in and out of the stuff and people were forever wandering in his way. The smoke was thicker, the fires closer and his neighbours fears were now edged with panic. Some of them tried to load furniture and family onto the lorry before Jimmy got it stopped.

Sam came running with the crowbar. He cracked it down on the lorry bed. 'None of that nonsense, there's room for all.'

Jimmy nudged Doc. 'Bring the beds and the bedding. And some clothes this time, school uniforms don't grow on trees.'

Doc flashed a smile and went off, he was wheezing badly in the smoke.

Jimmy turned to find himself facing the most wonderful pair of dark eyes.

She was older than him by nearly two years, and when you're eighteen that's a long time. The skirt hung close to the ankles, the cardigan to the knees, they were colourless in the poor lighting, and the white blouse was stapled to her neck by a cameo broach. She was holding a plate of sandwiches.

'God bless you.' He went to take one.

The plate was pulled back. 'We are going to wash our hands first, aren't we?'

He looked at her stupid. His body reeked of sweat and effort and his hands were black. He could have died of embarrassment. 'You're quite right, missis, though yours look clean enough to me.'

'Pardon?'

'You did say "we."'

'Really?' She flounced off and offered the plate to somebody else, she didn't ask them to wash first. She looked back and smiled. For that smile he would do anything. He went off and washed his hands and his arms and his face and his neck. He found a fresh shirt in the kitchen press and put it on.

He couldn't find her when he went back into the crowd. He fixed a smile on his face and helped Doc and Sam load their things onto the roof of the cab. He felt angry with her for being a tease. Somebody shoved a mug of tea into his hand and he gulped it down.

She was standing right behind him; the plate was well depleted. Her voice was tart. 'You did remember under the nails?'

His smile became real. 'And ears.' He took a sandwich.

'My own,' she told him.

'Delicious.' He had no idea what he was eating. He was cringing, his shirt was un-ironed, he never bothered with such niceties, and he hoped she hadn't gone into the house to see how they lived.

He waved the mug in her face. 'I know you. You're Eleanor somebody from up the Avenue where all the posh accents come from. All front gardens and Venetian blinds.'

'And you're Young Jimmy Terence. At least your father had some manners. He knew to say thank you.'

He coloured, he choked. She offered the plate again and he took a second sandwich. He struggled to thank her through the choking. Her teeth gleamed as she laughed at him.

He caught his breath. 'You're awful tall for a woman.' She was on the pavement; he was standing in the gutter.

She said, 'There's not much to you. Five nine?'

'And a half.' The half was important to him.

She leaned forward. His hands were tied up with a mug and sandwich. He ached to hold her.

She said, 'Good kissing height.'

Their lips touched. He thought he would die of happiness.

The last trip was near dawn. They were tiring and the lorry had little petrol left.

Jimmy's eyes were burning with the effort of keeping them open. 'Talk to me,' he said to Doc.

Doc was sitting upright and alert. Only his eyes moved, searching through the yellow pall of smoke that hung over the city. He seemed to be enjoying himself. He said, 'I think everybody's gone.'

'Could be.'

'And the shooting's stopped.'

'They're tired, God help them.'

They were two turnings off home. Jimmy took the first and peered down a street he had known from childhood and was unsure if he was right. It was burning, house upon house, and a body lay in the gutters. He was shocked. The lorry jerked to a halt.

'What are you stopping for?' said Doc.

Jimmy pointed.

'Drive on,' said Doc.

'You're a cold bastard.'

'He's dead, it's dangerous. Drive on.'

They glared at each other. Jimmy said, 'You don't know that for sure.' He had his hand on the door handle.

'His head's half stove-in, take a look.'

Jimmy looked; with the moving darkness around the flames he couldn't be sure. 'I'll check anyway.' The sudden blast of heat from the flames as the door opened made him cringe back.

Doc leaned across and shoved the gun into his hands. 'You'll need this.'

'This is Belfast, head-bin, not the wild west.'

He stuffed the gun into his pocket and went on, it saved arguing.

The heat from the flames was intense. Jimmy had to hold his arms across his face as he approached the body and his trousers were uncomfortably hot against his legs. The man was dead and was cooking nicely. Jimmy backed off rapidly, what was left of the sandwiches heaved in his stomach.

Something smashed into his back and upper arm. He stumbled towards the flames. Another blow landed before he could turn to face his attacker. This one scraped along the side of his ear and caught the edge of his shoulder; his left arm flopped useless.

There were three of them and each held a curved stick with a large flat head. Shillelagh? Hurley? Jimmy wasn't sure which.

One of the men gave him a hard poke in the guts. Definitely a hurley, Jimmy thought as he doubled up in pain and went back a step.

'Cook the bastard,' said one of the men.

The hurleys jabbed again. Jimmy's foot turned on a cobble and he almost fell. He could feel the hair on the back of his head curl in the heat and his sweater was smoking. The men were laughing.

He remembered the gun and pulled it out of his pocket. They didn't see it or thought he was bluffing. He fired. The middleman flopped onto his back, his hurley somersaulted through the air.

A hand, Doc's, came out of the dark and caught it. The other two men were standing stupid. Doc stepped back and swung.

Jimmy closed his eyes but couldn't blot out the sound of bone crunching.

Doc was standing over Jimmy. 'I thought you were going to see Eleanor?'

Jimmy got an eye open. 'I am, I had my bath.' The words came out slurred.

'You need an early night. Or maybe that's what you had in mind?'

'Shut your face.'

The world started to clear around Jimmy. The kitchen with the old tiled floor and a couple of comfortable chairs came into focus. They had electricity and gas and a back door to come and go through. Everything was as clean as they could make it because he was thinking of inviting Eleanor round.

Doc shoved somebody forward. 'Whippet's here.'

Whippet made Jimmy feel tall. He spoke high-pitched and quick, it came out like a yap. 'The Man wants you.'

'Does he?' said Jimmy, thinking that it wasn't his night; Eleanor wouldn't come anyway, she wasn't that sort of girl.

'You and your lorry, something's come up.'

'I'm busy.'

'Best advice, come at once.'

Jimmy came fully awake. 'Is that a threat?'

Whippet backed off rapidly. 'I'm only saying what I was told.' He sidled into the scullery and slipped off into the night.

Jimmy was raging with frustration. He had not heard from the Man in a year, not directly, and now this summons, and on a Friday night too. He slammed his feet into his boots, grabbed his coat and went out. Doc followed.

The old lorry was in a bitchy mood. 'I thought you could drive this thing?' said Jimmy, after Doc stalled her the third time.

Doc looked amused, Jimmy got more uptight as they neared Eleanor's house.

Eleanor wasn't too pleased especially when he could only talk vaguely about business and the Man. She stood in her hallway with a full-length dressing gown held tight to her throat. It was a nice dressing gown, all roses and flowers and things; Jimmy wished she would open it wide. He left as soon as he politely could; the chill was getting to him.

Doc quoted:

*Her voice was ever soft, gentle and low, an...*

Jimmy pinned him to the door by the throat. 'Listen, smart ass, if I kill you let it be for something you made up yourself.'

The Man was equally aloof. There had been talk.

'Not me,' said Jimmy.

The stare he got matched Eleanor's for coldness. 'If it had, you wouldn't be here... You wouldn't be anywhere.'

Doc stood silent at Jimmy's shoulder. His hand slipped to the knife he carried. It was made of fine steel with a tip like the point of a needle.

If the Man saw the movement he ignored it. 'As I was saying, when I was so rudely interrupted, there's been too much loose talk. Certain items have to be moved. Tomorrow will be too late.'

A pulse beat Jimmy's head. 'When you say certain items?'

'Yes.'

'I haven't asked the question yet.'

'Don't.'

They stared at each other. Jimmy felt he would always be looking up at the Man even from the top of a stepladder. He compromised. 'If I don't know?'

'It won't save you.'

'Fuck.'

Jimmy wasn't sure that he wanted to get involved, not that way. He was glad to break stare with the Man and look back at Doc as if asking his opinion. There was a gleam in Doc's eye.

It was the same gleam Jimmy had seen as they stood over the dead bodies in the burning street. They had never discussed that night, let alone told anyone else, though the Man suspected something. He had checked the gun when Jimmy returned it and saw that a bullet was missing.

'Yes,' said Doc.

The smell of the burning buildings and the fear of the women and children still haunted Jimmy. He nodded and felt chill.

'Right,' said the Man, and gave his orders quickly. He had a map of the city already spread out on the table. The finger pointed. Jimmy was to collect here, deliver there. Then...

Jimmy swallowed hard. 'How many runs?'

'Three should do it.'

'I'm not a Kamikaze, you know.'

'And I'm not a chicken, I don't put all my eggs in the one basket.' Jimmy pointed to the jail on the Crumlin Road. 'When you're sending the cake with a file in it. I like marzipan.'

'Icing too,' said the Man, and led them to an old stone warehouse near the Oranmore Bridge. Craig was waiting for them; his face was as sour as the twist in his shoulder.

Doc reached for his knife. Jimmy stopped. 'Wait a minute.'

'Have you and Craig a problem?' said the Man.

'Yes.'

'Not tonight you haven't.'

Doc's hand was on his knife. Jimmy glared at Craig. 'If anything goes wrong there'll be more than me not around.'

Other men waited in the near-darkness, cigarettes cupped in their hands. They were all family men because this was no night for young Turks with loose mouths. Jimmy hung around and checked for weight distribution while nondescript packages and boxes were loaded onto the lorry; he tried not to touch them. There was a lot and yet...

'Hardly enough to go to war with,' he said.

The Man's nose pinched at the implied criticism. 'Nobody likes us.'

'Aye,' said Jimmy. 'It's easy being a revolutionary, everybody can empathise with that.'

The Man put a friendly hand on his shoulder. 'Empathise? Empathise? Where do you get all these big words?'

Jimmy shrugged, casual. 'Doc has all these books. Sometimes I forget to buy the paper and you've have to have to read something while you eat your tea.'

The lorry was loaded at last. The Man said, 'Good luck.' He didn't ask insulting questions like: if things went wrong, did Jimmy know to keep his mouth shut?

The lorry was running like an angel. 'Don't forget the marzipan,' said Jimmy.

'See you in hell,' said Craig.

The first run was short. The number of army and police Landrovers loitering in the area made Jimmy nervous but they weren't stopped.

Back at the warehouse the Man and Craig had disappeared. 'They said they'd see you around,' said the new loading boss.

Jimmy paced nervously while the second load was being hoisted aboard. The night might be quiet but the darkness hung over the city like a pall and he felt cold. He was glad to be off. Their destination this time lay across everything that was dangerous, into a wasteland of crumbling houses on the Crumlin Road. They detoured by the city centre, it seemed safer somehow and there was less chance of running into a checkpoint. Jimmy's heart was in his mouth every inch of the way.

Doc looked at the Landrovers stacked around Carlisle Circus. 'They're heading into the Shankill.'

'Don't be daft, it's the Taigs they're after.'

They turned into the Crumlin Road.

Doc said, 'So far...'

'Don't even think it.'

Something caught Jimmy's eye as they passed, a movement in a side street. 'Did you?'

'Yeah.'

He hesitated, the lorry stalled.

They came out of the lorry running. 'This is crazy,' said Jimmy as they turned the corner into the side street.

They were right, they had seen the dark shadows of people against the poor street lighting. Two were on the ground, a third was standing over them. Jimmy shouted and two of them, men, ran off, one at little better than a hobble as he pulled his trousers up. Jimmy held an arm out to stop Doc from following.

The third person lay on. A woman's voice was gasping, 'Jesus was lost and Jesus was found. Jesus was lost and Jesus was found.'

By the time Jimmy reached her she had managed to push her dress down as far as her knees. White underwear and a shoe and other bits of clothing lay nearby. Her hair was dark on the pavement and was as long as Eleanor's.

She groaned.

'Are you all right, love?' said Jimmy. He wanted her to be. The last thing he needed was to get involved.

He struck a match, her hair was rust red in the uncertain light and her face was dark with blood.

'Fuck,' he said. He added, hastily, 'Sorry missis.'

She was a nun. He had never spoken to a nun before, he wasn't sure if they were really human. This one was beautiful.

'Cover her legs, you're not supposed to see them,' said Doc.

'You do it.'

'I'm not snogging Eleanor.'

'Shut up.' Jimmy's hand hovered uncertainly over the material.

'Don't you dare,' said the nun. She burst into tears.

They looked at each other, helpless. Jimmy was sweating. If anything happened to the lorry, if the police came...?

'Missis, I don't want to rush you but we've got our own problems.' The sobbing stopped. 'Go away.' It started again.

'Oh f...' said Jimmy.

They gave her a minute then Jimmy risked taking an arm and encouraging her to her feet.

Doc said, 'A couple of cars just passed the bottom of the street.'

Jimmy used the word internally and gave the nun a handkerchief to wipe her face. The handkerchief was clean; he had taken it out of the drawer especially for his date.

'I think they've stopped,' said Doc.

The nun shook herself free of his hand. 'Go away.' She meant it this time.

Jimmy understood. 'We'll wait at the corner.' He doubted if they'd get much further. He wondered how many years Eleanor would be willing to wait.

They walked slowly; Doc dumped his knife down a grating. They got to the corner. Men were all round the lorry. Jimmy said, 'No matter what you say, say nothing.' Doc was silent, Jimmy felt him tremble. 'You'll be all right. Blame me for everything.'

A torchlight swung in their direction, they blinked and squinted in its sharp glare.

'Do you own this lorry?'

'I do, officer.'

'It's a bit late to be out with a load.'

'Are you telling me?'

Doc nudged him hard. It wasn't the police, it was the IRA, and they had guns.

'What's your name?'

'Paddy John Joe,' said Jimmy. He was sure he knew that voice from somewhere.

Strange men crowded them, objects, some hard others prickly, were pushed against their bodies and torches glared in their eyes. Another torch, the men seemed to have an unlimited supply, was played along the load on the lorry. Hands searched their bodies. They found the driving licence in Jimmy's hip pocket and weren't particularly gentle around the crotch. Jimmy choked back a cough.

The voice said, 'Jimmy Terence, a good Prod name if I ever heard one. And from the Shankill.'

One of the other men said, 'We haven't time for this.'

'Now now, boys, we talk to them first then we shoot them.'

Jimmy bit his lip and wished he was somewhere else and wished he had found time to make it with a woman, any woman. Eleanor. A gun barrel was pushed in under his cheekbone. He wanted Doc to make a run for it. He knew the stupid bugger wouldn't go without him anyway.

The beam of the torch focused on a long box. 'What's in there?'

'Sten guns.'

The beam next settled on to a squat box. 'And that?'

Jimmy was sweating hard. 'Dynamite.'

A gun barrel stabbed his guts. 'Smart arse Prod.' Air hissed out of Jimmy.

The voice said, 'Take a look, Sean.' The lorry springs squealed and the dark shadow of a squat man stood out against the sky.

A knife was pressed hard against Jimmy's throat. 'What are you bastards up to?'

'Helping me,' said a voice. Jimmy jumped, he'd forgotten about the nun. It was a relief when the lights swung in her direction.

The nun stood at the corner, she was nearly as tall as Jimmy and had shapes and curves without being in anyway fat. Blood still stained her face and her wimple.

'I fell.' She looked hard at Jimmy delivering a message. 'I fell and hurt myself. These two gentlemen were kind enough to stop and help me.'

Jimmy was impressed; the nun lied like a well-seasoned trooper.

The atmosphere changed immediately. Attitudes became friendlier and relaxed, hard men were suddenly gentle and considerate; handkerchiefs were offered. They wanted to rush her to hospital, she insisted the convent was fine, and they vied with each other to have her in their car.

Jimmy and Doc edged away from the group. Jimmy didn't know where to look first, at the guns or the Sean still hoaking about on the lorry.

Sean straightened with something in his hand. 'Mi...'

Doc's hand snaked out, caught his ankle and twisted. Sean yelled and hit the ground hard. He lay groaning. Jimmy bent over him, by the way helping. Sean had a gun in his hand; Jimmy scooped it into his belt.

Their questioner stepped out of the shadows and hauled Jimmy back, he was a big man. 'Fuck off Terence.'

Jimmy grabbed his licence. 'I'll see you again, Quinn.'

'You and which army?'

The nun came between them. 'I can't thank you enough.' Her hands were pushing Jimmy to the safety of the lorry even as her eyes pleaded for his continued silence.

Jimmy could see that they were lovely eyes, some light colour. He said, 'It was a bad fall missis. I'd see somebody about it.'

'I shall. And I'll write and thank you,' She indicated Mick who was helping Sean into a sitting position. Sean's head lolled and his mouth hung slack. 'This gentlemen will know your address.'

'God I hope not,' said Jimmy.

The pubs were long closed when Jimmy got home. The lorry engine died before he could touch the ignition. 'Old bitch,' he said, and gave it an affectionate pat. He killed the lights and climbed slowly out of the cab.

'Still!' said Doc, and disappeared into the night.

Jimmy stopped and listened, forcing himself to concentrate in spite of the weariness that clogged his mind. He realised that the lights in the house were on. He had switched them off as they left, he was sure of it, or he thought he was.

He saw Doc's shadow slide along the wall and look in the kitchen window. Doc straightened, laughed and walked openly to the back door.

Jimmy caught him up. 'What?'

'Goodnight,' said Doc. He said 'Goodnight,' again to somebody in the kitchen and went into the hall, closing the door gently behind him.

Jimmy found himself alone with their guest. They had been there long enough to put a match to the fire and use a bucket of coal to keep it burning.

'You must take me for a fool,' Eleanor said.

Jimmy was wide awake now and dieing of embarrassment. 'You shouldn't be here.' He looked around, feeling there must be something he could do to make the place look better.

She stood up from the settee. 'When did you ever put work before me? Helping somebody? Yes. Doing a friend a good turn? No problem.' She flung herself at him. 'Don't get involved. Please, please. I'd die if anything happened to you.'

'I don't want to.' He said it into her hair.

'Then you won't do it again?' She looked up at him; there were tears in her eyes.

He felt he was betraying her. 'I can't.'

'Let the police do it, that's what they're paid for.'

He held her gently. 'They're only good for belting drunks on a Saturday night.' The fear he had felt earlier that evening when surrounded by the IRA men was still raw in his mind. 'This is war, the bottom line is our survival.'

She hugged into him again and they held each other a long time. Eventually she said, 'You weren't so quick to come to my rescue the night the Troubles started.'

He was glad to get back to an old battle. 'I did, I cut round by your house. Your dad's car had gone so I knew the rats had left the sinking ship.'

'I'll give you rats.' She punched him and squealed as he up-ended her onto the settee, her skirt went above her knees. It reminded him of the nun, he stopped there.

She struggled into a sitting position, her hand went to her dress and touched the hem but left it high. He gulped. She said, 'In your dreams, how do you see me?'

'Like that. Lovely.'

She slipped a hand under her head. The movement flexed her breasts and did things to his stomach. 'Exactly like this?'

Having her there, not criticising the house was like a dream in itself. He was wondering how he was going to get her home; the lorry wouldn't start again that night. 'Exactly like that.'

She knew he was lying from the blush burning his face. 'The truth.'

He licked his lips, he looked anywhere but at her. When he spoke he could hardly hear the words over the pounding of his heart. 'Well... without.' His hands fluttered at his buttons.

She unclipped the cameo and laid it safely on the ground, then took off her cardigan and undid the buttons of her blouse, the sleeves first. The skirt was loosened, the bra undone and everything slipped off and put aside.

'Well?' she said.

He licked his lips again. His hands started at his shirt buttons, the easiest to get at and the most innocent. He nearly fell getting his trousers and boots off.

He stood over her, afraid to do something that would spoil the moment. 'Is this your dream of me?'

'No,' she said.

Her arms were out for him before he could feel disappointment. He was grateful she seemed to know what to do.

She guided him into her. 'This,' she said. 'This.'

# RENDEZVOUS
## Howard Wright

Five minutes. I look stupid, suspicious or both. Five more minutes. I can't wait here all day. I love it though: the sea, the paths, the spiky trees; the summer seats for God sake! And what a time: the sensible hour in the middle of the day, the unrushed hours when the sponge of work, the dead-land of office stacks and shopping villages, has absorbed the commuters. She's not so slow. And yet a crowd would have helped, somewhere to lose ourselves.

Yes, I understand her difficulties, but I don't know what I'll do with her. The day has arrived to take responsibility. My choice, all the way. And here I am accepting it as if it were normal, and as I do I realise she frightens me. I'm out of my depth, out of my mind. She walks all over me. She decided and I agreed. My cock, my prison and escape. Where do we go from here? From here? I've made plans she will scrutinise like the gambler she is. When we leave here, is it right or left? When we settle on a future, is it hers or mine? How much will we have to pay? What's the price for getting out? Those sirens could be for me.

The railway, the landscaping, the house-backs, the insensitive sculpture signed by the artist (local). Ornamental shrubs and the broken clock. Sharp borders, pollarded trees, a duck pond. I never thought I'd feel such nostalgia for council workmanship. At another time this would be a place to explore. Five minutes more, then another five. All right – I'll wait all day for her.

A gust of air, an angel passing, the dead returning... The rails twitch and sing. They *twang*. What a great job, to watch trains arrive. Is there a job doing that? The train decelerates, the tracks wincing at the delay, the interruption. Amazingly no litter, graffiti or fly posters. This pleases me as I've an eye for such things: I arrange photographs in their albums and correct spelling before checking there's anything to say. Yet I'm inviting her in disturb all of this. I should walk away. I shouldn't be here.

A minute more and I'll go, pre-emptory and on the spur. I mean it.

I'm hungry with impatience. She has all this before her. And what of me? The faults, foibles, the undoubted strangeness she will bequeath. Untidiness, drink, bad skin? Ortho-creme taken for toothpaste? I don't know her. I run the risk of not being anything. After all, hers is only the third *real* vagina I've met. So what am I doing here, in this park, waiting? Seems I've been waiting all my life – at lights, harbours and doors; outside hospitals, schools and banks; in front rooms, back rooms, waiting rooms; at checkouts and bars; in beds and cars. I hated it and here I am, still waiting; waiting for this moment, a moment that will change everything. And here it is, or soon, entering the station, the ordinary bustle, the engines warming up, the fearless greetings for the public to savour.

Keep moving, that's the trick. Maybe it's not her train. The ducks are starving and time's slipping away. She's late. Twenty minutes, half an hour. The path loops behind the car park to the station. I'm half-hoping she won't appear. That case, that coat. Everything I own is in the car. It's still there, its back to me. How much has she brought? The train pulls out with a sigh. At that moment all paths lead to this place, here to me. She's on her way, loquacious and affectionate, cool and unprepossessing, and no one will stop her. She loves me. But I'm not so sure. How can we be together? What way is it? Five more minutes. This is the exit. The main road's the problem.

# BROKEN THINGS
## Katherine Martin

Her husband is a fix-a-holic. The black-and-white TV stored in the back garden that's been rained on one-too-many times, the neighbour's rusty blue tricycle that their eight-year-old long outgrew, old computers, broken latches, out-of-steam kettles and corroding toasters – he fixes them all. Whether it's barely hanging together with scotch tape or simply needing a wipe with a cloth – he fixes it. She doesn't begrudge it. Her broken thing was how they met....

'I have this CD player,' she ventured.
He nodded with assurance then took a drink of his tea.
'I've tried CD cleaner, but it still doesn't work.' She reached for the pot of tea, even though she hates the stuff, thinks it's like strange-tasting water.
He continued to nod.
'The CD spins, but it doesn't seem to read it,' she said, pretending to know more than she did, as she poured tea into her mug.
'I'll have a look.'
She was just glad it was settled before she actually had to drink the tea.

They'd met before, at a friend's housewarming party. But it was the hi-how-are-you-I'm-fine-my-name-is-I've-forgotten-yours-before-I-said-my-own kind of meeting. It was only while he leaned over her CD player, parts piling on her dining table that they really met.
She should have seen his bulldog persistence then, but at the time, she didn't mind that he kept coming back. Every day after work, he would arrive with his black toolbox in one hand. He'd push up his glasses when she opened the door and ask if he could come in and work on 'the project.'
She'd motion him in and he'd sit down at the table with a cup of tea always on the left-hand corner. He'd stare at the pieces, swear occasionally, but he always kept on working.

She was sometimes able to distract him with food. She'd make his pickle and pastrami sandwich and her tuna and onion one and they'd sit in the grandmother-quilt-covered chairs of her one-bedroom flat and talk. He'd tell her about his neurotic stepfather who was obsessed with banana pudding and golf. She'd talk about her sister who was ten years younger, but acted like she was her mother. When the conversation wilted, they'd just sit in silence, he with his tea, her with her legs curled under her, both with half-smiles on their faces. After awhile he'd insist he must get back to fixing the CD player.

He finally did fix it...two years later.

She's still not sure if he didn't know how to or if he just wanted to keep seeing her. Either way, they're married now and the fixing comes in handy. On New Year's Eve, someone threw a rock through their window while they were playing cards with friends. She jumped up so quickly she knocked over her chair, the arm breaking off its base as it fell. He fixed the window and the chair. They were given a new-used oven that didn't fit in the kitchen, so he sawed off the ends of the counter to make room for it. When she broke the handle off the teapot her cousin gave them as a wedding present, he glued it back on. He fitted locks on the windows when they first moved in and changed all the light bulbs when they burnt out.

She appreciates it. She does. She really does. She just fears he might start taking it too far.

She's wanted to just ask him about it for awhile now, even gets as far as clearing her throat to begin. But the words just stick in her chest like month-old bubble gum. One Saturday afternoon, while he's fixing the washing machine that she clogged with too much laundry, she starts to ask. She gets as far as distracting him from his work. As she searches his eyes, she wants to ask why he fixes things, why he never stops. She wants to ask if what he really wants to fix is her. He looks at her for another moment and then silently returns to his work. She touches his shoulder and just walks away. She fears squelching him, fears discouraging him from his persistence.

She fears she might be right.

Tonight he is fixing their CD player. This one's part of the new stereo system he received for Christmas. She hadn't meant to jam it. She'd been distracted by the news and put the CD in without looking. She hadn't seen the one already there, still doesn't know how it closed with both of them in place. She doesn't know how she does most of the things she does. She just does.

He is crouched over the dinner table, gripping a piece of the CD player with one hand and a screwdriver with the other. His cup of tea is on the left-hand corner of the table. When he stops to drink his tea, she's coming towards him, looking down at the ground thinking about the broken player. He takes another sip and watches her carry a plate of pickle and pastrami sandwiches, like she did during those days in her one-bedroom flat. In the other hand, she holds a bottle of White Sauvignon and a wineglass. She is trying to balance another glass on top of the plate of sandwiches. He gets up to help her.

As he does, he startles her and her hand shakes. It shakes just enough for the glass that is balancing on top of the sandwiches to shake. The glass shakes just enough to topple to the ground.

She watches as the glass, seeming to fall in slow-motion, hits the cloud-gray tile floor, the gold-rimmed shards shining. She doesn't move. They both just stare at the broken glass. She waits for him to tell her she was carrying too much. She waits for him to say she should know better. She waits for him to start fixing it.

He looks at her biting her lower lip, staring at him. She has the same look in her eyes she had at the washing machine. He reaches over and takes the sandwiches and wine and sets them on the table. She doesn't flinch, but just stands motionless clutching the remaining glass. He looks at the glass and then at his wife. A flicker of realisation flashes across his face.

He grabs the glass from her and throws it against the wall. They watch it smash, the shards leaving marks on the clean magnolia paint as they fall. Stunned, she stands silent. He reaches out to her, takes her arms and draws her towards him. Standing together in the middle of broken things, he kisses her.

## *TACE* IS LATIN FOR CANDLE
### Marie O'Nolan

When John thought of Lucy, he thought of her hands. They were small and delicate yet strong and purposeful, graceful in motion, expressive even at rest. He imagined them in many lights, spread wide as if to encompass a high drifting sky or folded inward in a room full of moving shadows from many candles... When he had first seen them they had had blood on them, not from violent crime but from a simple accident to a finger with a folding umbrella on the way into an art exhibition. He seldom attended such showings himself as he found them pragmatic affairs. At this one he was also easily distracted so, instead of viewing the pictures, he chose to follow her blood, as it were, minute traces of it, that she left behind as she passed, on doors, walls, the backs of chairs, a wine glass, her catalogue. He lent her a handkerchief to staunch the small flow but the words they exchanged were but a formal few and lost in the general buzz of conversation. Not that he had expected to get to know her there and then, however much he wanted to. He believed that you didn't get to know people properly at art exhibitions as everyone is metamorphosed to some degree in the presence of art. They drifted apart but before she left she returned his handkerchief with gratitude and he took it home with him in his breast pocket, her blood close to the source of his own.

The next time he saw her was equally unproductive, on a crowded early morning train going to work. He was never upbeat himself that early in the morning and was easily put off by the fact that she did not appear to notice him. He watched her at a distance, one hand holding the upright bar of the rocking, speeding train, the other linked into the strap of her large black leather shoulder bag. Her eyes were fixed on the rapidly changing scene beyond the window. Although her stare on the surface seemed vacant he suspected that it was hiding some secret inner preoccupation. He had a sudden urgent wish to be there with her in the innermost recesses of her mind, even more intimate than having had her blood in his pocket. He tried to get through to where she stood but there were too many people in his way. By the time he got near enough to speak to her the train had stopped at a station and she was about to get off. For a fraction of time their eyes met and a flicker of recognition in hers sent an unexpected *frisson* up the back of his neck. He had an unexplained urge to follow even though it was not his stop but he was too late and was held back by a fresh influx of commuters. He stared after her through the window as the train moved on but she did not turn her head. It was only when viewing her retreating figure that he noticed her tote bag was bulging with candles!

He had thought about her constantly for three days when he unaccountably found himself in a lunch queue with her. She looked taken aback when he greeted her with a warmth arising more out of his own frame of mind than the actual slightness of their acquaintance. Since his fantasy that had gone far beyond just holding her hand it had seemed tame to him to mundanely have to exchange names and tentatively suggest that they share a table in a busy fast-food restaurant.

'I should have taken it home and washed it,' she said when they were seated.

'Sorry..?'

'Your handkerchief. Instead of giving it back to you all covered in blood. I should have...'

'Forget it. Anyway I come from a long line of vampires.' Jesus, did I really say that? he asked himself silently.

'Sorry..?' It was her turn to look mystified. 'Oh, I see what you mean. Funny...'

'Not very funny,' he admitted.

After a short pause he decided to move things closer into his own orbit.

'Did anyone ever tell you have beautiful hands?'

To his surprise she blushed, laid down her knife and fork and twisted her hands in front of her face. The mere impulse of the action had its own instinctive grace. He noticed a small healing scar where she had nicked her finger at the gallery.

'I know someone who would love to sculpt them,' he went on.

She seemed taken aback at the suggestion but her effort to respond was quick and polite, too polite perhaps and she avoided looking at him momentarily.

'That's very flattering but there isn't time really.'

'Too busy for art?'

'It isn't that.'

'What then? Are you going away or something?'

'Yes. That's it. I'm going away,' she said as if by rote, taking up her knife and fork again.

'Far?'

'Pretty far'

'For a long time?

'Oh yes... for good.'

He waited for her to name her destination but she didn't.

'So then I had better hurry up and get to know you.'

'Well, maybe that would be a mistake.'

' I also come from a long line of people who make mistakes.'

That was true enough anyway but this time she didn't think his remark funny. Instead her brows drew together and her mouth tightened before she spoke.

'Why are you doing this?'

'Doing what?'

'Talking to me as if, well, as if you really do know me.'

'Because in a way I feel I do.'  He paused to take a deep breath. He was not usually so forthright with girls so early on but, as she had warned him, time was short.  He leaned further across the table and lowered his voice.  'Look, I haven't been able to stop thinking about you since I met you. I want to know things about you, where you live, what you work at, what you like to do in your spare time, oh and why you carry all those candles around in your bag?'

Her frown deepened.

'What do you know about my candles?'

'I saw your bag full of them as you got off the train the other morning.'

With this added admission of intrusion into her privacy he expected her to take further offence, maybe even rise from the table and leave him stranded with his half-eaten quiche but instead her expression relaxed and the beginnings of a smile lit her eyes.

'But that's what I do?'

'You mean you make candles?'

She nodded somewhat doubtfully.

'You seem disappointed.'

'No-no, of course not. I thought that you might have been planning some big celebration and that I might wangle an invitation.'

To his surprise she dropped her head to one side almost in a parody of coquetry but he felt it was more as if she were mocking herself than him.

'Do you really want to spend time with me in the next five days?'

'There's nothing I want more.'

'You may regret it.'

' I'll take that chance.'

'Well, all right then. What will we do?'

'I'll surprise you.'

But in the days that followed it was she who surprised him and went on surprising him. She brought him to parts of the city that were unknown to him or so it seemed because he was seeing them through her eyes. There was an almost surreal quality in the way she could draw the essence from every moment, highlight the extraordinary inner glow in ordinary things. They found themselves in corners where the light played on old stone and moments of suspended stillness reigned, in alleyways where bits of history lingered, at gaps through which the sun made oblique pathways on the river on which people might even walk... At first he thought that it was the actual limit on their time together that gave it its unique luminance but as the days passed it felt like something deeper. He did not know if it was love on her part but it wasn't just that on his. He had been in love before but it hadn't been like this. This was more. This was a tight rope, a place where joy and fear met, where he found himself on a pitch of elation balanced precariously by a constant fear of falling. It was intoxicating, like skiing without skis. She filled his days but, like the horizon, was always beyond him, just out of reach, drawing him on, yet, at the same time, holding him back. Their talk was different too, not the light banter of lovers but about fundamental things like God and life and truth and beauty, subjects large enough for friendship but too big for intimacy. They touched but they did not become lovers. Their arena was too wide. Love needs smaller, tighter spaces. Yet they craved each other's company. After they had separated they would talk on their mobiles well into the night, sharing what seemed to John a time warp of communication. Yet with all that he didn't feel that he truly knew her. It was as if the essential core of her personality was frozen in some secret place he had not yet penetrated. Perhaps if he were to see where she lived... But when he suggested that she take him to her flat she put him off repeatedly by describing it as drab and not worth seeing. On the other hand she spent many hours in his, fingering his accumulated possessions, pouring over his books, his CDs, even his clothes. He would watch her caress a jacket of his on a hanger in his wardrobe with her delicate hands in a way she never caressed him. It made him long to do the same for her. As time ran out he asked to be allowed to come to her flat but she went on refusing, that is, until the evening before she was due to go away.

Finally she consented and said she would wait for him there and that she would also let him know her destination, something she had withheld from him despite repeated requests. 'You will know soon enough,' she would say.

She had left the door on the latch so he entered without knocking. He did not call out in order to surprise her. There were low sounds of music and a bright light coming from what must be her living room. He moved towards it, his excitement mounting... The room looked luminous when he entered it, very different from the drab place that she had described. There were lit candles everywhere, all sizes, all shapes, all colours, all fragrances. So this was what she planned for their final celebration... Was it the climax he had been waiting for...? Since the moving flames from the candles dazzled his eyes from every level, even the floor, it was hard at first to make out any other objects in the room. Besides the wavering light, the many perfumes pervading the air made his head swim. It was some time before details came into focus. Finally he saw her. She was lying on a couch, her eyes closed, her hands folded inward. He picked his way though a sea of light towards her. Her body seemed naked except for a loose wrap of many colours. He called her name softly but she did not answer. He touched her hand but she did not move. In an endless, frozen moment he realized everything...

# CASSANDRA
## Csilla Toldy

Cassandra asked for admission to the literature club of the university and was warmly welcome by everybody. We liked newcomers. We liked to believe that we were expanding and it meant joy to have a new companion who shared our sophisticated passion.

Cassandra was a pail faced, rather pretty girl. She had long, brown hair, a little bit Jewish looking face with a characteristic, rather noble shaped nose, but I could only suspect this, for she never talked about her background. Her big intelligent eyes made a disturbingly brisk, even too clever impression, and any time she started to explain something, they jumped out of her face, mesmerising her listeners. This might have been the cause, as I believed, that she was favoured in most of our discussions. Her presence often created an austere atmosphere within the group. She had some wild air around her that revealed hardships in her circumstances or past experiences, but she was the youngest in the group, she could have become the pet of the company with time, if she had been more patient, or had had more faith in herself.

The boys were very pleased with her, especially one of them. Chris studied at the Faculty of Medicine, his main interests were science and new technologies, not literature, but he enjoyed our group meetings. I always thought that he only joined us on a holiday-basis. He must have found compelling the irresponsible play we often experience in the company of artists and bohemians. We provided a safe environment for him, in which his first romantic attempts in writing poetry were respected and not laughed at.

Chris showed the most enthusiasm for Cassandra's short story that she read the night she was admitted. The story featured a lonely girl, who whilst doing the dishes in the kitchen, talks to the pots and plates, entrusting them all her sorrows. I was moved by this tale myself, because it revealed the elementary need for love and understanding in all of us that I have never seen explored in such a disturbing way before. She touched a wound that I was not willing to look at that time, therefore I decided that Cassandra had a troubled relationship with herself and probably with her environment, and her neediness was too tacky for my taste. As it was our custom, we discussed her story. I advised her to rewrite the story, so that we can understand the reasons for the girl's loneliness.

Chris fell in love with Cassandra, as it seemed and Jack, my dear friend Jack, who admitted it and was proud of being a Jew, used to make jokes about them. He thought they really were Cinderella and Prince Charming, especially because Cassandra's strange, theatrical ritual was to leave the literature gatherings before we all have had finished.

On the other hand, Jack's favourite rite was to phone me every Sunday afternoon in the campus, on which occasions he used to recite erotic poems that he had written to me. I was listening to him for hours, in a peculiarly stiff manner, but with widely open ears, being too embarrassed, but also very tempted to imagine his hands fiddling to the rhythm of hot hexameters.

Once I was on my way home from a lecture, when Cassandra caught up with me and started to entertain me. She talked about a rumour that I knew myself. Somebody claimed to have overheard a discussion between our dean and the head of English studies about a guest lectureship of Harold Pinter. We all assumed that our dean consciously omitted inviting him to be a guest lecturer at our University. Cassandra's monologue bore a tone that was in no way different to the fashionable decadent style we all applied, when we moaned about the establishment. I was rather bored to hear the gossip again and did not look impressed enough, for she suddenly changed the subject. She became agitated and gulping for breath she lamented her young wasted life. To my amazement, she also told me that she had TB.

When I expressed my doubts assuming that her perception of the world and her life might be a bit too bleak, she started coughing forcefully and even managed to spit a little, but real puddle of blood on the concrete. I saw that I had to take her seriously and instructed her to go to see a doctor immediately. In her response she unveiled her wish to die, because she did not feel loved. Suddenly I was alarmed. I thought she was mentally disturbed and I felt responsible. I tried to address her conscience arguing that TB was contagious. I prompted her that she meant danger to the community, especially to Chris. Cryptic and menacing, like a black raven, Cassandra just laughed and coughed at the same time and left me behind on the pavement.

I was perplexed and very angry by her ignorant behaviour, by the drama she had performed to impress me, as I thought. I decided that Cassandra wanted to be noticed at any rate and the best reaction to her madness was non-reaction from my side. In my confusion I believed that if I ignored her she would forget her craze and leave me alone.

Some time passed and I did not talk to anyone about this encounter, I wiped it out of my memory. I simply forced Cassandra to disappear from my mind. Fortunately, she stopped coming to the club, and nobody missed her except for Chris, perhaps, who started to turn up less frequently as well. We were preparing to publish a new literary magazine, this activity gained momentum in our lives.

In the Christmas holidays I travelled home. In our little town I was invited to a party of an old friend of mine who studied at another university. We had a cause to celebrate. The oldest and most reputable publisher house in the capitol had agreed to print the first volume of his poetry, which he proudly presented to his friends and old companions. It was a smart looking little book, with a very limited number of copies but nevertheless... I was ashamed to discover a hint of envy deep in my soul that I tried to hide with an uncharacteristically noisy jubilation of my friend's success. I was honestly glad for his art being acknowledged, but the lurking impatience with my own achievements had come to the surface with a sudden push.

When I arrived back at the university, I could not wait for our club meeting I was so excited to get on with the magazine and see my first poems published. I ardently wrote and wrote.

The first provoking news after my arrival at the campus, that forced me to look at myself, was waiting for me in a letter from Jack. My friend, the old clever Jack informed me with great regret that he had to stop attending our university, on the wishes of his parents. They faced sudden financial hardship and had to send him to a less expensive college where he could finish his studies faster and become independent from them. That shiny brown envelope also contained the last erotic poem he ever wrote to me. To my utmost surprise I shed tears on that letter and later, I reluctantly had to admit that I missed his hot and intelligently wrapped desire, reaching me through the telephone cable on Sunday afternoons.

I was reminded of Jack on the first meeting of the literature club again, that we held in our favourite cafe in the town centre. Every old member came up with something newly written piece of work, except for Jack. Some new students came to us as well who were accepted without hesitation. All of us read their works one after the other. Cassandra asked to be allowed to read before nine o'clock saying that she had to go earlier as usual. The minute she started reading, an air of awe encapsulated the company. In contrast to me, everybody was listening to the beautiful music of her poetry with great pleasure as if being under a spell. After the second line she read aloud I started to feel unpleasantly aroused, and my anger grew with each word, until it became overwhelming. There could be no doubts about it: Cassandra was claiming my old friend's poem for her own, that I had just seen myself in that newly published volume during the holidays in my home town. It had been ruthlessly taken over by Cassandra, without any change.

When Cassandra finished, everybody thanked her and she left. The students were praising her progress that she had made in the holidays. It took me a while to gather myself, until I could spit out my unnaturally nervous horror over her behaviour and told my friends that I had known this poem and it was written by a friend of mine. Cassandra had committed the unforgivable: plagiarism.

I was appalled. I exaggerated it even more and fought to protect my friend from my hometown, until I realised that I did not have to prove the truth of my words, everybody believed me. Observing my dissonant feelings at the time I can see now that my ardent struggle for my friend was to hide the dishonesty of my statement and emotions. Because of that ill feeling of jealousy that was deeply hidden, but present in me, the lurking snake that poisoned my sentiments for

Cassandra, and even for my old friend in my home town. Though I was not lying, my words did not sound true to me and I fearfully hoped that I was the only one to notice the dissonance.

The members of the literature club instantly decided that Cassandra's behaviour was a cause for dismissal. We asked Chris to go after her and tell her that she was no longer welcome in the group.

I saw her only once after this night, on my way home one afternoon. Cassandra ran after me, and grabbed the sleeve of my coat. She stopped me, but then I had to wait until she finished coughing. Eventually she spat a little patch of blood into her handkerchief. Then she said to me:

– You are cruel, but you'll pay for it.

I could not reply, I was too perplexed. I found her childish threat ridiculous, but for some inexplicable reason I felt guilty. Although the law and moral had been on my side, I had been cruel and showed no mercy. She wished recognition and love, and I was the bearer of her secret, the only one to whom she lifted the veil that hid that painful desire. Why did I refuse to give her what she wanted in the first instance? Did I envy her charisma born out of suffering?

These are the questions that have been haunting me since that last chance meeting, like nasty, recurring dreams. Even now, when I vigil Joey, my four years old daughter. Sitting at her bedside I have to witness her spitting blood again and again. She suffers from a rare lung disease, which was caused, as an irony of fate, by the very vaccination itself against TB. Its occurrence is one to a million. Nevertheless, my husband and I are confident. He got his degree at the best university of this country. I trust my husband's abilities as a doctor. Chris knows what he is doing.

# NEW YORK
## Sam Millar

It was hot and sticky in New York. Stained shirts and biting underwear. Ninety in the shade and rising. A record was in the making. They said this muggy, claustrophobic weather made New Yorkers strange. Sometimes it made them do strange things.

I was feeling, for the first time since my arrival in the city, isolated. Above me, the sun floated on a ghostly haze as I entered the narrow street with its army of homeless people covered in liquid shadows, their slim belongings nipping at their feet.

An old, dilapidated church was now their 'home'.

"Yer axin' fer trouble, pal," said a deli worker, watching me walk towards them. "Moiderin' moither foickers, dem. Da woist." He pointed accusingly at the homeless as he denuded a tiny runway of *Juicy Fruit* and popped it in his mouth. His jawbones balloon nervously, as he chewed, like Norman Bates in *Psycho*.

I nodded, but otherwise ignored him. As one who had traversed the streets of Belfast, New York or its people held little, if any, fear for me.

The abysmal conditions of the homeless, in this the richest city in he world, never fails to shock. Their growth is cultivated by an obscene madness where, a few streets away on Park Avenue, the affluent feed and pamper their pets with apathy. Worlds overlapping; rarely touching.

At one time these people were the salt of the earth, pillars of society. Now they were the dregs, witnessed but unseen.

One man, both his legs amputated at the knee, was ensconced in a dilapidated wheelchair. Older than his years, his face sagged, as if the dogs of poverty and depression had stolen every bone from it, highlighting tiny dark webs which etched his eyes.

Near the end of the street, a bulging garbage bag lay gutted, revealing a shrivelled sanitary towel protruded from it like a bloody tongue panting in the heat. The stench oozing from the bag was stomach-churning to most passers-by. Not me. I've encountered worse.

As I side-stepped the bag, a man covered in a shadow of rags bumped me, mumbling: "Dirty my skin with bruises, punk? Ya betta kill me - cuz I'm cumin' fer ya! See? *See?* Whaddya hear, whaddya *sssayyyyy?*" He stuck out his tongue, which was carpeted in baked bean sauce and sores.

"Leave the man alone, Jo Jo," said the one in the wheelchair. "He done you no harm."

Jo Jo glared at me, then his friend, before walking backwards into the shadows.

"He don't mean no harm, really. Just suspicious of folk some."

I didn't know if I should get out of the street as quickly as possible, say my thank you and be gone. Instead, I opted to put my hand in my pocket for some change.

"Don't do that. Don't insult us."

My face reddened.

"Sorry…"

"No need for that. Your face already done apologised." He laughed, galvanizing his entire body into coughs and shakes. "Don't laugh enough. Out of practice."

"You don't sound like a New Yorker," I said.

"Neither do you, if you don't mind me sayin'."

The coughing didn't come this time, only the smile.

"Ah come from Tennessee, if a man can say he came from some place. Ah write, mostly, but do can-gatherin' to survive. You?"

"I'm from Belfast. I work in a casino - when it's not being shut down by the cops, that is."

"Well, Ah learned somethin' today. I didn't even know that New York had casinos. Must put that in my writin'."

"They're illegal," I explained.

"Nothin' wrong with that. Hell, being homeless in this city is illegal, if you were dumb enough to listen to the Mayor!" He pulled the wheelchair up to me. In his lap rested a bag of empty cans. "Belfast? That's a tough ol' place. All that killin'. Sheer crazy."

Now it was my turn to laugh. There are more people killed in New York on a weekend than there are in a year in Belfast. It seems everyone creates a bigger monster so as to diminish the one in his own head.

"Must be tough," he repeated, wondering.

"Not as tough as trying to survive in a wheelchair in New York," I said.

"Could be worse. Wheels could be gone," he smiled, not meaning it. "Ah'm not a regular at this can-gatherin', you know, but it's part of a strange adventure Ah fell into since comin' to New York City from Tennessee this last Christmas time."

He searched his pockets for something, found it, give light then inhaled it, deep down into his lungs. He squeezed his eyes tight, savouring the taste.

"Ah did have a better Saturday, myself, on account of the eight bucks plus Ah got for the cans and an idea came to me that same mornin'."

He blew a small amount of smoke into the air, as if not wanting to waste any. It had the sweet sickly smell of marijuana. "Usually Ah get just enough cans for cigarettes and coffee so Ah can set awhile inside and look over the ideas and writin' that Ah've been workin' on for going on eleven years now. In all that time Ah've travelled all over America, truck-ridin'. Ah rode all across the edge of Canada on freight-trains and went painting on a ship out of Montreal that took me to Hamburg in Germany. That was when I lost my legs, on board a rusted old whaler. A message from God not to hunt His creatures without feeling His wrath."

I thought he was going to tell me he had lost his legs in Vietnam, and in a perverse way I thought the truth more fascinating, almost romantic, as if ever one should lose his legs this was how it should be.

I was late for work, now, but I no longer cared. Along the avenue people were waving down air-conditioned cabs to avoid the oppressive air. The cabs' metal skins shimmered nervously, like stranded salmon – all silvery and scaly.

"Ah spent almost eight years in Dublin City, Ireland," he continued, "and travelled all up and down over there lookin' into the folk-music traditions that together with the Blues and Baptist gospel singin' was the roots of our country's rock'n'roll music. Then, living as hard and rough as I mostly did, got me interested in the people at the bottom of society and in all the strange wanderin' homeless ones who live on the streets of cities and out in the hobo-jungles. Living with these people and watching them has taught me many ways to survive and a whole heck of a lot besides about society."

The sun baked the back of my neck, burning it, making it peel. But I couldn't move. His voice had captured me, and I didn't struggle.

"Then my Grandpappy, who half-raised me, was a reading man. He got thousands of books, all kinds bought out of the moonshine he makes and sells. He planted some seeds got given to him by a biker club from Philadelphia. They come down every year on their 'cycles to collect the weed and bring him a two-pound sack of speed from the 'crack-capital'."

Jo Jo mumbled, somewhere in the shadows. I wondered if he was searching for a knife.

"Same as my Grandpappy, Ah also have a deep interest in mechanics, electronics, science, inventions and technological innovations. He's all but disowned me now because of the way Ah've been livin' and my areas of inquiry. He and Ah've had a feud goin' on because he never did tell me who my Daddy was or how he came by me for certain. He tells me versions until Ah don't know who to believe."

He inhaled once more on the butt and it disappeared between his finger and thumb. There was a smell of skin burning in the air and once again it made me think of Vietnam and an incident in Belfast.

"Ah got a draft-version of my book just about hammered together usin' a lot of songs Ah'd written, when it all got burned in a fire in west Philadelphia, October last. This, along with every other thing in the world Ah had and carried, guitar, too. A beat-up and beautiful guitar that almost broke my heart. Ah did go back to Tennessee then, but Ah could not stay and listen to Grandpappy telling me 'Told you so! Temptin' fate.' He's retirin' and wants me to stay there and learn 'the mixture' – moonshine - and tend him 'cause he's old. Hell Ah will if he'll last, but Ah gotta burnin' to do my own work. Besides, he could buy himself a nice old lady nurse if he really wanted."

He spun the wheelchair in a semi-circle, faced the sun, then said, "Say, Ah'm sorry. Ah guess Ah just had to open up to someone. Ah can tolerate hunger; but silence has always been a mean torture for me."

I said nothing, fearing I would ruin the stillness of time. Even the old church seemed to be swelling in the heat, listening, casting shadows further down the street. Long gone were its begging tongues and burning candles, but somehow it still infused the imagination with agonizing-angels whose alibi faces were all majestically attuned to a vivid tapestry.

"Ah know you gotta go, but Ah may as well finish what Am'm on. Ah decided to take my own final challenge of this journey – to come to New York City with no money or nothin' and see if Ah could make it through the winter and find the people that live so hard all the time and learn their way and see what songs and ideas this gave me. Ah've done this now and it was pure hell mostly because of the attitudes of 'normal folk' and because of the hopelessness felt on the streets. Now Ah've emotional scars and a bunch of new songs and ideas, but Ah've gotta get above this condition to get a little distance, if Ah'm to write about it or try to help these people. And Ah hope then to find a business manager so Ah can sell some of the material."

The silence of the street became eerily beautiful, like a symphony performed by ghosts of fallen warriors. You could fall right into it and be carried away, for ever and ever.

He had talked for an hour but it seemed barely a minute. An hour ago I had been wrapped in self-pity, now it was gone. He was telling me, a stranger, his life story of family intrigue and dirty dealing, of the rusted hopes of life's oppressive deepness and the unassailable belief that acuity of hindsight conquers all the dark guilt that clings stubbornly to our souls.

I wanted to tell him of a life I once knew, of madness, brutality and death, where whispers recruit the emotions, destroying them forever. But before I could answer, rain was upon us, stinging. Potholes became pregnant with it, gurgled as they choked on it. Yellow cabs navigated the slick, aqueous streets while the homeless squeezed their backs tight against the church walls, preventing most of their 'belongings' becoming waterlogged.

The cabs drenched me with their power of indifference for I, also, had become invisible, a nothing. I turned to say goodbye, but he was gone – they all were.

"Hey!" shouted the deli worker, wiping his massive hands on a powdered apron. "Ya really shouldn't be down here on yer own. Dat scum would cut your throat and think nothin' of it. Go on, now! I'll watch yer back…"

The deli worker was still there, when I looked behind, shaking his head in disbelief, obviously thinking of how lucky I was to have got out of there with my life. In a way I *was* lucky. Lucky to have met a man whose name was unknown but who put things, for me, in their perspective and suddenly my isolation in the great city was no longer complete.

I was free again.

# TAOBH THIAR DEN AGHAIDH FIDIL: GIOTAÍ AS AN SEOMRA SCOILE
Claire Dagger

Is criathar mór é an fochoinsias.
Scagtar an fíor ón mbréag ann.
Ní ligtear tríd ach an bhréag.
Coinníonn an fochoinsias smacht docht ar an réalachas. Dá scaoilfí na laincisí phléascfadh an domhan réalachas anuas orainn.
Anois is arís, áfach, éiríonn poill an chriathair níos mó ná ba chóir iad a bheith dár gcompord.
Tháinig an séu bliain isteach sa rang ag fiche cúig tar éis a trí, an rang deireanach tráthnóna Dé hAoine. Sheas siad go ciúin don phaidir mar a sheasann siad ag tús gach ranga gach lá sa tseachtain.
Glóir don athair, agus don mhac, agus don Spiorad Naomh, mar a bhí ar dtús, mar atá anois, mar a bheas go brách, trí shaol na saol, Amen....
D'imigh fuaim a nguthanna amach tríd an fhuinneog oscailte ... ag meascadh le fuaim an lomaire faiche. Bhí boladh milis an fhéir nuabhainte ag foluain ar an ngaoth. Cruthaíodh atmaisféar an tsamhraidh agus na laethanta saoire fada a bhí le teacht.
Agus am na scrúdaithe ag druidim leo arís, bhí an amisir ag imirt a cleas míchneasta ar na scoláirí, mar a dhéanann sí ag an am seo chuile bhliain. Bhí sé deacair orthu luí isteach ar na leabhair agus an ghrian ag spalpadh anuas ó ard na spéire. Ach do Bhean Uí Mhurchú, ba ghnáthrang é agus bhí obair scole le déanamh!
"Tógaigí amach bhur bpáipéir scrúduithe agus déanfaimid ceist a haon, cuid a dó, den phrós roghnach sa rang," a d'ordaigh sí. Tógadh amach na leabhair go drogallach, agus chrom siad ar a gcuid oibre. Thug Bean Uí Mhurchú faoi deara nach raibh an leabhar tógtha amach fós ag an bpleidhce, Séamas.
"Suigh suas díreach sa chathaoir, a Shéamais, nach bhfuil do leabhar tógtha amach agat fós? Tóg amach anois é!"
"Tóg amach é!," a dúirt Séamas á chaitheamh féin siar sa chathaoir,

"tóg amach é, cén rud atá i gceist agat, a mhúinteoir?" ar sé, a theanga ina bhéal aige.

Phleasc an rang amach ag gáire.

"Níl uait ach go gcaithfinn amach as an seomra thú, bhuel, ní shásod thú."

"Ní fhéadfá mé a shásamh, a mhúinteoir."

"Amach leat agus síos go dtí an bpríomhoide!"

Amach an doras leis.

Mhothaigh sé fós an phian sa droim mar ar chiceáil a athair aréir é nuair a rinne sé dearmad na ba a ligean amach as an bpáirc. Mharóinn é dá bhféadfainn, a mhóidigh sé, ach go dtí sin ní ligfead don bhitchseach siúl orm mar sin.

Bhí smacht iontach ag Bean Uí Mhurchú, le dearcadh crosta ar an rang, laghdaíodh an ruaille buaille agus chromadar ar a gcuid oibre arís.

Sheas sí in aice na fuinneoige. "Cad ba chúis leis an ráiméis lofa as béal Shéamais? Níl ciall dá laghad ag baint leis, agus an fheirm bhreá agus an teach mór atá ag a athair, agus gan dabht ar bith ach go bhfágfaidh sé chuile rud aige. Tá saol róbhog ag déagóirí inniu," a smaoinigh sí.

Tharraing sí anáil dhoimhin isteach ina cuid scámhóg. Ba bhreá léi an boladh ón bhféar nuabhainte. Chuir sé laethanta a hóige féin i gcuimhne di. Bhi an lomaire faiche imithe as radharc, ach chuala sí fós é. Mhothaigh sí teas na gréine ar a haghaidh agus ar a lámha.

Ní ligfeadh sí don phleidhce sin an lá a mhilleadh uirthi, ach fós lean sí uirthi ag smaoineamh air. Cuma dhathúil amuigh ach bhí an taobh istigh lofa. Stán sí go géar ar an fhéar nuabhainte. D'eitil a hintinn faoin chlúdach mín bog. B'fhacthas di go bhfaca sí na péisteanna agus na seangáin agus feithidí eile ag borradh agus ag ithe a chéile. Thángamar ón gcré agus rachaimis ar ais inti, tháinig na focail duairce ón mBíobla chuici. D'airigh sí ait. Níl cearr liom ach an diabhal Séamas sin. Nárbh eisean an boc ceart!

Thug sí faoi deara na scamaill dhubha ag cruinniú siar sular iompaigh sí ar ais don rang.

Bhí Áine, scoláire ciúin, seacht mbliana déag d'aois, ag stánadh amach an fhuinneog go smaointeach

"A hÁine, coinnigh d'intinn ar do chuid oibre, níl aon rud níos tábhachtaí ná na scrúduithe anois."

Bhí a guth tuisceanach. Ní fhaca sí sochraid chomh truamhéileach le fada, buachaill chomh ciúín sin, a shaol ag síneadh amach roimhe, conas a chuirfeadh éinne lámh ina bhás féin? Ba shóiléir go raibh Áine fós ag fulaingt, ach ar an iomlán, tá sí ag déileáil go maith leis, a cheap sí.

Bhí rún bhás a dearthár fáiscthe go doimhin i gcroí Áine.

Cén fáth a ndearna sé é? Ní dhéanfaidh mé dearmad go deo ar an scread uafásach sin a lig Daid as nuair a fuair sé é ag crochadh ón gcrann ag bun an ghairdín. Níor lig sé do Mham é a fheiceáil mar sin, ach chonaic mé é, a shúile agus a bheola ata. Ceapann Mam gur uirthi féin atá an locht, ach tá fhios agam cad a mharaigh é; nár tháinig mé air ina sheomra agus an t-insteallaire ina láimh aige? Cén fáth nár inis mé dóibh é? Dá bhfaigheadh sé cabhair níos luaithe, b'fhéidir go mbeadh sé beo fós. A Thiarna, an bhfuil mise mar eisean, an bhfuil an gealtachas céanna ag sní tríd mo chuisleacha?

D'fhéach Bean Uí Mhurchu timpeall ar na cloigne cromtha ar a gcuid oibre, smaoinigh sí ar na deiseanna iontacha sa saol a bhí ar fáil don aos óg inniu. Chuimhnigh sí ar an ioncam suarach a shaothraigh a hathair ón talamh crua. Ní raibh aon Chomhphobal Eorpach ag cur seiceanna chucu gach ráithe.

Bhí siad uilig anois ag maireachtáil ar an gComhphobal Eorpach. Dúirt Séamas Ó Sé léi inné go n-íoctar é gan obair a dhéanamh ar an bhfeirm ar chor ar bith. An tóin ag titim as an saol, ní nach ionadh, a cheap sí.

Chonaic sí Pádraig. Bhí a lámha trasna a uchta agus cuma trodach ar a aghaidh.

"A Phádraig, cén fáth nach bhfuil tú ag scríobh?"

"Tá mé ag smaoineamh, a mhúinteoir," ar seisean ag cogaint barr a phinn. Cinnte, bhí a éadan fillte suas amhail is dá mbeadh sé, ach ní ar a scríobhfadh sé ar cheist a haon ar an bprós roghnach a bhí a intinn.

Bhí fhios ag an saol go raibh an dara bean ag a athair sa teach. Ní raibh sé chomh dona sin. Cheap a chompánaigh gurb iontach an t-éacht é. "Ní leor bean amháin do lucht Seoighe, eh a Phádraig!," a deiridís leis. Cheap sé féin go raibh a mháthair amaideach cur suas leis, ach níorbh é a ghno é. Bhí a shaol féin aige, go dtí aréir. Bhí airgead de dhith air agus chuiagh sé isteach i seomra Mhaim chun iasacht airgid a fháil uaithi. Chonaic sé an bheirt acu sa leaba. Níor thuig sé ar dtús cad a bhí ag tarlú. Níor chuala siad é. Ba le mam a bhí sí cairdiúil! Rith sé amach sa gclós. Chonaic a chara Pól é ag caitheamh aníos.

"An iomarca ceirtlise aréir, a mhic?"

"Bí chiallmhar! Ní raibh tada cearr leis an ól ach is ar an diabhal borgaire a cheannaíomar ina dhiaidh sin i MacDonalds a chuirimse an locht." Dá scaoilfí an rún, bheadh sé ina staicín áiféise ceart.

Shiúil an múinteoir thairis.

Tá ciall ag an mbean sin, a smaoinigh sé. Dá dtosnódh sí ag tabhairt fúm...

Dhún Bean Uí Mhurchú ceann de na fuinneoga a bhí ar oscailt. Bhí an aimsir ag éirí beagán níos fuaire. Shiúil sí timpeall an ranga ag bailiú na n-aistí. Bailíonn Bean Uí Mhurchú aistí gach Aoine.

"An bhfuil an aiste réidh agat, a Mháire?"

Is cailín deas ciúin í Máire. Ní hé go bhfuil sí cliste, ach oibríonn sí go crua.

"Sé leathanach! Tá seo go hiontach. Ní raibh mé ag súil ach le cúig cinn."

"Bhí am le spáráil agam aréir, a mhuinteoir."

Bíonn am le spáráil agam gach tráthnóna Déardaoin. Téann Mam agus Áine go dtí an Bingo. Fanann mise sa teach chun aire a thabhairt do Dhaid agus a shuipéar a réiteach dó. An bhfuil a fhios ag Mam? Cuireann sí suas leis gach oíche eile. Nach gcloisim iad?

"Faigh gloine fuisce dom, a Mháire, agus suigh anseo in aice liom. Tá's agat bím uaigneach."

"Tá neart obair bhaile le déanamh agam, a Dhaid."

"Suigh," a d'ordaigh sé.

Chuir sé a lámh thar mo ghualainn. D'ól sé an fuisce go tapaidh. Leag sé a lámh chlé ar mo ghlúin.

"Éirigh as, a Dhaid. Ní maith liom sin."

"Nach tusa atá ag fáil mór anois. Tá bronntanas agam duit sa seomra."

Tá scoilteanna móra ar shíleáil an tseomra chodlata. Tá fhios agam, cúig cinn díbh. Comhairim iad gach oíche Déardaoin. Nuair a thosaigh a lámha ag baint mo bhlúis scoile díom, thosaigh mé ag pleanáil m'aiste. Scríobhaim sár-aistí. Thóg sé tamall fada air é a féin a shásamh aréir agus sin, a mhúinteoir, an fáth go bhfuil sé leathanach ann in ionad a cúig. Bheadh sé leathanach níos faide ach bhí orm cnaipe a fhuáil ar mo bhlús, timpiste a tharla nuair nach raibh mé sciobtha go leor á oscailt dó.

"Is tú an dalta is fearr atá agam, a Mháire."

"Go raibh maith agat, a mhúinteoir. Munar mhiste leat, an bhféadfainn an fhuinneog a dhúnadh?"

"Cinnte, ní dóigh liom go leanfaidh an dea-aimsir seo."

"Ó a Dhia," arsa Antaine, nuair a d'fhéach an múinteoir ina threo, "rinne mé dearmad ar an diabhal cóipleabhar sin arís." Bhí mé ar mo bhealach go dtí an seomra suí chun é a fhail ach chuala mé iad ag ithe a chéile, ag troid arís, fúmsa ar ndóigh.

"Nach dtuigeann tú nach bhfuil an buachaill cliste go leor fanacht sa scoil. Is am amú é. Tá sé uaim anseo ar an bhfeirm."

"Cén chaoi a bhféadfadh sé coinneáil suas leis an dream eile sa rang? Gach ré seachtain coinníonn tú ó scoil é ar chúis amháin nó ar chúis eile. Tá a sheans tuillte aige, rogha eile a bheith aige ná fanacht anseo ag streachailt leis an saol. Níl sé mar tusa."

"Is é mo mhac é, sin sin. Fágfar an fheirm aige."

"A Thiarna, fágfaidh sé cinnte, ní hamháin an scoil ach muid féin freisin. Ní chuirfinn locht air."

Ní raibh sé de mhisneach ag Antaine dul isteach sa seomra chun a leabhar scoile a fháil. Níorbh fhiú é ar aon nós, bheadh an focal scoir ag a athair i gcónaí. Bhuail an clog. Lig Antaine osna. Bhí sé a ceathair a chlog, deireadh an lá scoile tagtha.

"Deireadh seachtaine maith agaibh." Bheannaigh Bean Ui Mhurchu dóibh mar a bheannaíonn sí dóibh ag an am seo chuile sheachtain sa bhliain scoile.

Bhí said ar a mbealach go tapaidh. Bhí sí léi féin sa seomra. D'fhéach sí amach an fhuinneog. Bhí an bháisteach tagtha, drochthuar don deireadh seachtaine.

Thit ciúnas na deireadh seachtaine ar an scoil.

Bhí na guthanna ina dtost.

Ar feadh tamaillín eile.

# TALES OUT OF SCHOOL
## Claire Dagger
*Trans by Frank Sewell*

It's a giant sieve – the subconscious. Separating what is true from what is not. Only what is false is allowed to filter through. It really does keep a firm old hold on reality – the subconscious. If it let slip, reality would come crashing down on us. Sometimes, the holes in the sieve get bigger and wider than we would like.

Year six filed into the room at 3.25; last class, Friday afternoon. They stood quietly for the prayer, as they did at the start of every class.

Glory be to the Father, the Son, and the Holy Spirit, as it was in the beginning, is now, and ever after, world without end, Amen....

The sound of their voices drifted out the open window and mingled with the whirr of the lawnmower. The sweet smell of freshly cut grass hung in the air, reminding everyone of summer and the long holidays ahead. But the weather was only playing its annual schoolboy tricks, for they were still only in the run-up to exams.

The sun beating in through the window made it hard for them to concentrate. But as far as Mrs. Murphy was concerned, this was a lesson like any other, and there was work to be done.

Take out your past exam papers, she commanded. Today we're going to do question 1, section 2, prose. Slowly, reluctantly, they took out their books and papers, and set to work. Mrs. Murphy noticed that the class messer, Seamus, hadn't opened a single book.

Sit up straight in your chair, Seamus. Have you not even taken your book out yet? Take it out now!

Take it out!, said Seamus, leaning back in his chair. What is it you have in mind, miss?, he said, tongue in cheek.

You just want me to throw you out of this class. Well, I'm not going to please you this time.

You couldn't please me, miss.

Get out and go straight to the Principal!

Out he went.

He could still feel the pain in his back where his father had kicked him last night just because he forgot to let the cows out of the field. If I could kill him, I would, he swore to himself. Till then, anyway, I'm not gonna let that bitch walk all over me.

Mrs. Murphy had remarkable control over the class; with one cross look, the uproar subsided, and the whole class settled down to work.

She stood by the window. What was behind that stupid dirty talk Seamus was always coming out with? There was no call for it. Didn't his father own a big farm and house? And there was no doubt he would leave it all to Seamus one day.... Teenagers have it too easy these days.

She a took a deep, deep breath. She loved the smell of a new-mowed lawn. It reminded her of her own young days. By now, the lawnmower itself had moved out of sight, but she could still hear it. Her face and hands felt the heat of the sun.

She wasn't going to let that messer spoil her day. But even so, she couldn't stop thinking about him. Fine on the outside, but rotten within. She looked hard at the newly cut grass. Her mind delved beneath the smooth soft surface. She seemed to see worms, ants and bugs swelling up and eating eachother. Earth to earth, ashes to ashes – the sombre Biblical words echoed in her ears. She felt strange. I'd be alright if it wasn't for that rascal Seamus. The cheek of him!

Noticing the sky growing dark, she turned back to the class.

Áine, one of the quiet pupils, 17 years old, was looking out the window, lost in thought.

Áine, keep your mind on your work. Your exams are the most important thing right now.

Mrs. Murphy sounded understanding. She hadn't seen such a sad, tragic funeral in a long time. Such a quiet boy; his whole life ahead of him. How could anybody take their own life? Clearly, Áine was still suffering. But overall, she was handling it alright.

What lay behind her brother's death, however, was a secret Áine kept deep in her heart.

Why did he do it? I will never forget Dad's terrible scream when he found him hanging from the tree at the bottom of the garden. He wouldn't let Mum see him like that; but I saw him, his swollen eyes and lips. Mum blames herself, but I know what killed him. Sure didn't

I catch him in his room with the needle and all in his hand? Why didn't I tell them? Maybe if he'd got help earlier, he'd still be alive. God, am I like him? Does the same sort of madness running in my veins, too?

Mrs. Murphy cast an eye over them all with their heads down to their work. She thought about all the great opportunities open to young people today. Compare that to the pittance her father scraped from the barren bit of earth he had. There was no European Union then. No regular cheques in the post.

Nowadays, they were all in the E.U. Séamus Ó Sé himself told her just the other day that he got paid for doing nothing on his own farm. The world's gone mad, and no wonder.

Then she saw Patrick. He was sitting with his arms folded over his chest, looking like a wee tough guy.

Patrick, why aren't you writing?

I'm thinking, miss, he said, chewing the top of his pen. His forehead was wrinkled, and he did indeed look as if he was thinking – but not about question one on the prose excerpt.

The world and his wife knew that the boy's father had moved another woman into the house. It wasn't that awful, was it? His mates all thought it was a great achievement. One woman's not enough for the Shaws, eh Patrick?, they said to him. As far as he was concerned, his mother was stupid for putting up with it. But it was none of his business. He had his own life. Till last night. He needed some money, and went into his mother's room to ask for a loan. That's when he saw the two of them in bed. He didn't understand at first what was going on. And they didn't hear him. It was mammy she was sleeping with! He ran out into the yard. His friend Paul saw him puking his guts up.

Too much cider last night, boyo?

Wise up! There was nothing wrong with the drink. It was that bloody burger we got afterwards in MacDonalds.... If the secret got out, they'd all be laughing at him.

The teacher strolled on past him.

That woman's got sense, he thought to himself. If she started going on at me....

Mrs. Murphy closed one of the windows. It was getting a bit colder.

She walked around the class, collecting the essays. Mrs. Murphy collected the essays every Friday.

Have you finished your essay, Mary?

Mary was a nice quiet girl. Not that clever, but she worked hard.

Six pages! That's great. I was only expecting five.

I'd some spare time last night, miss.

I've some spare time every Thursday evening, thought Mary. Mum and Annie away at the Bingo. Me stuck at home to look after Dad and fix his supper for him. Does Mum know? She puts up with him every other night. Don't I hear them?

Get me a whiskey, Mary, and sit down here beside me. You know I get a bit lonely.

I've a lot of homework to do, Daddy.

Sit, he ordered.

He put his arm around my shoulder; knocked back his whiskey; and put his hand on my knee.

Don't, Daddy. I don't want you to do that.

You aren't half growing up. I've got a present for you in the room.

The bedroom has big cracks in the ceiling. I know it has. Five of them. I count them every Thursday night. When he started taking off my blouse, I started planning my essay. I write really good essays. It took him a long time last night, miss, and that's why there's six pages. There would've been another page, only I had to sew a button onto my blouse. You see, I wasn't quick enough, last time, opening it for him.

You are my best pupil, Mary.

Thanks, miss. Please can I close the window?

Of course. I don't think this good weather is going to last.

O God, said Anthony to himself, when the teacher looked over in his direction. I forgot to bring my bloody book in again. I was going into the livingroom to get it when I heard them arguing and fighting again – over me, as usual.

Can you not see the boy's not smart enough to stay at school? It's a waste of time. I need him here on the farm.

How can he keep up with the rest of the class? Every week you keep him off for one reason or another. He deserves a chance, some other choice than to be just stuck here struggling to get by. He's not like you.

He's my son, and that's that. The farm will be his.

He'll leave alright, I'm telling you. Not just school, but us as well. I wouldn't blame him.

Anthony couldn't bring himself to go in and get the book. It wasn't worth it, anyway. His Da always had the last word. The bell rang. Anthony breathed a sigh of relief. It was four o'clock and the school day was over.

Have a good weekend everybody, said Mrs. Murphy, just as she did every week in term time.

They soon got on their way. Standing alone in the room, the teacher looked out the window. The rain had arrived – a bad sign for the weekend.

That familiar weekend silence enveloped the school.

The voices were silent.

For another while.

# SLOW LEARNER
## Gordon Williams

"Ah! Hello Sean," the elderly man greeted him.

"Who are you?" asked Sean, puzzled by the man's familiarity.

The elderly man lowered his clipboard and told him: "Nathaniel. I'm Nathaniel. We have met before but you probably won't remember me. I'm your reviewer and you're here for another review."

"A review?" asked Sean. "A review of what?"

Sean still looked bewildered and the old man realised that his usual introduction would be needed.

"You're here because your life has ended and you have to review what lessons have been learned during that life before you can go back and start another one," Nathaniel told him.

"Why do I have to go back to another life?" asked Sean. "Why don't I have just one life?"

"Ah," said Nathaniel, "one of the big questions already. Perhaps we would be better going through some easier questions first." He picked up his silver pen and asked, "How old were you when you died?"

"Twenty four. I was killed when a bomb we were carrying exploded. What happened to Danny?"

"He's still in hospital. He lost part of his arm and he'll be having some plastic surgery to his face and shoulder but we won't be seeing him just yet. What were your last thoughts as you died?" the old man asked as if he already knew the answer.

" I hoped that Danny was alright. And that it's all ended for me. My war is over."

"Yes," said the old man. "It's over for you now. Why were you making bombs?"

"To destroy symbols of British Imperialism and to liberate the people of Ireland from oppression by a foreign power."

"And how many people did you kill trying to liberate the people from… from this oppression by a foreign power?"

"I don't know – eight, ten - something like that. We didn't keep score."

"You killed fourteen people, alone or in your efforts with others. Seven service personnel, two people that were actively involved on the other side of the conflict, and five civilians who just got in the way. You also injured another eighteen people who are still on the Earth."

"There are always casualties in war. How do you know it was fourteen?"

"The records are here," the old man pointed to the shelves along the walls of the room. "Everything is recorded and everything is here."

Sean stared at the long rows of boxes on the shelves that reached up to the high ceiling. "What are they?" he asked, pointing at the boxes on the shelves. "Are they the records of everybody's lives?"

"Yes, they are the records of everybody's lives, but each box is for one person," the old man told him. "These are just the lives of those that I review. There are lots of other rooms with records in, too. And yes, everybody's life *is* recorded, even if it isn't in this room: every detail, every action, every thought. The records are complete."

"Are these records like the files on a computer?" asked Sean.

"Well, I don't work on the technical side of things," replied the old man, "but you could say that they are similar to computer files, only a lot more sophisticated. There's a lot of information – more than you could get on your simple computers."

Sean looked again at the shelves and asked, "Could you show me a life from one of the boxes?"

"No," replied the old man, "but I can show you parts of your own life if that becomes necessary. Like the fourteen people that you killed if you were to dispute that."

"No, no. That could be right – I wouldn't know the exact number."

"And how do you feel about having killed fourteen people?"

"It was necessary because I was fighting for the freedom of my people – fighting against the British oppressors. Fighting so that we would have our own free Ireland. Fighting to give our children...."

"What did you achieve by fighting?" the old man interrupted him.

Sean looked deflated, having been stopped midway through his stream of justification, but continued, " We showed the British imperialists that they could not continue oppressing the Irish people and we destroyed symbols of that oppression and attacked those forces that..."

"You see that drawer – the top one in that desk?" Nathaniel interrupted him again, pointing to the desk near Sean's left arm. Sean pulled it open and asked him, "This one?"

"Yes. You'll find a head-set in there."

"This thing?" asked Sean, holding up something that looked like a crash helmet and goggles combined.

"Yes," replied the old man. "Put it on your head and pull the eyepiece over your eyes."

"Why do you want me to do that? What's it for?" Sean questioned him again. "Is it like virtual reality?"

"No – it is reality, but recorded."

"Can you play videos on it?" Sean asked.

"Something like that. Try it and see."

Sean examined the helmet and eyepiece for a short time before putting them on and adjusting them slightly.

"Comfortable?" Nathaniel asked.

"Yeah, OK. What are you supposed to see with these?"

"Just a moment," Nathaniel got up and switched on a small console. "Any pictures yet?"

"Yeah. Wow, it's really clear. There's this funeral with a tricolour draped over the coffin. And there's Dessie – and Paddy Joe and Jamesy. And that's me Da. And there's me Ma ...and our Nuala and me Auntie Josie are holding her up. And the boys are carrying the coffin... and they're firing a salute... It's *my* funeral.... *my* funeral... and there's lots of people there to pay their respects... and there's the oration at the grave as they lower the coffin down. Wow – look at all them people. All here just for me.

And there's another funeral. I don't know the people at this one... there's a lot of RUC officers... and some women crying....And there's another funeral.... And another one... and another one... it's just funerals – is there nothing else on this programme?

Now there's a man walking down a hospital ward with crutches... one of his legs isn't on the ground ... because it's not there. And there's another man having an operation on his knee... and another one...and there's a man walking with a limp – I know him - that's Declan McDonagh, the bastard....And there's a woman crying in her bed at night... and a little girl asking where her Daddy is...and two boys putting flowers on a grave...I don't know who they are...and a man taking tablets for his nerves... and three men in a car going out looking for Catholics... anybody...that they can shoot because of what's happened. And there's a family leaving their home because it's been attacked twice before and now it's burning...and they can't go back. And more shootings....That's it – the pictures have finished... it's gone blank.

What is all this? What are all these pictures?"

"It's a record of all your achievements during your lifetime," the old man replied. "What you did and its results."

"I never did all that," replied Sean, pulling the apparatus off his head. "You've made all this up. It's a fabrication."

"You know it's all true," said the old man. "It's what you did."

Sean jumped up from his chair and tried to grab the old man, shouting "You've made all this up, you lying bastard" at him, but his hands went straight through the old man's form.

The old man was completely unmoved, and he remained still as Sean tried to hit him, with the same result: Sean's hand went straight through him. Sean stood staring at the old man as he told him, "You don't have a body here – it's not the same as on the Earth. Attacking me won't achieve anything here, just like it didn't on Earth. Do you want to sit down again?" he offered, gesturing towards the chair out of which Sean had leapt.

Sean sat down slowly, staring at the old man before shaking his head in silence. He sat thinking for short time before asking, "What happens now? Will I be going to Hell?"

Nathaniel smiled at this question and then answered it. "There is no Hell. No fire and brimstone; no souls roasting in perpetual torment. It was invented as a concept by officers of the church to keep their subjects in fear of transgression. And it was very lucrative, too: you could give large sums of money to the church in previous times in order to avoid Hell or Purgatory, or buy yourself a place in Heaven. One of the reasons why the church became so wealthy and so powerful. But nobody ever bought their way out of Hell or into Heaven: they all ended up here whatever they did and whatever they paid."

"So, what do you do here – in this place?" Sean asked.

"As I said earlier, we review lives that have ended, and assess whether any lessons have been learned so that they won't need to be learned again in the next life."

"What next life? Will I have another life?" Sean asked, sitting forward on his seat.

"Well, yes you will have another life – in all probability several or many more lives, depending on how your learning proceeds. Which is why you are here now: to assess what you learned in your last life…. and looking through the records…" Nathaniel flipped through several pages on his clipboard, "…that appears to be nothing at all."

"Nothing? Nothing at all?" Sean shouted at him angrily. "I learned about our history. I got four GCSEs…"

"Not that sort of learning," the old man interrupted. " I mean what spiritual lessons did you learn? Did you learn about love and respect for your fellow men and other living creatures? Did you learn to accept responsibility for your own actions? Did you stop blaming others and yourself for your situation and for the events on Earth? Did you seek out any spiritual teachings or ask for any advice in order to understand God better?"

"I went to church every Sunday."

"And what did you learn there – thou shalt not kill? Thou shalt love thy neighbour as thyself? These are codes to follow in your daily life – not empty words to repeat like your six times table. Words are of no value if they are not matched by actions. And your actions indicate that you learned *no* spiritual lessons during your last lifetime. None."

"So what happens now? How am I going to learn any spiritual lessons?"

"You will go back to the Earth and be provided with the circumstances to allow you to learn what you did not learn in your last life," the old man replied.

"And what will they be?"

"I don't know exactly, but it's likely to be a lifetime in a place of conflict where there is opportunity for resolving that conflict to some degree without violence, even though violence may look like an attractive proposition to some of the people living there."

"Does that mean that I'll be going back to Northern Ireland?" Sean questioned him.

"Probably not," replied the old man, smiling. "Things are winding down there; by the time you are old enough to make choices there will be a lot less scope for violence than there was during your last lifetime. It's not perfect and there's still some way to go, but no, it's not likely to be Northern Ireland. Probably the Middle East, or Central and South America: much more scope for violence there. And consequently much more scope for choosing another approach as an alternative to violence."

"Are you going to be sending me there?"

"Oh, no," replied the old man, "I don't make any direct transfers - I just compile my report. I do make recommendations, which the Transfers Committee take into account, but they decide where you will go next time. I just assess each life and see what progress – if any – has been made."

"Why don't they teach you about the next life in church? Why do they tell you that you only have just the one life?"

"Well, some religions do recognise the doctrine of reincarnation – mostly the Eastern Earth religions like Buddhism and Hinduism. There was a time when Christianity used to recognise the possibility of reincarnation, too – which should not surprise anybody familiar with "the life everlasting, and the resurrection of the body" - but it was abandoned at the Congress of Constantinople about five hundred of your years after Christ died.

When you have advanced spiritually you will have to consider the possibility of reincarnation and what Buddhists would call The Law of Karma."

"What's that all about?" Sean asked.

"Well, the Law of Karma states that what you do in one lifetime is held to account in the next lifetime – or lifetimes – and that you have to live with the consequences of your previous actions. So, if you had stolen something from somebody in one lifetime then something similar would be stolen from you in a subsequent lifetime. Which means that whatever you steal in one lifetime you are effectively stealing from yourself."

"Well what about if you get caught stealing something by the police and get punished in Court? Does that get taken into account if you have another life?" Sean asked the old man.

"Yes, to some extent it may do; but the real lesson is whether you will want to do it again. If you get away with stealing in one lifetime and don't regret it or change your actions then you will have to learn about it from the other side – usually by having your own possessions stolen – another time around. The same goes for killing, too."

"Does that mean that if you kill somebody in this lifetime that you will be killed yourself in another life?"

"That's one of the possibilities. Another one is that you will have to experience the loss of somebody close to you who is killed by another person, just as those close to your victims would have experienced that loss."

"So even if you think you have got away with it in this lifetime – if nobody catches up with you when you're alive – then you will still have to face up to what you did sometime in the next life?"

"Yes – that's the way it works."

Sean sat there quietly shaking his head as he took in the implications of what the old man had told him. After a long pause he asked, "So what am I going to have to do in my next life – or the one after it? Am I going to have to be killed because I killed people last time?"

"Not necessarily. Your last lifetime was ended because we didn't want you responsible for any more deaths."

"You mean that it wasn't an accident? That you did it?"

"There are no accidents, Sean," said the old man, smiling. "It was arranged that your life ended so that you could start again because you had ignored the opportunities for learning in your last life. It's a routine procedure when lives don't make any progress."

"So you bastards killed me?"

"No, your own actions killed you. And we had to protect others who are still trying to learn... with varying degrees of success. You *will* get another chance to learn - which you showed no signs of taking during your last life. That's the way it works: you always get another chance. And another. And another. Lots of chances until you eventually learn how to love your fellow men and women on the Earth."

"And then what?"

"Then you don't have to come back to the Earth to live again...but that's some way off just yet. You won't remember but you have been trying to learn these lessons for some time already. You were here after the war in Cambodia, the Spanish Civil War, the Taiping Rebellion, the American Civil War.... and other wars, too that didn't have a proper name. Altogether you have been involved in eighteen wars."

"Eighteen wars? *Eighteen?* Why do I keep fighting wars?"

"A good question. A very good question. And one that you are still looking to answer when you are on the Earth."

"So what is the answer? Why do I keep fighting wars?"

"Because that is the pattern that you have got stuck in: killing, and being killed by those in your own country that you see as enemies. The Hindus have a word for it: *samskara*. A samskara is the rut that a wheel forms in soft earth. It's a rut that you have to break out of - a pattern that you have to end."

"And how do I do that?"

"By choosing another approach to hating and killing your fellows on the Earth. And then you can move on to learn other lessons. Your time on Earth is just a learning experience – that all. And some people take a lot longer to learn the lessons of Earth than others. But everybody will learn eventually. It might seem to take a long time in Earth terms but that's just the way that you would understand time on the Earth. There is no time here: everything happens at the same time."

"I don't understand... what do you mean, 'There is no time here'"

"Sorry. I'm getting ahead of you. You don't really need to know about that now. Perhaps we should concentrate on your current lessons: choosing alternatives to violence and killing. It can be done; there are examples of people on the Earth who have abandoned those approaches and still achieved what they have set out to do."

"Who do you mean? Who has managed to do that that I'd know?"

"Mostly they are people whose names you would never hear – people in difficult circumstances that don't get any recognition or publicity, although their achievements are no less for that. But there are a few names that you might recognise: Mahatma Ghandi, Rosa Parkes,

Nelson Mandela..."

"Yeah, I recognise them apart from the second one."

"It can be done. And as more and more people on the Earth find other ways of dealing with conflict instead of blaming others, fighting and killing them, then it becomes easier for everybody else to learn, too. The more people that choose other approaches then the less scope there is for violence to influence others. Just as violence creates a mass effect that means more are likely to be involved in it, so a culture of non-violence influences everybody that lives in that culture. Everybody that chooses to live without violence influences everybody else on the Earth in some small way and makes it that little bit easier for everybody else to learn, too. Example is a powerful influence – I'm sure you know that from your last life."

Sean thought about this for a while and considered the people that he had looked up to during his last life: the people who had influenced his beliefs and his actions. "So I followed bad examples in my last life, did I?" he asked the old man.

"You made choices. And all choices have consequences. You could have made different choices and the outcome would have been different: you might not be talking to me now if you had made different choices."

"So what should I have done in my last life?"

"It's not a matter of what you should have done: it's always your choice."

"Well, what mistakes do you think I made?"

"There are no mistakes. Something is only a 'mistake' if you don't learn from it. Mistakes offer you a lot of opportunities for learning: once you have learned that something is a 'mistake' then you won't need to do that again."

"So mistakes are part of this learning business that you keep telling me about?"

"They *are* the learning process."

"So why can't we just be told all this and then save us all the trouble of living and all the upset and grief and hassle that goes with it?"

"You *have* been told many times. You and I have had this conversation many times before. But you forget it when you go back to the Earth to start another life so that you can learn yourself by making your own choices and living – and dying – with the consequences. If you get told all the answers then you stop asking questions. You do have some free will, although it will be limited at times. And you have to experience everything that living on the Earth has to offer: every thought, every action, every feeling, every consequence. Until your choices are limited to love and it's no longer a choice but the inevitable outcome of experiencing every other choice and realising that love is a better choice."

"It's getting a bit complicated – I'm not sure that I understand you."

"Well, I could give you an example that should demonstrate what I've tried to tell you. Put the headset on again."

Sean held up the headset but asked warily, "I don't have to watch any more horror films, do I?"

"No – no more horror films, I promise. Put it on," the old man gestured.

Sean slowly put the headset on and Nathaniel went to the console again to start it. "Ready?" he asked.

"Yeah."

Nathaniel sat down again and asked Sean to tell him what he saw.

"Wow – who's that? I don't know her but she's gorgeous. And she fancies me, too." Sean was silent for a while.

"What's happening now?" Nathaniel asked.

Sean laughed and replied, "I don't want to say."

"Do you think I would be embarrassed?" the old man asked. "Do you think that there is *anything* that I have not seen or heard?"

"Well you'll have to guess – it's a lot better than the last film. We're getting married now… all dressed up in church…all our families are there…and now there's a baby…it's a girl, she looks just like her mother…and there's two boys as well…and I'm working as a builder…there's a lot of work about now that things have improved. There's more money and there's less violence than there was…it seems to be coming to an end because most people have had enough of it…. and I'm playing football with my two boys… the oldest lad is really good, he plays for the local team… and I'm coaching them…I'm coaching the team and they've won the local league…they've given me the trophy to hold and they're going wild...and the young fella's really upset because he's having trouble at school...he's a bright kid but he can't read and everybody thinks that he's a slow learner but it's just that he can't read...and I'm sitting with him every night, helping him...I was never that interested in reading myself but I've got interested in helping and we've formed a group for kids with dyslexia and we're all helping each other...and he's improving slowly but it's a long, slow business even with me and his Ma helping him.

And their sister is going to violin lessons...it sounds awful at first when she's practising...but she's just won a second prize at the first Feis that she goes to...and she's got all these certificates now, and lots of trophies in her room...and she's going to music college now, and me and her Ma are watching her get her degree...and she's got a job playing in an orchestra in England.... and the oldest boy is playing for the county and me and his Ma and all our family are cheering him on...and the young fella has got seven GCSE's because we've all encouraged him so much and he's really proud of himself. And me and his Ma are proud of him, too.

And I'm getting too old to do the football coaching now...I'm bald at the front just like me Da...but I'm involved in running the club teams, sorting out the fixtures and the transport and the equipment and fund-raising...the club is expanding and it's doing really well...and I'm the chairman of the committee now... and my eldest lad has just finished doing a degree in sports science, and he's got a job as a games teacher. And my daughter's getting married... I'm giving her away and she looks beautiful...and my youngest lad has got a degree in engineering...*he's done it, he's done it*...I always knew he wasn't thick like they all thought – he just needed a lot of help.

And there's grandchildren...and I'm getting older and slower but I'm still involved in running the club...I've got more time since I retired...and my wife is still there...we've had our ups and downs but we've always loved each other, always stuck together even when it was difficult.... and now I'm lying in bed in hospital and all these people keep coming to see me...and there's another funeral... all my family are there and lots of other people...the boys from the club...the ones I coached are all grown up but they're all there...there's hundreds of people...they've all come to my funeral....I can't believe it...

That's it – it's ended."

Sean took off the headset and sat with his head in his hands. He looked up for a short time and asked the old man, "Is that what my life could have been?"

The old man replied, "Yes, it could have been like that, with some different choices," as Sean put his head in his hands again. "Most people seem to be more upset by that second experience – the one that shows what their life could have been – than whatever actually happened in their life," he told the man who still had his head in his hands.

Sean looked up, his eyes wet, and asked, "Could I really have done all that? Could I have had a wife and children and ...and all that love and respect?"

"Yes, all that was waiting for you. It still is," the old man told him. He paused for a while before asking, "Do you want to ask me anything else?"

Sean answered, "No – I think that's enough for now."

"Well then, I'll send this file on to the Transfers Committee and they will make the necessary arrangements for your next life on Earth."

"Thank you."

"Thank you, Sean. Goodbye and... I'll see you again."

# FURNITURE
## Howard Wright

I moved the covered armchair closer, sat down and toasted my hands. The room smelt of sulphur and fresh paint, and a bare unlit bulb dangled from the center rose. The decorations wee cleared away early, leaving sprigs of glitter deep in the carpet. Sonia apologized for the mess and the cold, and admitted this was the warmest room in the house. She said she could happily sleep inside the fire. Her voice warbled between the four blank walls, and our shadows jittered ceiling to floor to the rhythm of the flames as I pictured her nestling like a baby on the top of the yellow coals.

Pulling back a dustsheet, Sonia sat on the other armchair and approached the fire, using her behind to waddle the chair forward on its castors. I had arrived early and interrupted her renovation; she did little to conceal her irritation.

Gwen, she explained, would be late, what with the roads, so I could watch telly if I liked. She moved to switch on the set.

I protested; "Please don't bother. No, really. Talking's better."

"Okay. Suit yourself. Nothing on anyway."

She sat down again.

I made a point of looking round; "The place looks well. Some work. The holidays must have come too quickly for you."

"There was a rush towards Christmas. A bit of unpacking and shifting things about to do yet."

"Must be hell to heat."

"It is," she sighed, "That's why we got the heaters."

Sonia raised the hackles of a velour cushion with her finger-nails, all of which were speckled white. She drew a spiral, then flattened it. The white flecks indicated a deficiency of some sort. Iron? Calcium? I couldn't remember.

"Life's treating you good then?"

"Good enough. No complaints. Can't speak for Gwen though."

Even Gwen doesn't talk for Gwen, I thought. Sonia, by this time, was visibly impatient. "Look, it's a pain, I know, but there's lots of stuff still to tidy up before her ladyship comes home. Do you mind?"

"No problem. I could give you a bit of a hand. Or a whole one."

"Whatever you want,. We're upstairs. You can do Gwen's room"

"Might as well sing for my supper." I said, getting up and following her out from the flickering bareness to the rest of the house.

The carpet in both bedrooms had been laid the day before, and Sonia was taking time to re-arrange the furniture without Gwen under her feet. Though the heaters were switched on, Sonia climbed into another sweater. I could have done with something heavier myself.

The spare room was at the back, facing the top road and the exposed newness of the most recent development. Some lights glimmered, all quiet in the dropping-down fog. The return of Gwen's wardrobe from the room would, unfortunately, have to wait on Gwen.

First I carried out the empty drawer-chest, then the drawers themselves heaped with cotton and lace. The chirping bed frame was next — a rickety skeleton, too broad for an one-person, and certainly not a double. The passion-killer had to be bolted to the head- and footboards, both of which were cut from veined oak. I had suggested Gwen buy a new bed in the sales, but she was always busy. Or just couldn't be bothered. She could think of many reasons.

Too wide for the door, only by crab-walking the unholy contraption did I get it back into the room. Slowly I set the frame down after joining it to the respective boards and tightening the bolts with pliers provided by Sonia, then bounced on the assemblage to prove its worth.

The mattress followed, like a huge slice of bread, so saggy and dead heavy it fell over, taking me with it in a slack grip, onto the screeching frame. Sonia came running. She laughed, and wondered if I was practicing for the night. I bounced again, and sprawled across it in a comfortable position, hands under my head on the tough, shiny mattress.

She called me a fool. Fair enough, I said, but I did put up the bed.

"You did, of course," she said, and tested its firmness with a hand.

"Nice and steady, eh?"

"Yes."

"I only wanted you t see my workmanship."

"Yes, well …. Good work, my man, damn fine craftsmanship there," and kicked the headboard, this time giggling at herself.

I told her again what a nice place she had; I even ventured a question about the other man, asking her to trust me because we were all friends. She saw no reason to tell me anything, but confessed the other man was dead and gone. Caput. As was any further talk on the subject. Instead, she offered me a drink.

"Okay—what've you got?"

"Beer …tea ….. water…."

What the hell. "The beer will do nicely. Ta very much, kind madam."

Sonia went down and fetched two long cans from the fridge. She didn't hand me one right way; she asked if I deserved it. When I said I did, she gave me the weeping tin. It fizzed wildly when I broke the seal. I let it settle, then drank, head back, too quick to taste it, only wanting the kick. To open her own, Sonia sat cross-legged further along in the middle of the bed. It must have been the jog for her lager spluttered out and upwards as well, splashing her sweater and jeans

"Shit!". She rubbed furiously at the spots with her sleeve. I took little sips and watched her speckled nails scrape at the blue denim. Her hair dropped like a curtain across her face.

"So it's over with this other guy, this … what's-his-name?"

"McBurney." She glanced up, and the hair re-established its structure.

"That's him --- McBurney. Couldn't hack it, eh?"

"All over bar the shouting." She knocked back another gulp, one eye still on her jeans for any sign of staining.

"And what would it cost to be part of the shouting?"

"About a tenner … but saying it's you, a couple of quid."

"You know what I mean." My can was now half-empty.

"I can guess."

"Guess; go on."

"Well, if it's what I think it is, it has to be twenty at least.

I considered her offer for a few moments then nodded towards the door. "You aren't really happy with all considering of this?" I emphasized the words with another gulp of lager.

"All what?"

I nodded again. "All this here the carpet, furniture, all the decorating; being house-proud."

"What do you think?"

"No. Not much. It's not you."

Wrong again. Hope her ladyship hasn't blabbed. I'll kill her if she has. But then we're all friends, aren't we?"

I drank you remainder of the beer. "Yip we are that. All palsie-walsie."

"Life's a bitch then you die, if that's what you want to hear. Only the lazy have the gumption to be happy. And I hate laziness."

"Yeah, so I noticed,"

"You do what you can but who's to care, so just make the whole thing easy on yourself. Stop me if I'm going too fast."

"No, you're fine. I hear what you're saying. Only you'll be telling me next that love makes the world go round."

"Yes; I mean. But like the right furniture it should be comfortable." She stroked her wedge of hair back into shape. It needed little encouragement for it had the perfection of a machine part.

"Comfortable?"

"I wasn't comfortable with Lawler."

"Enough said."

The can crushed and disposed off, we went back to work. Sonia drifting from room to room or downstairs to upstairs. I was tempted to have a look in her room, maybe her nightwear on the bed, the perfume bottles on the dressing-table, but we collided across the landing, and was offered a different opportunity.

I said; "I've got twenty pounds if you want it?"

"Sure, I'll have it. My mother told me never to refuse money or a window seat."

"Wisdom runs in the family; so what are you going to do for it?"

"Not a thing."

I handed her the vase I was carrying and crushed two tenners into the back pocket of her jeans.

"Twenty pounds, all for you; for any damage caused."

She thanked me, gave me back the vase and went into her room. A few moments later, while thinking if I should regret what I had done, a key turned in the front door, and Sonia was racing downstairs as if Gwen had come from the other side of the world. I listened over the banisters for treachery.

Gwen was exhausted. Gwen was this, Gwen was that. She removed her coat. Then came the questions; was I here? How long was I here? Where? And doing what? As they moved from hall to living-room to kitchen and back to hall.

When the phone rang, Sonia disappeared into the fire-bright living-room on the other end of the flex, shutting the door behind her, allowing Gwen to thump up to join the party, so to speak, to satisfy herself I was seriously occupied.

Like all women, I said, Sonia could find work for a man. She tried her newly-reconstituted bed.

"Sonia said something about a wardrobe."

"It will need the three of us."

When I suggested we have a go anyhow, Gwen refused – she was in that sort of mood.

"You've been drinking."

"Only a can as payment."

"And your woman?"

"She joined me. Only a can though. Not much."

"'Only a can'; 'not much'. Never is."

"That wardrobe of yours is an awful size." I spoke to the back of her head.

"I need somewhere to hide, don't I?"

We went across to the spare room where the monolith swung out from the skirting. I made an attempt to edge it further from the wall and failed. Gwen sat on the end of the bed and peered through the blinds to the top road where the chain of yellow lights lit the hill. They were hazy like dandelion ghosts in the freeze as if the light itself was unwilling to move far from its source.

"How's it going out there?" I asked.

"Fog's coming down. Black ice everywhere. Not very pleasant."

"We'll just be careful. Take a bit longer. There's nothing that can't wait on a night like this. We could even stay in and test-drive the bed. I can guarantee its safety."

Lying back on the coverlet she rubbed here eyes. I moved closer.

"Hard day, love."

"So bloody so."

Apologizing for the beer, I got on the bed, took off her shoes, kissed her damp feet, and moved up to massage her stomach. Obligingly, she turned over and I did her back, pulling away her blouse and unhooking her bra to sit astride her waist and push in at her spine and shoulder-blades, and cup and lightly squeeze her small cold breast, pink her nipples, until a door opened downstairs and Sonia was climbing the stairs.

I leapt off the bed and made myself look busy while Gwen, with soft mutterings quickly did herself up. Guilt hung on our clothes like hearth-smoke. It had been there ever since I arrived.

Sonia found us suspiciously separate. She, however, was in a good mood, grinding her hands like an insect. Some people need little cause to be happy.

"Right, my little love-birds, are we going to have a go at this thing?"

Half-joking, I said Gwen didn't feel up to it. She was putting on her shoes.

"Oh, come on. It'll have to move some time. And it is your wardrobe."

Gwen, suitably admonished, consented, and the three of us, one to a side, managed to raise the monster about an inch off the carpet and take Chinese steps, through the door, minding the paintwork, across the landing, to Gwen's room.

In the middle of the journey, Sonia divulged it was Oliver on the phone. "He's collecting me, so yous can have the house."

"Sounds good, eh Gwendolyn?"

She looked hurt. "Can we set this thing down for a rest?"

"Nearly there," encouraged Sonia. "Come on, three more steps." But Gwen let go anyway and collapsed on her bed, the bed I had put together with such care and consideration, the bar mattress still with the imprint of Sonia's knees, leaving me and her to wheedle the wardrobe closer, against the wall, and home.

Being in that sort of mood meant Gwen suddenly decided she was going to have a both. Her words sounded strong and flat as she ignored Sonia's pleas about the emersion heater; she said, as she slid from the bed and out of the room, that she hated hot baths; they were not good for you.

Sonia looked at me and pointed to the side of her head. I shrugged and, with nothing better to do, tried again to push the wardrobe snug to the wall.

"Oliver would never know," I said.

"Oliver knows everything."

Defeated, I let the thing swing out again, the door leaving a sliver of shadow running top to toe, I mentioned that all the walls must be crooked.

"An old house and an older wardrobe," said Sonia. "Anyway they'll have to do. Unless Queen Guinevere comes up with more money." She moved a few things around. The sound of running water came from the bathroom along with the scent of pine.

"She's a lot of help, you Gwen."

"It was the bear." The fog was thickening on the road and blanking the rooftops. I wiped the glass and was reprimanded. The lights were swathed in wool. Nothing moved. "She's not one for too much excitement. A hard day, I suppose ... and she's not my Gwen; she's her own and anybody's who can get hold of her. Anybody that wants her.."

I was twenty quid down on the evening. I asked Sonia again, and again she gave me the old tomfoolery:

"Twenty quid? For what?"

"A cup of tea what do you think? In your pocket."

"Where?" She patted her hips and bum, then her front pockets. "Nope, nothing there."

Just then Gwen wandered through, hair in straggles, a half-open blouse, with an air of bewilderment cutting through the conversation.

"Excuse me." She moved between us for something. "Sorry, she said, finding a brush.

Sonia yawned at me and stretched and smiled that smile; "A cup of tea, then, for all your hard work."

"Will it cost?"

Now she laughed. "'Course not." She looked at Gwen. "And one for her ladyship?"

Why not," she said, "I'll take it in with me. Thanks,"

Sonia went downstairs and put on the kettle. I carried the last of the stuff into Gwen's room while she stripped off her blouse with her back to me. I got the zip of her skirt.

"'Her ladyship'," she mumbled, letting the skirt fall, "I hope this isn't going to become a habit." She leaned forward to reverse out of her tights.

"What? Undressing you? Hardly."

"I don't trust you,."

"I know you don't. Nothing I do will change that. Have your bath, and I'll have my tea. Then we'll see what happens."

Gwen pulled away from me and stepped out of her cluster of shirt and warm nylon. "Which won't be much, I'm sure, so make the most of your tea.

She threw the bundle on the bed and, in matching bra and knickers, hurried from the room, banged the bathroom door and turned off the taps. I switched off the light and went downstairs. Sonia appeared at the kitchen door.

I said "I don't think our Gwen will be having any tea, and I'll not both either. Sorry."

"Oh, come on, you two were getting along find. You can't, in that minute …"

I put on my coat and opened the front door which was still on the snib. Sleet dotted the pavement and flecked the bare, uneven gardens. Higher up, flakes swirled like pale moths around the street lights.

"I'll head on. Tell her whatever you want. And don't spend the twenty all at once. Don't go wild."

"Here," said Sonia, pulling the crumpled notes from the sleeve of her sweater. You might need this."

I first protested, then accepted. The evening had not been without profit.

# HELPING HAND
## Brian McNulty

I was dead three days when they offered me the job. No pressure they said. No one will think badly if you say no. God knows it's a thankless task. I remember how I stood nervously in his office that first morning, my head spinning with the thought of what it would mean.

"Think about it, take your time" soothed the tallest of the three spirits from the personnel department who'd brought me the details. But I knew even as I told them I'd let them know tomorrow what my answer would be. I could no more have refused them than told God he could keep his Heaven.

Which was why two days later I found myself standing invisible in Susan's garden. Watching as she knelt by a flowerbed and pulled out the fresh weeds. Setting them in a little wilting pile by her side.

They'd warned me the first day was always the worst and they were right. I had to sit on her neatly mown lawn for nearly five minutes before the weakness in my legs passed and I was able to get up.

The urge to touch her wasn't as hard to resist as I thought it might be. Even if I had all she'd have felt would have been an icy shiver. If asleep she would wake with a start. The way one does from a dream where the last thing you remember is being thrown from a helicopter. And there was no way I could inflict that feeling on anyone. Especially someone I loved.

I wasn't exactly her guardian Angel. A long time would elapse before I'd get a shot at being an Angel of any sort. I wasn't really a guardian either although if I'm honest (and aren't we all in Heaven) it pleased me to think of myself as being slightly responsible for her. My orders were simple really. Just watch and wait. At first I thought the job would involve fending off death and destruction. Saving her from harm like some sort of celestial superman. But I quickly learned that like most things that sound exciting, the reality was surprisingly dull.

"You just will" replied one of the spirits when I asked them how I would know if I was doing the right thing.

"Have faith" whispered another, reminding me God was somewhere behind all of this.

So I did.

After that first day in the garden, which like the first day of any new job never quite lived up to expectations, things lapsed into a routine of sorts. I'd be there in the mornings when she got up and sent her husband Marty off to work. Sit in the back of the car as she drove Megan to school. I'd been told there was no need to stick beside her all the time. That I could do whatever I wanted as long as I was there when it mattered. But I liked staying with her. Being by her side was the best part of being dead. Almost worth my getting squashed like a rabbit under that lorry on the M1.

I learned a lot in those early days. I learned discretion. The art of averting my eyes when my view of her life was about to show me things I'd rather not see. During these times I'd go for a walk. Remembering why I was here and thinking about the price of my gift. Suffering the feelings the dead are rumoured not to have.

I'd remember how we first met. The way I'd watched her in the office and wished things were different. She was thirty back then. Dark haired and brown eyed, her body as light and delicate as a sparrow. She was, as I realised later when I watched them prise what was left of me from the remnants of my car, the only thing in my life I would ever truly love.

The fact she was married with a child made my hopeless passion for her a private burden. One I sometimes thought too much to bear. Especially after we became friends and she told me, in one of those rare perfect moments friends have sometimes, that she often wondered if she hadn't made a terrible mistake marrying Marty.

I thought about this for well over a year. Our friendship blossoming quietly. Helped by the chat in the bank where we worked and the social events we felt it important to attend in those days. Whenever she turned up at one of these dreary functions without Marty I'd gravitate naturally to her side. Pretending it was me she would take home later. I Worried constantly about getting too close. Causing tongues to wag and starting gossip that would ruin things.

There were even times I deliberately excused myself from conversations for fear I'd blurt out how I felt. That all I wanted to do was parachute into her life and rescue her from the unhappiness I imagined she only endured for Megan's sake.

But of course I never did.

I never regretted this until the day of the funeral. It gave me a feeling I didn't think a resident of Heaven should have watching her that pouring wet afternoon. I thought she'd never stop weeping. Marty, obviously embarrassed by her sobs stood awkwardly beside her, arms hanging uselessly by his side instead of around her. I did wonder, that wet afternoon, as I have done so often since, just what I had done to deserve this.

I got used to my new life. It had its ups and downs like any other life. There was a lot I didn't know yet which would, according to my supervisors, be revealed in the fullness of time. And I had plenty of that. I had no real influence over things yet. Not like the big boys who worked in the natural disaster department or the shadowy group I heard operated the global politics wing. But I was happy.

So time passed. I saw Megan grow up and pass her exams. I watched over Susan as her life twisted and turned. Wherever I went I could feel her presence. It ran through me like the lettering in a stick of seaside rock.

I learned my trade. Practiced my art in small ways they told me would provide valuable experience if I earned promotion in the future. I did little things I only discovered I could do once they were done. Locked her back door when she forgot. Guarded Megan, as she stood alone at the school gates when her mother was late. Checked the electrical sockets last thing at night after they'd all gone to bed.

I didn't know when my moment would come, or even if it would. The future was as much a mystery to me as it was to her. But come it did and like most moments that are important, it came when I least expected it.

I was sitting in a departure lounge at Heathrow airport. Susan and three of her friends from the gym were standing in line for a flight to Lyon and the fourth skiing holiday of her life. She was forty-nine by now and divorced eight years.

Megan had long since left home and was working as a cardiac surgeon in Edinburgh. Spending her off duty hours seeing an accountant called Peter. A person I thoroughly approved off even if, strictly speaking, it wasn't my business.

Just as Susan was about to disappear down the wide carpeted ramp towards the gate, at the exact moment I decided I would take a little holiday of my own somewhere warm, I was overcome by an awful feeling of unease. As if someone were standing on my grave again. I watched her throw her head back and laugh at something one of her friends said and then, as if a light had been switched on in my mind, I knew.

Four hours later I was sitting in the bar of a hotel high in the French Alps. Staying a lot closer than usual as Susan and her friends sipped their drinks. My senses humming with an energy I hadn't felt since the first time I'd gazed on the towering grandeur of Heaven's capital. A place, so I'd been told, I might one day work.

After a restless night during which my head ached incessantly I followed them to the cable car in the middle of the resort. Losing sight of them in the throng of brightly suited skiers I took a chairlift to the top of the mountain. Admiring as I rose the tiny figures weaving down the slopes like dancers in a vast brilliant ballet.

At the summit I stood for a while. Feeling a charge running through me like electricity. The tips of my fingers tingling from the power of it. The sun burning down from the cloudless Alpine sky seemingly meant for me alone. Susan, I realised, was over to the East, cannoning down a red run with that coltish grace of hers I'd grown to love even more in the years since my death. She was safe over there. The signal from her that had become tuned to the rhythm of my soul sounding loud and strong in the part of me born when I'd perished on that wet motorway.

A tall man in a purple jacket set off on his run and I watched as he wobbled and dropped out of sight. I took a deep breath, spread my arms and launched myself down the pristine white slope after him, the fact that I could suddenly glide through the air registering only mild surprise in the back of my mind.

I caught up and flew along behind him for a few seconds until he reached the junction with another run. He stopped and I landed beside him, scenting the chill air and sensing the movement around me of immense silent forces. I was sure he was the one now so I let him ski away, watching the sadness ribboning behind him like the smoke trail of some battered old aircraft. Susan and one of her group, swished past and I felt a burst of something blossom inside me as I set of in pursuit, the air carrying me as if created for that purpose. As she passed the man in the purple jacket I swooped down close beside her and, with a hand pulsing with something strange and new, gently touched her arm.

Her balance shifted off the tips of her skis and she fell backwards, vanishing for a second in spray of snow and flailing poles. I heard the splintering of her ankle as it snapped and I thought my heart would break. But of course it didn't. She screeched once with pain and then it was over. I wasn't supposed to find out what happened next. Strictly against the rules. There's usually a way though and years later I managed to sneak a look at the file when I was back in the office on some other business. Susan recovered from her fracture. It was a simple enough break and Philip, the man in the purple jacket who blamed himself for the accident, had used his training to immobilise the limb until the ski patrol arrived. He was a kind man. A man who had lost his wife and with her the will to live his life with the intensity it deserved. He held Susan's hand and reassured her and when he flew home to his quiet empty life waited longer than he should to phone and enquire how she was. When he did he found the courage to ask could he come and see her and when she agreed felt something stir inside him that he'd imagined as dead as a boarded up shop.

They moved in together the following spring and Philip took a fresh look at his work. The desire to do what he did best jumping in his veins.

A year later his research finally paid off and the disease that for decades had claimed so many lives was consigned to the history books like scurvy. And me? Promoted now. Involved in bigger, though not necessarily better things. I still love Susan though, and even though the rules say I can never see her again, I suppose I always will.

# WATCHING THE WIND
## Stephen McMurray

Martha sat and stared at the headstones. The fingernails of stone giants that slept beneath the earth. That is what she had said they were. Great, big hands poking through the grass to warm themselves in the sun as they stretched awake each morning. That is what she had told Erin, the first time she had saw a cemetery. That was at Alec's funeral. Now she was with them. Erin was lying with her father and those mythical slumbering giants.

A breeze blew through the graveyard, toying with her hair and cooling her tears. It scooped up a blue, plastic bag and tossed it in the air, flipping it this way and that. Martha smiled. It reminded her of Erin's kite.

They had lived in, 'Sea Breeze House.' A rather grandiose title for a run-down cottage out by Windmore Point.

She remembered the three of them, her, Alec and Erin, on the cliff top. She recalled the scene vividly. She was sitting on the blanket, picnic hamper beside her, whilst Alec and Erin launched her little, blue kite into the air.

She could still see Erin's wheelchair glinting in the sun. Still see her smiling face, beneath those auburn curls blowing in the wind. Still hear her voice screaming with joy, "Daddy, daddy, it's flying. Look it's flying." And then Alec stumbling and his glasses falling off and Erin laughing. All of them laughing.

Now here she was alone, staring at the newly dug earth, which held both husband and daughter. And that headstone. A little, gold heart, below which were the words, 'In loving memory of Alec, father, husband and soul mate.'

Erin's name would soon be etched into that cold, black stone. She knew the pain would come again when she saw it and she knew how potent it would be. Her daughter's little name. Large and permanent, cast in rock. This bleak graveyard marked for all eternity as her resting place.

The breeze had become boisterous and grew into a wind. It swirled around her, her black blouse and jacket offering only a modicum of protection against its cold touch.

Paradoxically, its more rowdy nature brought with it a softer side. Now, it carried the scent of flowers in its indelicate, gusty fingers. The smell of lavender.

Martha closed her eyes and inhaled, drinking in the sweet aroma. It was the smell of Erin's perfume, the first bottle her daughter had ever owned. She had bought it for her last Christmas to make her feel just like any other little girl trying to play at being a grown-up.

Martha had been sniffing it this morning, before the funeral, reminding her of how her daughter had smelled the last time she had saw her alive. Erin had been lying in bed, asleep. She hadn't washed her face like she had told her to and, as a consequence; still had the make-up on she had let her use earlier in the evening.

She had lay there, her eyes so overdone she looked more like a panda than a little girl. Her cheeks had so much rouge she resembled a sleeping, clown and she had applied the lipstick so over-enthusiastically it looked as if she had gorged herself on a whole jar of her favourite strawberry jam. And, of course, there was the smell. That distinctive fragrance of her lavender perfume.

The aroma brought the tears back and with them came the wind again and the blue, plastic bag, entangling itself on the legs of the bench upon which she sat. She found herself smiling once more.

The wind. How Erin had loved the wind. Being wheelchair-bound she couldn't go and experience things on her own like other children so she would ask to be pushed to the front of the house, overlooking the sea, and there she would sit for hours, letting the sea breeze play with her hair and dance upon her skin.

When asked what she was doing she would say, "Watching the wind. Just watching the wind."

Erin called the wind the breath of God. As she watched the waves, she would say that God was blowing on the sea to make it work. As she watched the seagulls spiralling on the thermals, she would say God was below them, blowing on their tired wings, keeping them aloft to let them have a rest. And, as she craned her neck skywards, she would sit in awe and tell them that God was painting the sky with his breath.

He was fed up with all the blue and was using cloud paint to make it more interesting. And at night, when the wind howled around their house, she would tell mummy and daddy not to worry because it was only God's guard dog, Rover, howling to let them know he was patrolling the house and watching over them.

The wind rose in intensity once more, sweeping up the leaves that had been shed by the trees that lined the pathways of the cemetery. They swirled into the air above the bench. She watched them as they rose and was amazed.

As the leaves were scooped up they began to form patterns. The reds and ochres, the golds and browns were coming together to make a shape, and that shape was a face. The face of Erin.

The colours had blended together to create her auburn hair and her brown eyes and her little, red lips. And it was out of those leaf-lined lips she heard it. The wind transformed into the voice of her daughter. And the wind said, "Don't be sad, I'm with daddy now."

Then the leaves rose higher, spiralling skyward. And as Martha craned her neck to watch their ascent, she noticed a solitary cloud amidst the blue. Her amazement suddenly turned to disbelief.

Above her now, was not just the leafy outline of her daughter's face but the face of her husband as well. His contours were formed by the grey perimeter of the cloud, his hair by the wispy nature of its surface and his distinctive glasses by two darker patches within its structure.

Then the wind blew across the surface of the cloud, rippling it and forcing puffs of it to part. The gap formed a mouth. It smiled down upon Martha as she gazed up in awe.

The leaf Simulcrum of Erin was so high in the sky now, her features were blurred but Martha could still hear her daughter's words, "Don't be sad, I'm with daddy now."

Then the swirl of leaves vanished as grey, fluffy, cirrus arms reached out and embraced them, gathering them into the body of the cloud. Then, both cloud and leaves drifted off towards the horizon, the consoling words of Erin still whispering in her ears.

With the sky, now clear and blue, the sun blazed down unhindered. Its beams fell upon the gold heart etched on to the headstone. The heart glistened under its touch as if glowing from within.

Martha smiled through her tears. The pain of her loss would never go, but neither would their presence. She would see their faces in the clouds and trees, hear their laughter in the breeze and smell their scent on a spring day. She would see them in the rain and the sun and the wind. She would feel the warmth of their spirit around her and within her forever.

She sat and gazed up at the heavens. She sat and stared at the sun illuminating and warming the little, gold heart. But more than anything, she just sat watching the wind.

# IMAGES of HEAVEN
## AF McKenna

I have chosen the killing ground well. Given the terrain the enemy will be forced to converge in a small, scrub clearing. To their left runs a river, but once the action has started, they cannot possibly ford it in time. To their right lies an impassable barrier; they are walking into a natural funnel, with the evergreen shrubs to the front providing the only real cover. As a sniper my elevated position is perhaps ideal. Although using an old bolt-action 303 rifle with telescopic sights, I remain confident that I can dispatch them with ease. About fifteen metres away, I see two of the shrubs move. An initial excitement at sending death hurtling outwards is quickly replaced by an icy cold calmness. Two heads appear, then a third and with practised action I squeeze the trigger repeatedly. Each has a punctured heart but they do not bleed or fall.

Jumping from the tree I yell, 'Got you all. You're amateurs!'

Standing there with a rifle as large as I am tall, school tie loosened, twisted awry and with both socks around my ankles, I fill with pride.

Richard Dixon, the spoiled child and runt of the pack rushes up, full of indignation and says, 'You cheated! You said you would stay on the ground. You cheated!'

His best friend, Alan McComb, vociferously lends his support to the allegation. In any group there are always dissenters, who cannot accept defeat gracefully. But also there is also a special buddy – someone with whom you bond closely. My ally, David Simpson, quiet and thoughtful demolishes them easily by interceding on my behalf.

'Jim's set-up was perfect. You two want to go home and get your nappies changed!'

Inevitably the vituperative retort leads to a schoolboy scuffle and the game is at an end…

These images are exact, fulfilling and soothing. I don't know how long I have been in this realm or indeed, where I am. It is not frightening but comfortable. There are no pressures of life; one is not forced to endure the dictates of society. In this timeless domain, one cannot be judged and the extent of freedom is immense. Pursuing atavistic thoughts are the major pastime now but not by choice. My otic sense appears to be the only one remaining in tact. Curious noises from another dimension are increasingly filtering through, but to date, remain incomprehensible. I drift languidly away into a universe of soft, welcoming darkness but when I emerge, I know another adventure will unfold...

A plethora of war movies are playing on the silver screen and those of particular interest involve the death-defying battles of air aces. They infuse notions of power, glory and class. Identification with the best pilot – the one with the most kills, is a simple matter. These men are from a higher social stratum and taking on their mantle elevates existence. It takes one from a happy but basic lifestyle in a small terraced house, to the opulence of a manor set in fifty acres of verdant woodland and sculpted lawn. Simultaneously with film release, plastic model aeroplane kits are being sold by the millions. Anyone of note in the street will already be the proud owner of at least two fighters and a bomber. Hours of careful construction are necessary and then there is the communal unveiling. Which is the best plane? Which is the best reproduction? These questions are of paramount importance to a fourteen-year-old.

The day is sunny, crystal clear and warm but it is the day! There is to be a dogfight and the venue is the lamppost closest to the park at the top of the street. Following the title of a famous Western, high noon is the allotted time. Out of my squadron I select the American Mustang. Its high speed, manoeuvrability and firepower will surely bring ultimate victory. I am the first to arrive, eager to demonstrate the prowess of my acquisition. Alone I practise looping the loop, flying out of the sun and banking in tight turns around the lamppost. Within ten minutes the venue is now a war torn field in France. The drone of aero-engines and the staccato pulses of machine guns rip the air above asunder. To me all is alive and real. Battles are won and lost, but the final contest is between David Bailey's splendid Spitfire and Dixon's grotesque Flying Fortress. The FF is more like a congealed mound of plastic with small-deformed wings, rather than the product of precision engineering. Dixon had left it in front of an electric fire to dry the adhesive more rapidly. The result was meltdown, yet despite noisy protestations, he is adamant that it can still fly. It strikes one that pigs would have a fairer chance.

Paul's Spitfire, suddenly coming out of cloud cover sees Dixon's malformed machine and opens up with all weapons. He screams, 'Kill! You're finished Dixon!'

'No I'm not! My top gunner got you!'

'What top gunner? He was melted by the electric fire you idiot!'

'No he wasn't! I'll show you.'

The dogfight recommences and Dixon, white with anger, smashes the mound of misshapen plastic into the beautiful Spitfire, its wings falling from the fuselage. Dixon shouts with glee, 'There! Head on crash. Now who's an idiot?'

Paul's solid right hook takes Dixon cleanly on the chin and the war ends with the resounding thump...

These episodes are most pleasurable but quite draining. Because I tire therefore I am. Why should I rock the boat by questioning further? My sanctity could be irreparably damaged so I shall desist. The external noises visit again and with concentration, a few sounds can be decoded. One single word yields a massive clue. *Hospital.* I am in hospital so thus I am injured, but how and to what extent remains a mystery. This is merely knowledge and does not evoke any stronger emotion. I refuse to jeopardise my state of grace. I suppose when I drift off again, I am sleeping and that often means recovery. But do I want to return, to face whatever is my due? I think not.

Summer days at the cinema are a real treat. Entrance to the Saturday matinee is a meagre threepence but yet that is out of the reach of many in the gang. A strategy to allow all to view is evolved. Four people pay for admission, then ten minutes into the movie, the emergency exit door is mysteriously opened and one's little friends, like elves in the night, silently steal in. Frozen orange juice, in one-third pint bottles, gives much slurping satisfaction particularly, when the screen action is slow. However, those days are quickly surpassed by the advent of dating. It is novel, exciting, holding promises of intimacy and indeed elements of power. Memory of one's first true love would bring a smile but one's lips do not respond. Her name is Mary Atkinson...

She is early and I am pleased at her fervour for encounter. Her sparkling auburn hair, earnest brown eyes and fine features make her a neighbourhood beauty. In the Belfast vernacular, she is a wee honey. For her sixteen years her breasts are well developed and the shortness of her miniskirt leaves little to the imagination. Her physical attractiveness promotes an abundance of tenacious hormonal impulses.

'Hi Jim, what have you got there?'

'It's for you Mary. It's our six-month anniversary, or had you forgotten? It's only a wee box of chocolates. Here take them.'

'Oh Jim, they're lovely. Thank you.'

Her soft hand takes mine as she moves closer and whispers, 'You know I really love you and always will. I will never leave you.'

'I love you too Mary, but let's go in. I'm sorry I'm a little late.'

We hold hands even while I pay for the cinema tickets. An usherette with feeble, darting torch leads us to an almost deserted back row. The overhead balcony juts outs like an ageing prominent chin but does not obscure the view. As the main feature starts we touch then kiss with all the passion that young, innocent love can muster. We disentangle as the interval approaches.

'Mary would you like an iced cream or something else? I've got money from my paper round so it's not a problem.'

'No thanks Jim. We can just sit here holding hands. I never want to leave you, always remember that.'

'I will my love. We will be together forever.'

As if by clockwork, usherettes with trays suspended around their necks, step in unison out of the ancient woodwork. A heavy pair of boots walks the length of the balcony overhead. A startlingly loud ripping noise ruptures the calm. Dust billows from the ceiling and settles in thick layers of dandruff upon the audience below. When it clears I see two unattached legs poking precariously through the plaster. But the show goes on. Hilarity and fits of spontaneous giggling put severe restrictions on any further petting. All too soon, the film ends and in the guise of Romeo and Juliet, we travel on a bed of light to her doorstep. She falls into my arms but her mother behind the curtain curtails extended contact. Besotted and in a dream state her words, *I will never leave you*, play in an endless loop.

These recollections initially appear to occur in random fashion, yet on reflection, this is not the case. It is similar to the order in which I eat from the plate. The essentials for nutrition are devoured first and the most delicious morsels left to the end. This is the way to extend the finest pleasurable moments. Concentration is improving and lucid periods are becoming more prolonged, although without access to a timepiece it is difficult to be sure. What will be next on the agenda? Will it be mere sustenance or an exquisite slice of memory? The exterior sounds return and I understand more. I listen with the rapt attention of the voyeur. The female voices are clear...

'His EEG signal is more normal and stronger. Do you think he will make a full recovery?'

'Perhaps but maybe he shouldn't.'

'Why do you say that? He was a brilliant surgeon and he saved that little girl, didn't he?'

'Have you not been fully briefed?'

'What about?'

'So you haven't. However, you have certainly been told that there is a complete media blackout in existence here. This case is not to be discussed by anyone! Now that comes from the very top and way beyond the head of this hospital. Do you understand! Mum's the word. Now get on with it please; change the gunshot wound dressings.'

Today is my first animal dissection and the level of excitement I feel is inexplicable. Cutting up fruit was interesting but this will be fascinating. The preparation of cleaning the instruments and dissection board seems to take aeons, but finally he arrives with the fresh cadavers. He has a rat for each person in the class. The exercise comes in two parts; the first is to remove the brain, while the second involves an abdominal section. I opt to do the second part first. The creature becomes a person and is pinned to the board in spread-eagled form. I lift my scalpel. There is a slight tremble in my hand. My breathing is shallow, verging on the erratic. A hormonal rush similar to that felt in Mary's presence courses through my essence. The first incision brings an ecstasy of emotional, though primordial, satisfaction. I know at this moment that I shall be a surgeon. I cut deeper and find a foetus. I lift the little being and breathe upon it. But I do not have the power to restore life… not yet anyway. This will take study, endurance, practice and above all perseverance. I am in another dimension when he taps me on the shoulder.

'Come on Price, it's time to clear up and go home. Good gracious, what have you been up to boy? What a mess! I'll tell you what Price, you'll never be a surgeon!'

If I had a sword in my hand, I would decapitate him instantly. I regain control, look straight into his eyes and seethe, 'I will sir! I will be the best of the best. I will restore life.'

That was the start of my magnificent career. Promotion followed promotion until I became a surgeon of international repute. But as in all things there is always a dark side, a skeleton in the cupboard. I did conduct experiments but was it not for the benefit of humanity? Who are they to be one's accusers? Anyway this line of thought is not healthy. I have reached a station of purity, where clearly all sins have been forgiven. I have been shot but why and by whom I cannot remember. Yet from the nurses' chatter, I saved a little girl and that's all that matters. Mary's gentle tone unbidden, comes again and her ardent promise completes the fabric of heaven. New voices approach but one doesn't care for they cannot touch.

'How long has he been like this?'

'Four months.'

'You know he will never be brought to trial. Someone as eminent cannot possibly be. The ramifications would be extreme. Also this is costing a fortune.'

'You're not suggesting we terminate? Is he that bad?'

'So you too have not be told all. He is a monster. Before he was stopped, he abducted pregnant teenagers, some only in the twentieth week of their term and performed unsolicited Caesarean sections. The mothers bled to death and of course the infants were stillborn. He performed grotesque rituals with them. He is a sociopath. Do you understand now?'

I know even though they are filled with extreme anger and repulsion, that they are men of principle and honour. They will not destroy my bower of love and reverence. They will not switch the machine off. Mary's hand comforts again. The sound of a heavy-duty electrical contact being thrown open sends one's brain cascading frantically in all directions. As the death gene provides the numbing affects of dopamine, I am spread-eagled on a table. Mary lifts the kitchen knife and begins to saw at my innards. Is heaven only a state of mind?

# THE VALUE OF FLAMES
## Brian Kennedy

It was the sound of the downstairs window exploding into the street that first woke Aggie from her crowded dream and then she let out a roar when the flames started licking the bottom of the bedroom door "Oh Jesus get up Gerry, Get up for Gods' sake Gerry...we're on fire"

Her husband moaned "Whaa love?" But she was on her feet wrapping her housecoat about her and yelling for everyone to get up and get out. She opened the bedroom door with her head tucked under her other arm like she was expecting the flames to bite her but the banisters had distracted its' appetite momentarily and she ran into her son Freddie's room and shook him out of a drunken stupor. Her hair was standing on end and she frightened the life clean out of him. Another window exploded and she let a scream out of her, running back in the direction of her husband who was now frantically searching for his underpants but she grabbed him by the wrist and pulled him towards their back window that led on to the yard roof shouting for Freddie to follow. The smoke was filling the room so quickly that they only just got the paint encrusted window open in time and as they gingerly lowered themselves out and on to the ledge their Neighbour Mrs. Larkin shouted over "Your house is burning so I called the fire brigade love "

Freddie was the last to squeeze his enormous bulk through the window anddropped into the yard twisting his ankle and yelling "Fuck Fuck Fuck...mammy I think I broke my fucking ankle"

Aggie was over like a shot shouting "I'll break your hole Freddie Sloane if there's any more of that filthy talk. The whole street can hear, never mind our dear lord who died on the cross for all our sins"

When they got round to the front of the house most of the street had woken up and people began gathering in their night clothes, huddled in their doorways and the nosiest pulling on their slippers mid dash to the single storey bonfire. Aggie Sloane was now in full tilt screaming about her poor house and all her belongings being eaten by the devils flames as they watched, powerless and too afraid to go in and try and save anything. "Why us? Why us?" she kept sobbing over and over again. It was only then when she turned to hug her husband that she realized he was completely naked and attempting to cover his "Family allowance" with his cupped hands like a footballer about to block a penalty. Another round of "Oh Jesus" followed by sharp intakes of breath and a few of the older women began crossing themselves and looking heavenwards until Mr Sharkey from two doors down brought over his painting overalls that were a bit on the small side but anything was better than nothing.

As the first strains of the fire brigade could be heard slicing through the tiny streets people were asking what they thought had caused the fire and Mrs Sloane just looked Blankly at them. Old Mrs Stitt stood in her gable passage and shouted that she'd made tea for her and then started praying in loud slow phrases until the other women joined in.

The fire brigade woke up the surrounding streets and there was a huge crowd very quickly as the Firemen connected the hose up and aimed it through the shattered windows saying thank God it wasn't another fucking hoax. Aggie Sloane had gone quiet and just stared into the thick Grey smoke that was choking the front room and destroying the house that had taken them all of their lives to own, just recently bought off the priest who miraculously had managed to inherit most of the area. At least they were insured but there was so much that was irreplaceable and she just cried uncontrollably as the men went inside to deal with the source of the fire that appeared to be coming from the kitchen. The people either side were worried that their houses would be burnt too but the fireman kept saying that they had it under control now and they didn't think it was likely but they would check as soon as this one was definitely out.

It was close to morning when the chief fireman Presented Mr and Mrs Sloane with a black and charred Chip Pan that he was in no doubt was the "culprit"as he called it. She looked up at him with her face streaked in tears and said "But we never had chips last night, did we Gerry ?" She looked into her husband's eyes as if the answer was there and then they both roared "Our Freddie"

Their only son had slept in his clothes because he'd come home so drunk from the club. Unfortunately there had been a massive queue at the take-away so he'd waddled home comforted by the thought that his ma would still up and sure he'd get her to make him something. The front door key was on a string behind the letter box because he'd lost three in a row and Mrs Sloane had seen this solution on the TV program "Handy Hints for the home" He'd opened the door to a silent house and muttered under his breath before putting a match under the ancient Chip pan and then went to the toilet feeling too ill to stand up anymore, Then he just went on up to bed. The scalding lard bubbled over like a volcano and the plastic floor tiles were the first to catch, spreading quickly to the curtains and then the piles of freshly ironed clothes on top of the chairs.

The reason why Freddie Sloane was still living with his parents when he was nearly forty years old was because he'd just burned his own house down to the ground a few streets away the previous Valentines day. The fire officer had presented him with a burnt out grill pan saying someone obviously liked their toast well done. His next door neighbour had saved his life because he'd seen the smoke and kicked the door off it's hinges to drag a still snoring and intoxicated Freddie down the stairs. He was one of those people that left his body and the world behind when he slept so deeply his granny had said, "Just like your Grandfather god rest his soul" which had been a blessing when he was a baby but all through his childhood Mr and Mrs Sloane had to physically remove him from under the blankets and he was perpetually late for school.

He was by far the fattest child in the area and only got bigger as time went on. His saving grace was that he was funny and also managed to do the least amount of work but consistently end up in the top five of his class at school so he was left alone most of the time, especially when they were picking the school team for the embarrassingly competitive "It's a knockout" at the end of term just before the summer. He managed enough exams to get into college and from there into teacher training just around the corner where his mother was the cleaner at night.

With some relief he graduated and found a job teaching primary school kids in the very building he'd attended as a child. It was so familiar he could almost walk there in his sleep, which almost happened on several occasions. His parents dropped hints all through his twenties about how they had had him when they were his age and sure it was only a matter of time before he would meet someone who he wanted to marry. He would look at his Mother and then say "No-one could ever measure up to you mammy"

This would keep them quiet for a while but other people's grandchildren were paraded up and down the road and she burst into tears one day when she handed him a big pile of roast dinner one Sunday after mass. He was 37 and decided it was time to look for a house, not too close and not too far away either. His parents took this as a sign that he had met someone and they dropped hints that whoever the "Lovely wee girl" was they would welcome her and sure didn't everybody live together these days until they got on their feet. He just looked at them and groaned thinking suddenly how great it would be to live on his own and no have to put up with the constant questions. He didn't want to marry anybody.

Two streets away old Mr Black died after a bout of cancer and Freddie bought his house at the insistence of his ma and it was even closer to the school. He still went to their house for dinner most nights and the others he spent watching the TV and marking homework during the adverts. He practically had shares in the Chip shop and the off license.

A new teacher came from the country to fill in for Mrs Erwin who had taken Maternity leave. Her name was Josie O'Kane and she was an only child like himself. He went even more purple every time they met in the corridor because their classes were next to each other and she always said hello. Most of the other teachers were round her in the staff room at every opportunity and he stayed away swallowing Biscuit after Biscuit with pure nerves.

"Mr Sloane" she said one day as they unlocked their classroom doors, "Yes" he managed to reply but stopped because he wasn't sure whether she was married or what and he didn't want to offend her by calling her miss o?Kane if she was a missus.

"Do you think it will rain today Mr Sloane? My mothers' people were Sloanes from Belfast you know, we could even be related"

"Oh is that right" He replied uselessly and almost broke the key by pulling it so violently out of the lock. He felt faint on the other side of the door and immediately opened a Twix he was saving for that mornings' break and pushed the whole thing in his mouth. The bell rang and 28 kids swarmed into their seats giggling at the big rim of Milk chocolate that stained his lips. He brushed it off on the sleeve of his coat and Barked at them to behave.

The whole term went very slowly but Miss O'Kane seemed to be getting on well in the school with everyone, especially the kids who were always asking her to come and play with them. She was full of life and always said yes charging after them in the direction of the playing fields. Freddie got out of breath walking the short distance home so he refused any invitation that meant exertion, except walking to the off license for Beer most evenings.

They did bump into each other once in the super market when he was with his mother and he had tried in vain not to catch her eye but he could hardly have hidden behind the Baked Beans so he had to say hello and then endure the interrogation by his delighted Mother all the way home and all the way through that evenings dinner.

Christmas came and the teachers had to put their names in a box and whichever one you pulled out then that was who you had to buy a present for only. He got Mr Murphy the woodwork Teacher but she ended getting Freddie. You could see the look of disappointment on the other teachers' faces but she seemed pleased. The Monday before Christmas she gave him a beautiful brown woollen scarf and he gave Mr Murphy a bottle of Whiskey, which instantly cheered him up. She told him she was heading across the country to spend the holidays with her family and wished him all the best, then she was out the door, into her wee car and away.

He spent the holiday time with his parents eating for Ireland and drinking from the moment he woke up. On New Years Eve he met a few friends in town but they all had to be dug out of their girlfriends at the stroke of midnight so he submerged himself even further in the warm lake of booze surfacing only to mark a few ignored Christmas exam papers. Then it seemed he was back at school in the blink of a very hungover eye.

Josie called him Freddie when they met again in the staff room on the first day back and he was glad to see her. At the beginning of February Mr George the art teacher was saying how his class wanted to make their valentine cards themselves this year and so he was offering a prize for the best one. That was it. Freddie decided to make her a card. It was only a week until the 14th so he went to the shop and bought far too much stuff and made about five of them before he was convinced it was good enough to give her. He took it into school with him amongst a pile of exercise books and there was great excitement in the corridors with people declaring how many mountains of cards they'd had to wade through that morning to get out of the house to come to school and then someone shouted "Sir...How many did you get?" followed by hysterical hormonal tittering. Then another voice announced "Miss O'Kane got about ninety "

When he got to the staff room he had intended slipping it into her locker somehow but when he opened the door he walked straight into a commotion. Josie was standing in the middle of the floor with Mr Tumelty the PE teacher. She saw him looking a bit puzzled until Mrs O'Toole the head secretary turned and gushed "Oh Mr Sloane you should have been here minutes earlier it was so romantic. Mr Tumelty went down on one knee and asked miss O'Kane to marry him. Right there by the coffee table and she said yes. Oh isn't it wonderful. On St Valentines day too, isn't it romantic?"

Poor Freddie didn't know what to say and he managed to mumble congratulations while the rest of the teachers crowded round to see the ring and calling them "sly ones" Because they'd kept their romance such a secret. Josie was crying with embarrassment and delight all at once and said they wanted to be secretive because it had all happed so fast over Christmas and they had only been seeing each other just over six months.

Freddie felt sick and managed to leave the room unnoticed for the first time in his bloated life. He headed straight for the toilets and sat in one of the cubicles smoking. What a fool he thought he was thinking he'd had any chance at all with Josie, sure she probably only talked to him out of pity he told himself. The rest of the day was like purgatory and as soon as the bell rang he packed up his stuff and headed for the gates. The other teachers shouted that they were going to a pub down the road for a celebration drink if he fancied it but he said his mother wasn't well and he should get home.

He was never so glad to have his own front door and the house to himself. He opened some beer and lay down on the settee for a while distracting himself with the TV. His Ma rang him to ask was he coming round to dinner and when he said no she asked was he feeling ok. He nearly bit into the receiver and told her "No Mammy I feel fucking great". He put the phone down as she started quoting saints names at him for cursing.

That evening he drank everything in the house and had to go and buy more because he didn't want to stop. He bought a pizza and ate it half cooked because he couldn't be bothered to wait. Then when he was marking the books for the next day he noticed his home made Valentines card that was still being kept flat inside his roll book. It was after midnight now and he opened it up and looked at the message inside....

TO THE BEAUTIFUL JOSIE KANE
BE MY VALENTINE,
LOVE
XXXXXXXXXXXXX.

Just enough X's to spell each letter of his name. He had initially been worried about doing it but what did that matter now. He looked at the grill where the pizza had been and it was still lit. He staggered out of his seat and thought he might make some toast with the heels of the loaf that his ma always saved. He looked at the card and then again at the gas flames and just put the card under the grill. Then he needed to go to the toilet so he struggled upstairs and pissed everywhere but the bowl. He looked at his unmade bed in the next room along the landing and crawled in under the covers as best he could still fully clothed and exhausted. The next thing he knew his neighbour Tommy was dragging him down the stairs and the thick smoke was everywhere.

His Granny sat him down and told him no to worry because these thing happened for a reason that wasn't always clear immediately. It was a sign she said. "There's value in them there Flames son because something awful bad must have happened that only fire can clean away and make room for a new start. Sure isn't that what the farmers do with the fields and the travellers do with the caravans of their dead loved ones, And anyway love" She looked around the room to see if the picture of the pope was looking at her before she lowered her voice and pulled him close to her whisper "your ma never owned half the bloody things she put down on that insurance form"

# THE HAIRCUT
## Gary Allen

I stepped lightly from the bedroom to the landing. Past the sound of boozy snoring, the creaking springs beneath bodies turning in sleep, the cold bathroom, gurgling pipes and cistern. Down the stairs and into the death-silent living room caught in the throes of early morning as if in guilt, the stench of stale cigarette-smoke in the closed room, the careless half-drawn curtains admitting the grey light of the coming day.

Pulling on ripped jumper and stained trousers, sole-shiny hard socks infested with the odours of many days rough play. Forcing feet into scuffed shoes with laces still tightly knotted, and rubbing sleepy eyes, listening to the sound of the milk-float our on the street, the crunch of feet and the clink of bottles, tuneless whistled sounds. The poking, thumping noise from next door where the grate was being cleaned out and a new fire set – even in summer the old neighbour sat with her face to the flames, while her daughter traipsed off to chapel.

No breakfast till they had risen above, blaming their resurrection on my bumping around the house, cursing me for having gotten out of bed at all. Colin still sleeping with fingers curled to his open mouth, in the bed I'd left, dead to the beginnings of this Saturday.

When I was clothed and fully awake there was nothing to do, but wait, sitting on the edge of the flattened settee-cushion, hands in lap, yawning, bored already, looking for the first time at a room unchanged for seven years.

The flowered wallpaper turned yellow by decades of cigarette-smoke, coming unstuck at the joints, torn at child-level, marked by blue ink or smudged with leaning shoulders. Long, sweeping cobwebs high up like creepers on the cracked ceiling, hanging with dust from the pelmet. The hearth chipped and covered with ash, the remains of rubbish half-burned in last night's fire – old shoe, oilcloth, food-packages, peat – like the remains of a charnel house. An iron poker leaning by her chair, work-boots standing guard by his. A yellowed cigarette-butt behind the vase on the mantelpiece. Bills behind the ticking clock, a false pearl earring with a broken catch, a comb with missing teeth, bottle of pink nail-varnish, and a pen. Large, oval mirror on the wall above, a stranger passing through it. On the far wall hung a huge plate with a three-dimensional picture of a water mill and forest, steps dropping into a fast-moving stream. An old television heaved with its weight on a castorless trolley – only one channel was clear and the valves kept blowing – on top stood a picture of two, swarthy soldiers in uniform, their arms around each other's necks, their lips smiling, eyes shy – him and Jimmy McAuley. I looked away and yawned, stared at the first stream of sunlight gliding across the oilcloth covered floor, illuminating the million stiletto-heel pricks and the worn pattern. The finger-marks on light-switches and doors, the hardened drips of paint along the door-panels.

Then there was the jingling and creaking of springs as a body rolled over on the sagging mattress, a moment's recollection and a half-asleep cry before two feet landed with a thud from the high bed onto the floor above me.

I listened, by eyes turned to the ceiling, following the patter of bare feet across the room to the landing, to the bathroom and the sound of tinkling pee, the flushing of the toilet and a deeper creaking of more springs, a man's groan and someone raising themselves from the bed, a woman's voice, sleepy and mumbled. A child answering, then the sound of two feet tramping down the stairs.

'Go quietly down those bloody stairs,' a man's voice growled, 'and tell that other get I'll strangle the life out of him if he doesn't stay in his bed from now on...' but the voice stopped with the sound of her feet on the floor, her stifled yawns and their low voices murmuring to each other as she dressed.

The door opened. Colin came in and pushed it closed behind him. The sun was coming fully into the room, falling upon his bare, blanket-warbled hips, and he held his small penis with one hand, rubbing the sleep from his eyes with the other, as he scampered across the floor and climbed up into the armchair by the fire, drew his legs up beneath him and pulled down the soiled vest to cover himself. The golden curls stood an unruly mass on his head. He looked through half-opened eyes at me, before tossing back his head and yawning till his jaws cracked, then he closed his eyes, his head falling onto the armrest.

I heard her tramping slowly, carefully down the stairs, and I rose from the settee and walked through to the kitchen. Under the piles of old clothes heaped on the kitchen-table, I searched till I found my biscuit-tin of toy soldiers. I opened the back door and stepped out to the yard, the full glare of the morning sun making me narrow my eyes. A cat was lying sunning itself by the bins. It raised its head slowly and looked at me through slit eyes. I ignored it, and it twisted and licked its paw with sweeping tongue-licks.

I sat down on the rough stone of the path, spread my soldiers out on the door-step and played silently, ignoring my mother who came into the kitchen and looked through sleep-swollen eyes at me before lighting a cigarette, pulling a comb through the thick mat of her piled hair. She closed the door and as I played I heard her wash her face at the sink, clatter about among the dishes and cutlery as she set the breakfast things out.

'Do you want toast?'

She was hanging out of the open window. I didn't answer, and anyway she didn't wait but went back inside. To my left I heard the old neighbour's daughter out in the next yard filling a bucket with coal, humming a lullaby. She pad-locked the shed-door.

'Hello Eddie,' she called through the fence.

I ignored her, went on with my game, listened to mother scolding Colin, telling him to get dressed or to go back to bed if he was still sleepy, and no, he couldn't go to town with her later, she had too much shopping to do, couldn't be bothered dragging him around by the hand.

The door opened and a slice of toast and margarine was reached out to me. I took it without looking up, ate as I played. From beyond the yards the sound of a military pipe-band struck-up and carried through the air, from the barracks.

'Hear that?' a voice chirped from the open window,' they want me to re-enlist – sending the band out for me...' and he laughed as she told him not to be so daft.

'You can go up-stairs and get me some money our of your pocket-book,' she scolded, 'while I do my face up.'

'Ah Christ, love,' he groaned,' and how long are you going to be in the town?'

'As long as it takes,' she snapped back,' and I'm not taking those two up the town with me.'

'I can't sit around here all morning – Jesus,' he groaned pathetically, 'it's Saturday for Gods sake.'

'Just for a few hours,' she told him, 'you'll have all afternoon and night to throw it down your throat…'

'Now, don't be like that,' he mumbled.

A cigarette-butt – still smoking – came flying out of the open window, past me and onto the concrete.

'I'm surprised you were able to get out of bed at all,' she humphed, 'the amount of drink you had in you last night…'

'Well,' he laughed sarcastically,' it would be hard to sleep any length of time in this house…'

'That's not my fault,' she retorted bitterly.

'Now,' he sighed sanctimoniously, 'don't get ratty.'

There was a moment's silence, then he laughed, changing the course of a collision, 'Was I really that drunk?'

After another moment she answered haughtily, 'Don't you know you were, sure auld Edna from next door was out on the step, worried because you had fell through her hedge into the garden…'

'Oh well, he sang sarcastically, 'I must have been bad then – to have that auld bat away from the fireside – the auld crow,' he whispered beneath his breath,' I suppose she made the sign of the cross over me?' he laughed, and then there was silence as both of them went through to the living room to have breakfast.

A little later I heard him in the kitchen again. I breathed-in, opened the door and watched as he stood at the sink in his trousers and vest, his face covered in shaving-cream, as he took away the foam in great sweeps with the razor.

He stopped in mid-action, looked at me and waited. I couldn't find my voice.

'Well?' he asked, with a strange lisp, out of the side of his mouth, 'What do you want?'

'I want my money,' I mumbled.

He straightened, and relaxed his face muscles, looked at me coldly and let his hands fall to his sides.

'What money?' he asked.

'The money I saved-up for my soldiers,' I went on, and then, when I saw his growing impatience, 'You-took-a-lend-of-it-last-night-for-you-said-you-had-no-change-to-go-to-the-pub-and-you-said-you-would-give-it-back-to-me-this morning...' I got it all out in one stream.

'Jesus Christ,' he hissed as he rushed towards me, one hand darting into his pocket, 'Keep it quiet for God's sake, you wee shit, if your ma...' and just as he reached me several shilling, my mother came into the kitchen.

'You make me sick – bloody sick,' she cursed, throwing her make-up bag onto the table and striding back to the living room again.

I took the money with a sigh, glad that he hadn't forgotten or tried to deny it. He rushed after her, already pleading the innocent nature of what she thought she saw.

I got down on the ground again and played with my soldiers, just as the door opened and my father looked our, his face drawn and angry.

'Could you not keep it to yourself?' he scolded, 'now look what...'

'Mr. Adair,' she called through the fence.

My father's lips broke into an immediate smile as he stepped carefully over my soldiers in his bare feet and looked over into the next yard.

'I'm afraid this is yours,' she cooed, 'it fell our of your pocket last night – I found it in the garden this morning.'

'Oh, thank you now,' he beamed, 'it's kind of you to return it...'

'Not at all Mr. Adair, not at all,' and there was much giggling and polite thanking.

'The snooty bitch,' he growled under his breath as he steeped back into the kitchen.

Then he looked down at me, his face almost vacant, and suddenly he cleared the step with one sweep of his foot, sending me tumbling back, soldiers scooting off in every direction.

'Damn things under your feet,' he cursed, 'everywhere you set your foot...' and he went in and slammed the door shut.

Early afternoon. He was restless. Losing. Flickering from the good channel to the bad one, from race to race, thumping the television-set trying to get a better picture, without success. Cursing. Mouth dry, dying for a drink. Woodbine after Woodbine. Swearing and screaming at us to be quiet, to sit still on the settee and don't move.

'Can I go to the toilet?' whined Colin.

'Give bloody over,' he shouted back, flinging himself forward in the armchair, 'you've been earlier – how many times do you have to go? Now, shut-up.'

I wished it was later. I wish she would come home from the town and release him – release us – but the hands on the cheap clock moved slowly, hardly at all it seemed. I wished I was allowed out in the yard to play. I wished I was allowed to move. And the sound of the commentator's voice yakked on and on. The horses raced round and round, trotted in the paddock past ladies hats and bored punters, and he cursed and smoked, screamed at us to be quiet, to stop fidgeting, to stop talking.

'No – you can't have a glass of water – sit down on your arse – stop looking our of that window – what the hell'[s keeping her anyway?'

Even he was getting bored. The racing was over. He was fed-up with the Saturday sport.

'Can we watch the cartoons?' I asked him.

'No – a load of rubbish – waste of electric,' he shouted back.

He rose from the chair and went down to the kitchen, came back with a stool, a towel, and the blunt scissors.

'Right – who's first?'

We looked at each other, then at him, and I thought – Oh God.

'You,' and he pointed at me.

With no choice I rose and sat on the stool. He stuffed the towel into the neck of my jumper, spat on his hands before clipping. I closed my eyes. The hair fell around me. He pushed my head this way, pulled my face around. Clip, clip, clip – then he was finished. He spat on his hands again, brought from the back of his throat, patted down bits of hair that were sticking out. I wined from his touch. I didn't want to see what he had done, and I thought, Oh God, school on Monday, two days for it to grow into some kind of shape…

He pulled the towel from me and pushed me off the stool with a thud to the back.

'Next,' he cried sarcastically, like the barber, playing a game.

Colin rose reluctantly. As he ambled past his look told me everything I needed to know about my haircut. I felt close to tears, the only satisfaction being that there would be one hell of a row when she came home and saw what he had done.

'Sit,' he commanded, holding the towel ready.

Colin hesitated, almost crying.

'Sit,' he shouted, and Colin visibly jumped, his eyes turned to the shorn hair on the floor.

'My ma said you were to take us to the barber's,' he sniffed.

'Your ma's not here,' he grinned, then reached over and grabbed Colin by the collar, 'Now sit on that bloody stool or I'll pull the hair out with my hands,' and he flung Colin onto the stool, rammed the towel down into his jumper.

The scissors snipped in the air before descending on the mass of rich, golden curls, her pride, the object of many adults' comments. Snip, snip – all gone.

When he had finished Colin rose and pulled the towel away, ran to the settee and sat with his head down, trying to hold back the tears. And I thought, If my haircut is anything like his, then it's worse than anything I could have imagined – uneven, bits sticking out, bald patches – then I looked at the curls on the floor, at Colin's head, and cruelly I felt like laughing.

'Now, get that hair lifted and into the bin,' he ordered, and we got to our knees, swept-up the cut hair with our hands and carried it down to the rubbish bin in the kitchen.

He was sitting in his armchair, smoking a cigarette, watching the hands move slowly on the clock, his fingers beating time on his leg as he hummed a tune, closed his eyes, and waited for her to come home.

# COSAINT / DEFENCE
## Daithí Ó Muirí

Ba iad na teifigh a d'inis dom fútsa i dtosach: tháinig siad anoir an bóthar, fir, mná agus gasúir, traochta ag an siúl, a maoin ar iompar acu. Scéalta uafáis le hinsint. Go raibh na bailte i ndiaidh a chéile ionsaithe agat, creachta, scriosta. Go raibh na daoine uile maraithe: ar nós buachaillí a chéasfadh ainmhithe, francaigh, éin, cait, madraí, asail, agus nach mbeadh ann dóibh ach spraoi, chéas tú ainmhithe as spraoi, agus chun a thaispeáint do na fir, na mná, na gasúir céard a bhí i ndán dóibh. Bhí teipthe ar gach iarracht cur in aghaidh chumas d'airm; ní raibh sé de mhisneach an iarracht féin a dhéanamh le teann imeagla roimh do bharbarthacht. Ní raibh fágtha ach teitheadh siar.

Fúmsa a bhí sé cinneadh a dhéanamh: teitheadh, ár dtailte a thréigean, ár dtithe, ár maoin, nó seasamh. Rinne mé mo mhachnamh. D'fhógair mé go raibh íobairt ag teastáil. D'ordaigh go dtabharfaí ar lámh céad beithíoch.

Rinneadh amhlaidh.

Go trócaireach, mar is nós do mo mhuintir, cuireadh an scian lena muineál agus thit siad marbh. D'ordaigh go dtabharfaí ar lámh céad duine, fir, mná agus gasúir, daoine d'ardmhisneach.

Rinneadh amhlaidh.

Réitíodh an deoch nimhe, tugadh dóibh í. Tháinig tuirse ina súile, thit codladh orthu, d'imigh an dé astu. D'ordaigh mé go dtabharfaí ar lámh scór laoch de mhisneach neamhghnách. Sheas siad go cróga romham. Mhínigh mé: tugaigí na coirp soir, ainmhithe agus daoine, scaip ar dhá thaobh an bhóthair iad. Cuirigí an chosúlacht orthu gur céasadh iad: cuimhnígí ar a bhfuil cloiste agaibh ó na teifigh ach ní mór daoibh dul thairis sin–gach céasadh ba mheasa, ba dhíchéillí, ba bharbartha ar féidir le samhlaíocht an duine a chruthú, cuirigí i bhfeidhm iad.

Ag an bpointe seo ba mhaith liomsa–an scríbhneoir–labhairt leatsa–an léitheoir. Níl sé i gceist agam aon chur síos a dhéanamh ar an mbail a cuireadh ar na conablaigh agus ar na coirp sin. Ba mhaith liom go mbainfeá úsáid as do shamhlaíocht féin. Tá cúnamh ar fáil duit. Sna siopaí feicfidh tú irisí faoi dhúnmharfóirí agus a modhanna dúnmharaithe, tá leabhair faoi chéasadh sa stair, cur síos ar na fearais, na baill choirp, agus mar sin de. Agus, ar ndóigh, tá na scannáin ann, gheobhaidh tú iad ar fístéip mura bhfuil siad á dtaispeáint sna pictiúrlanna. Ach ní leor aithris ar a bhfuil ar fáil duit ansin. Má chuireann do chuid taighde olc ort, ní mór duit an t-olc sin a shárú, agus an sárú a shárú arís go mbeidh olc thar olc ort. Thíos faoi seo tá spás bán. Ba mhaith liom go scríobhfá an céasadh a shamhlaigh tú ansin, nó pictiúr a tharraingt, sula leanfaidh tú leis an léamh, má bhíonn an fonn sin fós ort.




Rinneadh amhlaidh.

An lá ina dhiaidh sin tháinig tú. Chuala mé tú sula bhfuair mé amharc ort. Drumadóireacht, béicíl, liúireach bharbartha d'airm. Chonaic tú an feic a bhí réitithe agam romhat. Stop tú. D'ísligh an gleo nó go raibh tost marbhánta ann. D'éirigh liom déistin a chur ort. Déistin a chlaochlaigh ina himeagla roimh an dream a dhéanfadh a leithéid d'uafás. D'iontaigh tú ar do sháil. D'imigh soir agus lean d'arm thú.

Ar an gcaoi sin shábháil mé an baile, agus na bailte níos faide siar. D'umhlaigh mo mhuintir roimh an scór laoch. D'umhlaigh an scór laoch romhamsa.

Ach sula raibh mí caite tháinig tú arís, aduaidh agus aneas, gan choinne. Rinne tú sléacht fíochmhar. Tá an ceantar ar fad faoi smacht agat anois agus d'arm i mbun foréigin ar gach taobh.

Tá barbarthacht dhochreidte curtha agat i mo leith agus i leith mo mhuintire. Ba chóir dom a bheith buíoch díot as an deis seo a bhronnadh orm míniú a thabhairt os comhair do chúirte, sula ndaorfaidh tú chun báis mise agus mo mhuintir uile, go mall agus go míthrócaireach. Ach an bharbarthacht a chonaic tú ionam, ní mór duit a admháil anois gurb é do bharbarthacht féin a chonaic tú.

## COSAINT / DEFENCE
### Daithí Ó Muirí
*Trans by Frank Sewell*

It was the refugees that told me about it first. They crossed over the road: men, women, and children, exhausted from their long walk, carrying all their worldly possessions. They had such horror stories to tell. That you had attacked the villages one by one, plundered and destroyed them. That the people were all killed. Just as boys torture animals, rats, birds, cats, dogs, donkeys, just for kicks, you did the same, not just for kicks but to show the men, women and children what was in store for them. Every attempt to repel your forces had failed; no-one dared to even try anymore, such was the terror at your barbarity. The only thing to do was withdraw.

It was up to me to decide: to draw back, abandon our lands, our houses, our goods, or else stand our ground. I thought it over. I declared that a sacrifice was required. I ordered for a hundred beasts to be set aside.

It was done.

With a sympathy, typical of my people, they put their knives to the animals' throats and watched them fall down dead. I ordered for a hundred people to be set aside: men, women, children, people of great courage.

The poison was prepared and administered to them. Tiredness entered their eyes, they fell asleep, and breathed their last. I ordered for twenty warriors of extra-ordinary courage to be set aside. They stood bravely before me. Move, I explained to them, the corpses, animal and human, and spread them out on both sides of the road. Make it look as if they were tortured. Remember what you heard from the refugees, and do even worse. Every bodily violation has to be as disgusting, as mindless, as barbaric as is humanly imaginable, and must be carried out.

(At this point, I - the writer - would like to speak to you - the reader. I do not intend to describe in any way the states that those carcasses and cadavres were left in. I want you to use your own imagination.

There is help at hand. In the shops you'll see magazines about murderers and their methods; there are historical accounts of torture, descriptions of the equipment, the body parts, etc. And, of course, there's the movies; you can get them on video, if they're not at the cinema. However, an account of all that's on offer in those places, will not be enough. If your researches make you sick, you'll have to over come that sickness, and go way, way beyond it until you feel something sicker than sickness. Below, there is an empty space. There, I want you to write out the torture which you imagined, or to draw a picture, before you read on, if you feel like it.)

And so it was done.

The next day, you came. I heard you before I got a glimpse of you. The drumming, screaming, barbarous yelling of your army. You saw the sight I had prepared for you. You stopped. The noise diminished until there was a deadly silence. I succeeded in filling you with disgust. A disgust that turned into terror of those capable of such atrocity. You turned on your heels, went back east and your army followed.

That way, I saved the village, and the neighbouring villages. My people bowed down before the twenty warriors; the twenty warriors bowed down before me.

But before a month had passed, you came back without warning and attacked from the north and south. The destruction you wreaked was ferocious. Now the whole area is under your control, and your army is unleashing its violence everywhere.

You have accused me, and my people, of unbelievable barbarity. I suppose I should be grateful to you for granting me this opportunity, here in your court, to give my explanation before you condemn me, and all my people, to death, slowly and mercilessly. The barbarity you saw in me, you now have to admit, was your own barbarity all along.

# THE EXPERIMENTAL GIRLFRIEND
Rosemary Jenkinson

She said she was from St Petersburg. Was she from the Ukraine? She wasn't educated. Of course she knew Dostoyevski but she didn't know Solzhenitsyn.

Liam stared across at the square-holed dovecotes, the balconies of the apartments opposite. A hundred TV's were on, flickering like a lightning storm in the building, a code of successive dusks and lights and darks, a holy blue. He was thinking about the old woman's story of the Russian soldiers coming to her home in 1945, how they were savages, stealing everything, shooting at the cuckoo clock. The Russians had had no fear because they'd been brainwashed into believing they were immortal and that not so much as a bullet could harm them.

Alex looked over and grinned suddenly.

Liam had met Alex three weeks after arriving in Poland when his Swedish friend, Tony, invited him to this 'club' out in the country. It was Tony who'd bought her for Liam for the night but even Tony and Tony was mad - he was dating two mafia girls behind their boyfriends' backs - even he'd said not to do it, not to let her get so close but for Liam 'don't do it' was a red light that had to be jumped.

Alex had brought her things round the next day in a pitifully small suitcase.

Right now she was wearing his t-shirt and his socks which made him laugh because the heel bagged out lumpily at her ankle. She was sitting on the bed with the nail file in her hand. Sometimes she'd dig it into her skin like a scalpel, peeling back the layers, tunicate as a Russian doll. At this rate she'd file her beauty down into a little pile of wood shavings. There was a black shine on her parted hair, catching the light bluely, soaking it up into its dark quivering puddles, that rim of snow gleaming under her bark-brown eyes. She never wore make-up in the house. Her face was pale brown like dry earth or dead bronze corn.

'Baby,' she said and beckoned him over. She got him to touch a tumid lump on her leg and sucked in the air with pain. He rubbed it better. Two years ago she'd jumped out of an apartment window in the Ukraine and injured it.

She couldn't speak English but her Polish was perfect and Liam's friend, Wojtek, had translated some things for him. Liam knew only a little about her, that her father had beaten her and her mother had tried to sell her to the first man. What had attracted him was her energy. 'My little Kalashnikov' he called her. She mock-fought him a lot and gave him a fireman's lift home from the pub when he was drunk. 'Russki,' she'd say proudly, flexing her arm. 'She says she will kill you if you don't go running with her tomorrow morning,' Wojtek had translated. 'She can win in any race. Tomorrow she will be running away from you.' 'Ah, but I'll be running away from her in six weeks when I go home to Ireland,' Liam had replied and she'd laughed but he'd felt guilty about that one.

He took another toke on the joint. Julian, who used Liam's flat as a post-pub drop-in, bolted a shot of vodka, dropped his jaw and screwed up his eyes, trying to hide his face in his shoulder which made Alex burst into laughter.

Alex's friend, Kristiane laughed too. She was curled on the bed behind them browsing through a Real magazine, murmuring about the delicacies she'd like to eat.

In three weeks I'm skedaddling, he reminded himself. He'd set up the office and recruited a lot of Polish labourers. It was now up to his brother in Ireland to get the contractors but the boys back home preferred cheapness of labour over quality and were happy enough with the workers from Nigeria, Senegal...

His mobile rang.

'Hi, it's Tony.'

'Tony! How's it going?'

'Not bad. Look, I found something out about Alex you're not going to like.'

'Oh?'

'Friend of Patricia's was supposed to fix up a flat for Alex in Warsaw but she didn't do it, so Alex sent round two men to smash things up.'

'No. It's not the sort of her to do that.' Alex was laughing again.

She'd laughed at a slapstick film on TV once, at the really cruel parts.

'I'm telling you, man, be careful how you break up with her.'

Sure, he knew she had friends who could hurt him. First night she came, a man called round to check up on her, even though she'd said her boss was a very good woman who was content to let her go. She was still nervous whenever the doorbell rang. At that nightclub the Russian doorman who'd shaken hands with him was covered in blood. At the Russian market, Alex's friends looked at him with shaded eyes, evaluating him.

Sure, she wasn't like that. Julian for one thought she was fantastic.

Kristiane opened Liam's litre of whiskey. She was a hard dark shadow behind Alex. Alex's fringe was soft; hers was not, though she had the plucked eyebrows of a saint. Some psycho called her yet again on her mobile and Alex grabbed it and deep-breathed down it, then she, Kristiane and Julian fell about in stitches.

Strange. Alex had shaped curvy lips from the front view but from the side view nothing. No substance to her appearance. She had a broad Slavic face but starved strait-leathered legs. She'd made those leather trousers herself. Funny, but Liam always noticed that the people with the most vices had the greatest talents. Or perhaps their bad past just highlighted the skills they were capable of bringing to the world. No, she was a good girl.

A plate of cold red watermelon lay on the floor. She loved ice-cold fruit and the old Russian fridge in the kitchen froze the life out of everything.

Her grey-valleyed eyes were closing again. She was often sleepy these days. Those long eyelashes like a broom sweeping away the truth.

Julian said he was going.

'I'll lend you money for a taxi.'

A hundred zloty was missing out of his wallet. It was the second time. He glanced at Alex. Her eyes were closed. He'd speak to her about it tomorrow. Only reason he'd let it go before is because she was kind. She gave leftover food to the tramp who slept by the bins. Or had he let it go because he expected it, accepted it as his punishment.

A hand was creeping up his thigh. No, he said, pushing Kristiane away. She swore at him, then ran into the bathroom and he heard her puking. He knocked on the door to see if she was okay and she burst out, screaming and slapping, then rushed back in and slammed the door on him.

He slipped into bed beside Alex. She was fast asleep, grinding her teeth, and he rolled her onto her side to make her stop.

At about three a.m. she woke him up. She was moaning and gripping her stomach. She'd had on-off pains for days but this was serious. He drove her to the hospital and she was rushed into casualty. While he was waiting, he kept thinking of his favourite image of her standing at the door long-legged in nothing but his t-shirt and pulling him to bed and it made him pray for her. When he was allowed in, the doctor told him that her ovaries had swollen. She showed him an x-ray and all he could make out was a big black patch in a swirling white galaxy of miniature stars. He went for a walk outside and looked up at the stars. He cried a little. There was nothing new under the sun but in other galaxies there was plenty. He remembered phoning his older sister the day after Alex moved in.

'I'm with a Russian girl now. Well, I'll tell you the story when I get back. It's a hell of a story.'

'Liam. Not another new girl.'

'You know me. I want to see it all.'

'For goodness sake. D'you know what you would say if you were on the way to heaven? Would you just let me off at hell for a minute to have a gawk?'

Alex was kept in hospital for twenty-four hours. Initially the nurse came to the flat to give Alex injections, then Alex did it herself. She stayed in bed all day while he went to the office. She painted her filed-down nails deep purple like the retracted buds of tree in winter and got him to dye her hair black. One night he was at his friend Karolina's when Alex phoned. She went crazy with jealousy, thinking the sound of the washing machine in the background was Liam and Karolina having sex. Liam laughed it off, putting it down to the heavy medication.

When she was feeling better, he took her for a walk. She was in the new clothes he'd encouraged her to wear – a tartan skirt and a jumper to her midriff and she was cold beneath her jacket and angry with him. It was a day when the sun's colours were being sucked out like a coloured ice cube by the fog's tongue. Black clouds passed over it highlighting its outline – a black resinous aureole. They walked along the path of the canal, its chunting dark blood in a white tube of snow. The path had been swept of snow as if gouged out by a finger leaving a furrow of white tissue on either side. But the day, though bleak, cheered her up and she laughed, playfully trying to get him to skinny dip with her.

'She's stealing from you,' said Wojtek when Liam complained about the amount of marijuana Wojtek gave him for a hundred zlotys. 'She only gave me sixty zlotys.'

He confronted her that night and she cried. He would have given her the money if she'd asked. After he stormed out, she phoned up promising to tell the truth about herself if he came home. She told him she used to smoke opium, she'd been to prison twice and she tried to explain something more but he couldn't understand and she lost her temper. She filed her nails and cut herself. She scared him. It was now a case of how to get rid of her without trouble. He could just leave her there and find himself another flat when he returned to Poland. He wouldn't find somewhere though with a better location. Maybe he could tell the landlord the situation and get him to pretend that they had to move out before Christmas.

The next night Liam couldn't have been more delighted when Alex mentioned she was thinking of taking a sewing job in a factory in another city. She went out to meet someone about it and was optimistic when she returned. It appeared that the situation was happily resolving itself.

She went out another time to see about the job. When he asked her how it went, she was non-committal. She slipped off her trousers and lay on the bed, tired again. He looked at her legs. She had a tattoo on her ankle of a rose surrounded by briars. The briars seemed to grow up her leg, to even peep out in the shadow of her neck. His hand holding the joint was shaking.

Her behaviour was changing. When he looked for a pen, she would shout, No,' and rush to get him one herself. She insisted on drying him when he came out of the bath. One night he woke up alone and found her sitting in the kitchen reading a book with the gas rings on for warmth. She was sitting up to ensure he got a good night's sleep because she knew her grinding teeth disturbed him. Finally he persuaded her to come back to bed.

The issue had to be ironed out.

'You know I have to go back to Ireland in a week, don't you?'

'Yes.'

She said matter-of-factly that she'd move out and spend Christmas with a friend but hoped he would contact her when he came back to Poland. He relaxed. It was that Tony's fault for making him paranoid. She was cool about it and now he didn't worry about himself, he worried for her.

She'd developed full-blown going-out-itis, complaining of pains in her eyes, sitting like a tired Madonna engrossed in a Mills and Boon type book. It unsettled him to watch her, her unsmiling down-tilted face in shadow except for her forehead touched by light. Reluctantly she got dressed to go out one night.

It was a disaster. They went to a club where Liam met some friends and spent time talking to them. Alex hitched up her skirt and danced sexily with any man she could grab, then when she failed to raise Liam's jealousy, ran out. Liam could have let her go but he thought that he should go easy, play the game. There were only a few days left with her.

She was waiting round the corner. More falsely brewed tears!

She'd tell the truth if he came home. Well, he was sick of this silver little hook of truth but would hear her out anyway.

The truth was she was on heroin. She'd started at the time she'd met him.

The syringes from her illness were still at home, that lump on her leg, her supposed sewing job, well, it was a different use of needles that fascinated her. He remembered listening to a Polish woman, a strong Catholic, singing the song, 'Californication.' She'd been lost in the beauty of the melody without realising the words... What was beauty if you didn't know what lay behind it?

He hardly slept that night. She was grinding her teeth and he sweated under a series of fractured nightmares in which he could see beneath Alex's skin to a liquid pattern of red plush and gold veined flower.

Of course he would come back to Poland after Christmas and help her. But he was afraid. To come back to her would be like reviving a dying flower by setting it in water. He locked her in the flat when he went to work. Later Julian called round.

'I'm stressed. Put me to sleep, Liam,' he said, so Liam made him a big soporific joint. Feeding the habit. Injecting everyone. He'd given the tramp some money that morning which must have been spent on cheap alcohol. Being giving and sharing didn't make you a good person.

Their last afternoon together, he took Alex to the Irish pub. Let it stand, he had to tell her because she was impatient to try the Guinness. It was her first taste and she loved it, so he bought her a Guinness t-shirt. 'Irlandski super,' she said, doing the thumbs up and kissing him. Then they had fun, bombing up and down the supermarket, throwing presents for his family in the trolley.

She hardly had anything to pack. The evening dragged and she tried to pierce her ear. She stuck a needle through it but became agitated because the earring was too big. There was blood everywhere. She phoned her Russian 'collega,' colleagues as she called them, to buy amphetamine for her friend to take to her husband in prison the next day. Or so Liam understood, but what was the difference if he fully or half understood. They could only get it to her the following afternoon and she flung down the phone, biting her lips, inconsolable. Liam gave her six hundred zlotys and drove to her friend's house in the country where they had an emotional parting and he promised continually to come back for her. She shoved lots of the chocolates that he'd bought her back into his pockets. Her friend was going to try and help her get off heroin. The final wave goodbye ended with a great buzz of relief.

He got up early the next morning ready for the long drive. There were thumbprints of blood on the bathroom towel and half a sponge heart blackened with her hair dye.

He phoned his sister at the Polish/German border.

'I'll stop over in Holland tonight and be home late tomorrow.' He told her about Alex. 'I didn't use precautions. I'll have to get a test,' he said. His sister began to cry and he thought of Alex locked in the house in the country, the princess in the tower trusting him to come and save her. Forever. Epidermally yours. Tired, so tired. He had just passed border control but he pulled over onto the verge.

He hoped to God his blood was clear. And Alex's. He kicked at a decaying leaf, detaching it from the bare ground with which it was merging. He remembered that story about the Russians believing themselves resistant to death and he thought of Alex not throwing herself into life but at it fearlessly. He'd wanted to look closely at a prostitute, lead the wild life while staying behind a cold observing screen but she'd chiselled her way through, file in hand. He laughed as it occurred to him that the Irish were descended from a race where immortals ran round with the mortals, were commingled. Maybe that was why he could be with Alex. All along she'd been looking to him to teach her about normal mortal life.

He was scarcely out of the country and he wanted to see her again.

It wasn't just a case of going round the world seeing things. It was about seeing things through.

# OFF THE HOOK
## Csilla Toldy

The high heels on Lidia's shoes produced a nerve-tearing clatter that was insensitively echoed by the staircase. She took the steps with a high pitched staccato, deeply sunk in thoughts.

"Yes, it is true. Andy had a totally different view on love, but I did not want to accept it. I chased myself into that passion. My own voluntary blindness threw our relationship into the void."

She arrived at the elevator. A carelessly ripped piece of paper, stuck to the lift door read: "Out of order." Lidia stopped; feeling instantly victimised by the circumstances.

"This too." She thought stepping to the bottom of the staircase, vigorously swinging her upper body over the marble balustrade. She turned her head upwards to stare into the darkness. Five floors gaped back at her. A cool draft from the lift shaft calmed her for a moment; instead of screaming she swallowed her rage.

"Is it worth climbing? What if he is not there?" A moment of hesitation gave way for another flood of uncontrolled thoughts.

"I walked into this doomed adventure as if it had been my birthright." she thought, turning to the steps with deliberation.

She has known Andy since they were fifteen, and in recent years they met more frequently, but the 500 miles distance between their homes provided enough space and a good chance not having to take part in each other's lives too closely, and allowed them not to get involved in each other's problems too seriously: only as much as it was convenient.

Curiosity drove her when she invited Andy to a short trip to Paris. She had decided to spend a week there on her own to take a breath of fresh air and relax, but at the end of the forth day spent in solitude she changed her mind. A quick phone call and Andy was there.

She admitted, after all that she was desperately trying to escape from her everyday marriage that seemed to suffocate her. During those days in Paris, she realised that in truth she was frightened of the responsibility and to make it more complicated, she had forced herself to believe that she was destined to stay in the golden cage out of a sense of responsibility. Whereas, in reality, this belief was the makeshift of common sense. By negating her needs, the desire for freedom had become increasingly strong in her, and at the age of forty, with two children and a loving husband, she was drowning.

They started the evening with a delicious meal, the best example of French cuisine with oysters, champagne and a long, teasing chat. Later, in a double room of the Hotel Dubois, they loosened up with a bottle of cognac. The ceiling over the bed was covered with a mirror, softly reflecting the mellow light. The owner of the hotel was a real Madame, a cultured middle-aged beauty, very kind and full of understanding for the special needs of her guests. Although the first kiss felt like a trap, Lidia offered the opportunity. She resisted him for a while, as long as she had ears for the foreboding whispers of her mind, the fatal certainly that her whole life was going to turn upside down. The blame of being selfish blocked her, until the ideas of doing or not doing became equally unbearable.

Deep in her subconscious she dreaded that she might lose control over her own life and it would run away with her like a mad horse. In her thoughts, she often played with fire, seduced it in thousand different forms, but when it eventually manifested and it was there in front of her, she did not dare to look into the glow and to take it for that what it was. Her cowardice bore fruit, her fears became reality and passion took control over her; while she believed she had fallen in love.

Shame accumulated at even higher levels. She was utterly disappointed by Andy, when he could not reciprocate her feelings. He did not even notice them. Fate showed an ironic face when it sent her a conspirator who never listened to his own heart. He behaved like a smoker who sets a whole forest on fire by carelessly throwing away a match, and then admires the "accident" with amusement.

"Teardrop by teardrop I found out about the other woman." She thought looking at her feet taking the stairs with a monotone force. "Although he mentioned his new girlfriend in Paris, I did not care about her then. I was more worried about going home and having to look into the eyes of my husband."

She was turning to climb the next fly of steps to the second floor when she heard a noise, the cautious opening of a small window on the door directly opposite her. She jerked, staring into an old lady's peeping eyes. They froze for a second, startled, then the old woman smiled, vaguely recognising her.

'Hello. I thought I should check who it is, you never know.'

'The lift is not working.' Lidia smiled reassuringly at the woman.

'Is your dog all right? She asked, for she remembered the old lady with the old dog they met in the lift one morning when they sneaked into the house.

'He's in hospital, but the vet tells me he'll be fine.'

Lidia smiled again, meaning to say good-bye. She carried on taking the steps like picking petals of a flower with melancholia. "Loves me, loves me not." She could not suppress an ironic chuckle.

Her pain had been devouring her life force until she understood that in reality she was deeply disappointed with herself. She could not blame anyone for her own naivety. Lidia found it most frightening that Andy could have carried on with this quartet until the end of times. He had a part for everybody, Lidia, the lover, Sandy the spouse and Charles the potential business friend. Yes, the French art of la vie legere that she admired so much. She had the opportunity to live it for a while, but eventually it transformed her passion into disgust. One day she woke up with the conclusion that she had to finish this relationship, just as the other one.

She could not communicate with her husband anymore. She could not and did not want to play parts, especially not in bed. If she could have taken it easily she could have enjoyed the security provided by Charles and the erotic pleasures from Andy. She could have talked herself into believing that she based her choice on respect for her husband and on the love of her children; taking the interest of teach family member into consideration, finely balancing family life with her natural need for freedom. It would not have been the first balancing act in her life. She did manage her profession and motherhood very well, too. This theory failed, however, because she ignored the power of male vanity. Charles only wanted her as his wife, to possess her, as Lidia thought bitterly now. He was not willing to descend from the classic marriage in any way and if she shovelled away the anger, deep inside she had to admit that she agreed with him. She was a desperate idealist herself.

In reality she was hurt be the fact that she did not mean everything for a man. She wanted a partner, after all. She yearned for the lover-friend-partner trinity, which according to the laws of the expanding universe, seemed to be getting out of reach with every breath. She started to doubt herself; her system of values became chaotic, too. She could not forgive herself, but perhaps only because she knew that her husband would not do so either. He could have forgiven a one-off adventure, but not a regular affair.

Climbing up the stairs she felt angry about her confusion, just wanting to finish, put the full stop to the end of a too long and pompous sentence. "The whole story sounds like a big nineteenth century romance. The woman desires eternal love, while the man is withheld by the concept of "honour" that can accept a lover, a mistress much easier than allow either of them to leave their families, their responsibilities their social status, the safe construct of their lives."

She knew that this cumbersome robe did not suit her soul's size, but her passion and the "perfect lover" confused her.

Though she knew very well that he was not perfect in any way. The only reason for falling in love with Andy was the emotional starvation she suffered with Charles. A delicate link of human weakness helped to create the atmosphere at home. Charles' aggressive approach was matched by Lidia' s passivity, although she silently resented her husband abusing her generosity by reacting out all the tensions of the workplace at home. With time their house became congested with unpleasant pickings, low-level criticisms, ironic battles with words. Charles was suffering from a mid-life crisis, but he forced it under the surface of a confidant image. Lidia withdrew with a hurt pride; she closed the doors in front of her husband, becoming more and more unhappy and inaccessible. She could have easily set the boundaries for his outrage; instead she allowed it to tear apart the emotional ties of belonging. She played the part of a suffering martyr with near perfection.

"This passivity" she thought "is such a nineteenth century concept, too. I feel as if I was the embodiment of the female image that Freud created. The gentle flowers of submission, who allow the males to dominate them. Their vulnerability is touchingly beautiful and sexually provoking. The only difference is that I do not escape to a nunnery, do not go mad, or do not commit suicide, but get a divorce. Society has progressed. We can solve all our problems in a democratic, fairer manner. We can divide the children, too. Only the underlying passions, fears and pains have remained the same."

Her feet tread the timeworn marble even faster, when she ruminated about the first night she spent with Andy. She could still remember that satisfaction, involving her whole body, the petit mourir she experienced in Paris then, for the first time in many years. Her soul flew away into the expanding universe and it was a miracle that it found its way back. For a small eternity Lidia disappeared, sucked up by infinite space. When she returned she felt a deep gratitude towards the man who presented her with this gift.

"I mistook this gratitude for falling in love. We were wide-awake during that night. Andy radiated so much joy and contentment, he must have been indulging himself in his success, honouring himself with the title of a real man." For some inexplicable reason Lidia felt no bitterness, she just uttered a short laughter.

"Seen often enough, even the most mysterious miracles become common place. The aftermath has been the games we played, the teasing, the power struggles. Nothing but delusions."

One day Lidia found out that Sandy moved in with Andy. The next time, when they made love at his place, while Sandy was out working, Lidia did not have an orgasm. Andy must have sensed the change, for he asked her whether she had enjoyed their lovemaking. Lidia evasively replied that she enjoyed being with him, but deep inside she knew that it was all over. Through her body, the subconscious gave her a sign that this relationship had its time and it was dead.

This was the moment when she realised that their link was only sexual; it could not be love. She cursed herself for being attractive. She remembered Andy's joke about sex being the least expensive and most widely used drug and she could see the truth in it. Now having gained distance, she could also see how well baited its hook was. People used their sexual success to fill the void in their human relationships.

Physical intercourse was the imitation of love and caring. A good sex life equalled personal freedom, yes; it all appeared like a mute, black and white pantomime of the vivid, bold bountiful soul. Having sex was the only cost-free, legal opportunity people accepted without hesitation that allowed them to become one with eternity for a moment, which was in fact, their essence. The liberation one experienced by letting go of one's personality and the happiness of non-existence meant more than pleasure. However, when people were frightened to open up to each other in other ways, they became prone to addiction. Lidia realised that she had been addicted and that it was time to rip herself from the hook.

When she finally arrived at the top floor, she was ready to yell: "That's it, it's over."

She was rather perplexed when Sandy opened the door and asked her in with a broad smile. She chattily explained how glad she was to have an excuse to open a bottle of champagne. After the first glass, however, she started to complain about Andy who regularly cheated on her from the first moment of their relationship.

Lidia listened dumb founded to Sandy who recounted an endless series of betrayals. Strange situations she experienced with Andy made suddenly sense to her and became understandable in the light of Sandy's story. She could see Andy's real drive now, the greed that made him want to possess every better-looking woman he met. His desire for being seen as the successful male was coloured by financial and sexual interests. With a collector's passion he made his lovers emotionally and sexually dependent. Knowing that women related to sex with emotional ties, he used their need of bonding for his own advantage, to have better business relations and helpful connections. Lidia began to see the deep fear hidden behind Andy's tactics, his ill desire for safety, his need for manifold securities in life. Lidia began to feel pity for Andy, recognising that he was a slave of fear himself. Lidia sensed a deep-seated rejection in him that did not want to see his own weaknesses, although by simply accepting them he could have turned them into strength. She felt pity for Sandy too, who seemed to love Andy despite all that happened, or perhaps she was an addict herself. Andy treated her like a piece of jewellery; he was proud and terribly jealous of her, wanting to keep her at any price.

Sandy was about to burst into tears, so Lidia made a quick joke:

'I hope, he has taken out an insurance on his penis. It seems to me that his livelihood is dependent on this important extremity." Sandy joined her laughter. Then Lidia went on:

'I don't know whether you know...'

Sandy's eyes reflected shy sadness. She nodded.

'Yes, but it's over I think. Am I right?'

'Yes, you are. How do you know?'

'He would never admit anything, and he ignores my emotional intellect. I feel it all here and here.' She pointed at her heart and at her stomach.

'Oh, Sandy, I'm so sorry.' I felt very bad about it myself.

'It's all right. Thank you for being honest with me.'

They remained quite for a while, in a warm and meaningful silence. Sandy opened another bottle of Champagne and they clicked their glasses: 'To our friendship.' Sandy said, and Lidia felt gratitude. Then she had a flash of a vision. She saw the beautiful, fine and vulnerable Sandy in black leather, with a whip in her hand. She giggled. She asked Sandy:

'What if we gave him a lesson with his own devices? We could dress up like dominas. We could beat the egotism out of him.'

Sandy smiled shaking her head.

'I'm not so brave.' She turned away for a moment to close her tearful eyes. 'But I guess I have nothing to lose.'

When Andy arrived home, he joined in with the last glass of Champagne. The women winked at each other and started to take off their clothes in unison. They seemed very excited, drunk and naughty. Andy could not believe his eyes. First he was excited, too, and then he cooled down. Somehow, knowing both of the girls he doubted his luck. Then he understood that they must have talked about him and felt embarrassed. He nervously walked up and down in the room. It was obvious that all his secrets were revealed, he was humiliated.

'What the fuck.' He said. The women burst out laughing. Sandy and Lidia hugged and kissed each other with a funny noise on the lips. They giggled and the twinkle in Sandy's eyes said more than Lidia expected. She looked at Sandy seriously and folded her arms around her thin waist tenderly. They stood there, talking with their eyes. The love and compassion they felt for each other was tactile in the air, and even Andy was moved by it for a second. He was stoned by surprise. Gazing at them he felt excluded, chased out of Paradise. He swallowed his rage and with his most impudent poker face he asked them:

'Are you lesbians?'

Sandy's answer slapped him:

'No darling. You will have to satisfy both of us at the same time. I want to see what a wonderful male you are.'

The women uttered a wicked laughter, but he could hear from Sandy's shriek that she was getting hysterical. Andy suddenly stood up, seeking an escape rout, but the girls, now more like black ravens, blocked his way. Feeling trapped between them, he bit on his lips. He seemed lost for a moment, then he gave a sign of capitulation, accompanied by a theatrical sigh. He looked weak and almost worthy of pity. The girls looked at each other hesitating, not quite sure what would be the right tactic to employ. They needed a moment to reflect. When Lidia looked back at Andy she froze from disgust and anger. Andy was slowly licking his lips, staring at her provokingly. In the same moment Sandy lost her control. She jumped to Andy and beat him where she could reach him. Andy caught her arms and pressed himself against her. With a voice that was filled more with the contempt of the defeated than with remorse he grumbled between his teeth:

'I'm sorry, I'm sorry.'

Sandy could not pretend to be strong any longer. She burst out crying in between his arms.

Lidia was already dressing up in the hall. She heard through the slit of the door that Andy and Sandy started talking. She was reminded of her husband by a gush of compassion. She could not trace guilt neither pain in her heart anymore. She tore open the door and ran down the stairs like a whirlwind. When she emerged from the dark staircase, she took a huge gulp of the light summer wind that was carrying the sent of streaming waters. Overwhelmed by a feeling of freedom, she turned against the wind and set off with long steps towards the riverbank.

# WHO'S A CHEEKY BOY
**Gordon Williams**

I blame that bloody Mynah bird.

It wasn't my idea of a pet – I just agreed to look after it for a few weeks while Dougie and his family were away at their cottage in Normandy. That's the best thing about working at a university: the long summer holidays. You can take your time and do what you want. That lucky bastard Dougie spent most of his summer in France. His family took everything with them in their Volvo estate – everything except Maxwell. Quarantine restrictions mean that he – or for all I knew it could be she – had to stay behind.

"He's easy to look after," Dougie had told me. "Just give him the special food every day, with some fruit and green leaves. Change the water every second day and clean the cage once a week. That's it. And talk to him – he likes people to talk to him." I asked Dougie if Maxwell was likely to talk back and he said, "Yes, he picks things up very quickly."

"No bad language, then?" I asked him.

"Of course not," he told me. "I've never heard him use any bad language. He wouldn't hear any in my house."

This was getting worse. I wasn't *that* enthusiastic about the idea of looking after somebody else's Mynah bird for two months, but not being able to curse in my own house, too? Well, it was the summer and there would be no football on television so that would be one less reason for swearing. And it wouldn't be a good idea to upset Dougie just now. Sally wasn't that eager to have a Mynah bird at home but I told her that *I* would be looking after it and I would keep it out in the hall where we wouldn't hear it if it did talk a lot.

Talk a lot? It never stopped. It didn't say much at first when I brought it home at the end of term – it may have been upset by the change of surroundings – but within two days it was chattering away without a break. It reminded me of Sally's Aunt Rosie who couldn't stop talking, either. She was bad enough but Maxwell was even worse. I had never tried putting a blanket over Aunt Rosie to see if it would keep her quiet, but it didn't work with Maxwell. He did stop talking at night, but only because he was asleep.

I told Sally that Maxwell had to be a female because only a female would keep talking like that. "Ha, Ha," she said. Like Aunt Rosie he kept on talking but he didn't make much sense: a few phrases that he had picked up at Dougie's house and a lot of gibberish. Did Dougie and his wife really call each other "Sweetie Pie"? How quaint. He was right about the lack of bad language, though – there was none – but Maxwell could do some interesting sound effects. Answering the phone for the fifteenth time because he had learned how to imitate it ringing soon became more than mildly irritating, and within three days he had even learned how to mimic the doorbell. Repeatedly opening the front door to find nobody there was even worse than finding double glazing salesmen or Jehovah's Witnesses, and I couldn't curse in case Maxwell began to repeat it. Twice I came close to shouting the "F" word to at him – and I don't mean, "feathered."

Sally was away at work so she didn't hear him during the day, but I had to listen to that incessant noise coming from the hallway. At least I did for the first six days before I gave up and put the noisy bundle of black feathers in the shed outside, suspending his cage from a hook on the ceiling. Another few days like that and I would have gladly suspended him instead of the cage. It was my holidays but I still had work to do, collating all the data for my research project and writing it up before the university year re-started in October.

It had to be finished before the second week in September, when Sally and I were going on our holidays. Two weeks in Crete may not have been as grand as two months in Normandy, but it would still be very welcome. I did not want to come back from our holiday with work unfinished, and expected that July and August would be more than enough time to complete it. And do some gardening, watch the Olympics on television, make some wine – and drink some, too. What are holidays for, if it isn't to enjoy yourself after working so hard? And, with one thing and another that summer, I intended to enjoy myself although it would have been easier without that bloody bird twittering away in the background.

I knew that I was stuck with Maxwell and it would be another seven weeks before Dougie returned to collect it. I had finished working on the project by mid-afternoon and after two glasses of homemade elderberry wine I was in a better frame of mind. Had I over-reacted to Maxwell? Would he be quieter if he could relax in these unfamiliar surroundings? He had been in the shed for nearly six hours; I wasn't missing him or feeling guilty about putting him there but I did wonder if there was some other way of keeping him quiet that didn't involve banishment to the shed, rat-poison or a shotgun.

I asked myself what would *I* do to relax and would it help Maxwell to keep quiet? No, the elderberry wine might make him fall off his perch and injure himself. It could even make him worse – just like those people who get noisier and more uninhibited with a few drinks inside them. Then I thought of those Relaxation CDs that Sally had bought last year. Just the thing, I told myself as I switched on the stereo. Well, that's it *exactly:* "The Wonder of the Rain Forest." Maxwell should really feel at home listening to that.

He wasn't sulking out in the shed, and I couldn't tell if he was pleased to see me again as he kept on chattering before, during and after bringing his cage back into the house and setting it down on the coffee table. "Right, you garrulous creature," I told him, "this is to help you relax."

"*Relax. Relax*," he squawked.

Relax? – He went berserk. All that birdsong in the rain forest and he had to join in the chorus. Maybe he had had none of his own kind to talk to for a long time but he tried to make up for it now. Relaxation? It drove him crazy, jumping from perch to perch and squawking wildly as he attempted to communicate with the speakers.

That was enough of that, so I tried The Mozart Effect. I played him the *Sonata in C, the Horn Concerto* and even some *Eine Kleine Nachtmusik* but Mozart just didn't seem to have the same effect on Maxwell as it did on people. Not content with the Mozart Effect, I tried the Tchaikovsky Effect, the Brahms Effect and – as a last resort – The Ride of The Valkyries Effect in an attempt to drown out Maxwell's efforts to sound louder than the orchestra. None of it worked.

"Back to the shed with you," I told him, "then I can listen to some music in peace." The No Maxwell Effect: very relaxing and I dozed off in the chair, only waking to prepare the evening meal before Sally came home.

"Where's Maxwell?" she asked, noticing his absence from the hallway.

"I had to put him out in the shed," I told her. "He was making so much noise that I couldn't get on with my project."

"Are you going to leave him out there?" she asked.

"Yes – it's the only way I can get any peace," I replied.

"Is that a good idea, leaving him out in that dusty old shed?" she questioned me. "What if he gets a cold or gets ill out there?"

"It *is* the summer, and Bangor may not be the sub-tropical paradise that was his birthright," I told her, "but I'm sure he'll survive."

"I hope you're right," she replied. " I wouldn't want to have to explain to Doug why he wasn't there when he comes back from France."

No, I didn't think it would be good idea to upset Dougie, either, so Maxwell came back into the house. At least he did when Sally was at home: he went back out into the shed half an hour after she had left for work and I brought him back into the hallway half an hour before she was due home. On sunny days when I was working in the garden, I put his cage out in the shade at the back of the house. This routine worked well throughout the summer and wherever he was he never stopped chattering away.

I fed him every day and checked that he was not getting a cold, although I wasn't sure what the signs would be in a Mynah bird. Would he sneeze or get a runny nose? I didn't know but everything appeared to be in working order – especially his voice. I did imagine having to take him to the vet if anything appeared to be wrong with him – I had even considered training him to say *"Give it me straight, doc: it's psittacosis, isn't it?"* – but Maxwell remained resolutely healthy and resolutely noisy.

Maxwell became a minor problem in a pleasant summer and I had finished my research project a week ahead of schedule, checked it through twice and had it all printed out before Dougie was due back to collect his pet. He came round to our house on a Thursday evening, looking tanned and rested, and he had brought us six bottles of French wine as a present for looking after Maxwell. It seemed rather generous until I calculated that it was less than a bottle a week for my efforts.

We brought Maxwell into the living room, setting his cage down on the floor while I opened a bottle of wine for Dougie. After eight weeks of Maxwell I had felt like giving him last year's damson wine but offered him a glass of decent claret instead. Sally and I also had a glass as we sat in the living room chatting about France while Maxwell chatted away to himself.

"He does talk a lot, doesn't he?" I asked Dougie, who agreed that yes, he did sometimes, before he himself resumed talking about Normandy.

The saying that pets become like their owners – or was it the other way round? - did cross my mind as Dougie kept talking about Normandy and he would probably have talked about it for longer if it hadn't been for Maxwell saying *"But of course I love you, Donna."* This may have been overlooked at first but when he had said it for the eighth time my face was nearly as red as the wine we were drinking.

"Who's Donna?" Sally asked us both.

"Friend of yours?" I asked Dougie.

"No – I don't think I know anybody called Donna," he told us, sounding a bit more convincing than I had been, but that wasn't difficult.

At this point Maxwell decided to join in our conversation too, adding, *"Sally wouldn't understand. Sally wouldn't understand."* He probably didn't understand what he was saying but the three of us certainly did. He may have never heard any swearing at Dougie's house but he heard some that night. I never saw him again after Dougie took him home rather hurriedly so I didn't discover if he ever included, *"You lying, cheating bastard"*, *"Have you been shagging one of your students?"* or, *"Tell me who this fucking Donna is,"* in his subsequent repertoire. I knew that he was good at imitating noises and I wondered if he ever managed the sound of a wineglass being thrown, a face being slapped or a door being slammed.

That was bad enough but I hate to think what he may have heard if Dougie had not taken him home so abruptly. In between several of her angry outbursts I did explain to Sally that Donna was *not* a student but a postgraduate research assistant. It made very little difference: nothing I said would have improved the situation. She carried on shouting for a while longer before going off somewhere that night with a hastily packed suitcase.

I could only think that Maxwell must have heard me talking on the phone when I had brought him into the hallway the previous afternoon. Donna had phoned and I told her that I couldn't really talk to her because Sally would be home soon. If she phoned tomorrow morning I could speak to her then: she knew that I couldn't phone *her* because Sally might see her phone number on the itemised phone bill.

I still had two places booked for a holiday in Crete the following week and when I told Donna what had happened she suggested that she came with me instead of Sally. It seemed like a good idea, and I made the arrangements for the transfer, but when we got to Crete I was still so upset about what had happened at home that even the impressive sight of Donna wearing a bikini – and less – couldn't keep me from thinking about Sally. Two weeks together was a week more than we needed as the excitement of brief and forbidden liaisons disappeared and was replaced by something too ordinary to survive.

Donna had realised this, too, and asked me before we came home if I thought things would be better when we got back to our usual routine at the university. I told her I was sure it would but I didn't believe it myself. And I couldn't tell her that I was missing Sally.

I had a miserable week at home: ironing my own shirts; sleeping alone and not very well; cooking my own meals but not feeling much like eating them. I didn't even have Maxwell to talk to me. I hoped that going back to work would distract me from the circumstances at home but I was wrong: it got worse there. Dougie seemed to be as incapable of keeping quiet as his bloody Mynah bird and I was greeted by *"Who's a cheeky boy?"* from several of the department staff when I returned. So it *was* a good story – and I've certainly passed a few around about other people – but I had hoped that Dougie would not have been gossiping after I had done him the favour of looking after his bird.

I only did it because I thought he had known about Donna and me. He kept seeing us together the previous term – nothing untoward at work, but I was sure he knew – and I didn't want him starting any rumours about us. After we came back from Crete it became more and more embarrassing to see Donna at work every day as our relationship disintegrated, and she still had another year to work there.

Dougie didn't ask me to look after Maxwell the following summer and nobody else in the department volunteered for the job. I don't know if he found anybody to look after that bloody bird and I don't care.

If it had been a hamster I might still be married.

# PERMANENT
## Anthony Toner

The lads had warned him about the shaking, the loss of control in the arms and the hands, but Brendy hadn't expected it to last so long. A week after he'd started, he would still come home from the car wash and sit trembling at the dinner table, like he had some old man's disease. His wrinkled fingers couldn't control forks or knives, teacups wobbled and spilled in his unsteady grasp. It would go on for over an hour.

It's the power hose thing, he told his wife. Holding it all day pulls at your muscles. She'd laughed at his attempts to steady himself, but by Thursday it wasn't funny any more. Don't worry, he told her. Something better will come along.

The money was good at the wash, but it was back breaking work, sore on the spirit. He and four other guys washed and lathered and sprayed and hosed and wiped the cars for four pounds a time at the side of the garage on the Screen Road. All around them, above their heads, edge-of-town pylons hummed with distant menace.

As the new guy, Brendy had all the stooping and stretching work to do on the first couple of days – washing the wheels, wiping the cars down with the chamois. He'd come back to the house each night exhausted, his hands squeaky clean and corpse-white, his feet squelching in his cheap trainers. He'd be asleep in the chair by ten.

But after a few days, they'd given him the power hose, and he would take aim and trigger the blur of high pressure water across windscreens and bonnets, relishing the clean run of the water, the revealed shine of the paintwork and chrome.

The drivers of the cars never knew how to react. Some of them would pretend to read newspapers, or stare straight ahead, or lean their heads back and doze. It was a brief but awkward master-and-servant relationship, Brendy considered. He was outside in the cold, stooping and rubbing and wiping, while they sat on their velour seats and listened to their Fleetwood Mac tapes or whatever. Putting his hand out for the money was an even more uncomfortable experience, especially if you had to run for change while the rest of the line waited behind.

At least he was outside, doing something physical. He could sense the tightening of his shoulders and chest muscles already, the work pulling him back into shape. On the first couple of cold days, he hadn't noticed the drop in temperature. The work kept him warm and the rain – well, the rain didn't matter when you already spent your whole day in a mist of water and suds.

They weren't a bad bunch to work with, either. When a couple of them took a smoke break or stopped for lunch, there was always some chat about the news, or a dirty joke or football banter. None of them really knew anything about each other beyond first names and the briefest of family details. That was the way Brendy liked it.

The autumn was fading, and it was tough going, but the money wasn't bad – the more cars they washed, the more they took home. And they took pride in the work, poking the sponge into the bars of the radiator grilles, enduring all kinds of little scrapes and gouges in their numb hands to make sure the cars were spotless. It earned them a steady repeat trade.

Louise was ashamed of the job, ashamed of the mess they'd both got into, and hated the fact that he was reduced to such graft. But Brendy was less worried. He figured it would do until a better job came up, and he scanned the local papers and the jobmarket, followed up every asshole recommendation from every well-meaning relative and found himself applying for jobs in fruitmarkets, warehouses, shoe shops, burger bars, nightclubs...

Both of them were acutely aware of what they'd lost, and they mentally circled each other in the flat every night, like wounded animals who didn't know who to blame.

You'll freeze to death out there by the time Christmas comes round, she said to him one night as they sat in front of the TV. On the screen, people were arguing with staff at an airport and their hysterical voices contrasted with the cultured voiceover of the presenter. Brendy felt awful for the people being filmed – their misery had become someone else's entertainment. Still, they were probably being paid for it in some way. You could even sell your own misery now, he mused, wondering who would buy his and how much it would be worth.

It'll be all right, he said to Louise. They have heavy gloves. And I can wear more layers.

She didn't speak.

Besides, he went on, by that time they might have laid a couple of us off.

Thursday was slow to start with, although lunchtime had got busy. But things tailed off a little by three o'clock, and when the silver BMW had rolled in, Brendy stepped forward and pulled the wipers forward, began to sponge the windscreen down. Looking through the toughened glass, his heart sank as he recognised Edgar Thompson. There was an exchange of wan smiles between them, each wracking his brain to put a name to the face, to sort through the memories of double geographies and pavilion changing rooms and morning assemblies. They nodded to each other. Thompson took out a mobile phone and made a call. Brendy got down on his haunches and began to soap the alloys.

His cheeks began to burn and he worked over in his head the many things he could say, the myriad opening lines that would make this situation look better. But none of them seemed adequate. He looked to the sky in misery, almost hoping that the car would burst into flames or roll down the hill without being noticed. But there were only the bruised clouds and the distant thrum of the high tension wires and the rumble of the power washer.

Hosing down the paintwork and wiping off the excess water took about ten minutes. Anticipating the end of the process, Thompson wound up his call and tossed the mobile onto the passenger seat. He hit a button and the window slid down.

Well, well... he said with an oily smile. How's Brendy?

Brendy managed a half grin that he hoped looked kind of rakish.

Oh, not so bad, not so bad. Working away.

Thompson took a sideways look at the puddles and the snaking rubber hoses, the half empty buckets. So I see, he said. Damp ould work.

Brendy nodded. Oh aye – but, er... It keeps me off the streets.

Thompson frowned. I thought-, he began, then stopped. Brendy's heart gave a little leap of fright. Here it comes, he thought.

I thought the last time I met you, you were running that... Photo processing place.

Brendy lifted the sponge and tossed it into a nearby bucket. Suds slopped over the edge. His stomach tightened and he could feel a cold rush of adrenalin down his back, a hammer blow of dread in his heart at the memory of the big policeman calling at the house.

Oh, that... Brendy said nonchalantly. Didn't work out.

Thompson continued to frown.

So, he said after a while, gesturing with his thumb carelessly at the forecourt. Is this permanent or temporary or what?

Brendy's cheeks burned with shame.

It's permanent, Edgar, he said, nodding gravely. He extended his palm.

Four quid.

Thompson lifted four coins from a scattering of money on the passenger seat and dropped them into Brendy's palm. They stared at each other for a moment, then Brendy folded his fingers on the cash.

All the best Edgar, he said.

Thompson nodded. Cheers Brendy, he said.

And the window slid up between them again.

Brendy turned for the office, hearing the engine starting up again behind him. He stood breathing in the gloom of the dirty portakabin, and dropped the coins into a tupperware container. He was surprised to find himself shaking, although whether it was cold, anger or the effects of the vibration on his muscles he couldn't tell.

When he told her about it in bed that night, she'd tried to pass it off as nothing.

You worry too much about other people, she said. He'll have forgotten all about it by the time he even pulled back onto the road.

But Brendy stared at the Artex pattern on the ceiling and pictured Thompson in social circles, chattering about this guy and that guy – where they are now, and who had met who and what they were doing. He hated them all and he envied them all. After a while the relief pattern on the ceiling would play tricks on his eyes and the tiny peaks would turn into craters and the ridges into troughs.

He turned on his side and the alarm clock winked 2.11 at him. The winter was coming. He could hear the whine of the wind outside, feel the bite in the draught from the windows. Somewhere up the estate a front door slammed. She could feel his wakefulness, his sense of being marooned somewhere, the wheel going loose in his hands.

Don't worry, love, she said, touching the small of his back. Something'll turn up.

# BALLAD OF THE CAFÉ CAPRI
## Niall McGrath

An old-fashioned Wurlitzer stood at the back of the musty-smelling joint like a shrine in an ancient Greek grotto. Teenagers were gathered around it – acolytes, offering gleaming coins as they poured reverently over the list of psalms to the god of popular music that were displayed. A rousing rock number was blaring out, promising true, uncompromising passion, unending devotion, uncomplicated, unconditional love. Already I had the intimation that this was a magical place, a place imbued with anticipation, longing and impalpable significance.   Certainly, it was a sanctuary from the December drizzle that was marring the Christmas-shopper-packed streets that dour evening.

Although it was late, there was still a good stock of pastries and cakes available at the counter. Chocolate goodies were exquisitely presented. They reminded me of delicacies I'd only seen in France: it was the 1980s, Belfast had still not opened up to the variety and tastes that would soon be ushered in as peace began to burgeon and the stifling weeds of internecine violence withered.

It was the early 1980s – the youths here were togged out in Ska gear: dark, narrow-legged trousers, white or chequered tee shirts, black Harrington jackets or anoraks and trendy hats. Their lapels were arrayed with columns of pin badges that draped like Orangemen's sashes – guitar-shaped ones, pop group-shaped ones, all kinds of exotic designs, all chequered.

The staff were two little old ladies, hair tied back in buns, wearing navy cardigans and long grey skirts, who looked like they existed in some pre-Second World War time warp. Cassie called my order across to Emily, who was deaf, so the chips and beans had to be shouted for more than once.  I wasn't sure yet whether the young Ska lads' amusement at the old women was malicious or amicable.

I asked a young couple, in a leather upholstered, high-backed seating area that resembled a bar snug, if I could share their table. They acknowledged my request offhandedly, engrossed as they were in their puppy love. The lad was puffing on a roll-up, the girl fiddling with her tight skirt absent-mindedly as they chatted about the movie they'd just been to see. She mentioned her folks would be expecting her home, so they got up to leave, draining their coca-cola glasses and wresting with jacket sleeves.

It was while I was looking at the sew-on patches and cool designs on the backs of their dark Harringtons that I noticed the photographs on the wall. They were of a band. The lead singer also appeared in one shot playing a sax. In one, a portrait, his clean-cut features radiated wholesomeness and perfection. That annoying red-spot that flash photography often produces was absent, his blue eyes shone purely, mesmerised me even though it was only a picture.

"Coke?"

Startled, I turned to smile at Emily. "Sorry, Fanta."

She had one on her tray, but had already gone away with it, not having heard me. I was about to follow her to get my fizzy orange when I glimpsed the pictures on the wall out of the corner of my eye and let it go. I waited patiently for my chips, sipping my coca-cola, relaxed by the vibes from the jukebox. Madness tunes which before had not appealed to me suddenly had depth to their lyrics. The Specials' *Ghost Town* had me nodding my head, eyes closed, as if in prayer, or chanting some cleansing rite, when I felt the table judder against my thigh. It was a couple of girls. They were slightly older than the couple who had just been sitting with me. They were sucking raspberryade through straws and giggling about some chitchat or other. Each had a huge pastry before her, which they began to devour slowly as if they were connoisseurs, licking blobs of cream from the corners of their mouths and the tips of their noses and their fingers.

I was beginning to feel warmer now, so I slipped off my raincoat. As I did so, I nudged one of the girls with the back of my hand.

"Oh, sorry."

"No bother," she remarked in a broad, west Belfast accent.

"That's the only chance Julie's gonna get of someone touchin' her up th' night!" her friend sniggered.

Julie cursed at her friend, but shared in the joke. She asked her pal, "Where's Jenny th' night?"

"No doubt she'll be here anytime now."

"Aff seein' a fella, eh, Claire?"

"Sure, she's only eyes fer one bloke," Claire responded, nodding at the pictures on the wall. "Drew."

"*Drew-ll!*" Julie squawked, leading her mate into a frenzy of innocent laughter. At last, she said, "Seriously, Claire, *is* there anything between them?"

"She'd like to think so."

"Wouldn't we all! Drew's a dreamboat!"

"*Dreamboat*! That's like somethin' yer grannie'd come out wi'!"

"Still an' all, he *is*."

"Aye," said Claire, bowing her head like a nun at confession.

My plate of chips and beans arrived then. I tucked in, to discover that it had taken Emily so long to shuffle from the kitchen with the meal that the beans had got cold.

Suddenly, the front door burst open. A panting lad, whose face was pitted by acne, came panting up to our table.

"Jenny's just been knocked down! By a car!" He caught his breath.

"She must've been on her way here!" Julie shrieked, cupping a hand over her mouth. "Where'd it happen, Steve?"

I was out of the café like a bullet from a barrel, while the two millies still sat stunned in their seats. I don't know exactly what drove me out into the cold night, but when I reached the scene an ambulance was already pulling up, so I merely whipped out my camera and began snapping wildly.

"Get outta here!" Steve snarled at me.

I had already got shots of the damaged car and the pathetic trails of blood that were trickling across the wet tarmac towards a drain, so I stuffed my camera beneath my raincoat once more. I stood hypnotised by the blue flashing lights as two paramedics bandaged up the girl's wounds and stretchered her into the ambulance. That was when I noticed an envelope lying on the pavement. Picking it up, shaking the rainwater off, I saw that it had scrawled across the front 'Drew'. Hurriedly, ruthlessly, I stuffed it into my raincoat pocket. Claire and Julie had arrived by then. Shaking, they pleaded with the ambulance driver for news of the victim.

"It's serious," was all he told them gravely before hopping into his cab and driving off.

"She doesn't deserve this!" Claire cried straight into my face, spittle masking her mouth.

Behind us, as the three of us wandered back towards the Café Capri, a policeman was restraining Steve, who was trying to attack the car's driver.

"I'll kill you, you drunken eejit!" he was screaming. "I'll kill you!"

When we got back to the café, my plate was no longer on the table. Emily appeared behind me, carrying it.

"I warmed it up for you, love."

As I thanked her, she asked Julie, "Who's your friend?"

"Isabel," I told all three.

I got a Fanta at the counter and came back to eat. The girls were sipping their raspberryade solemnly.

"Do you think she'll be alright?" Claire kept asking me.

"It didn't look too bad. There always seems to be more blood than there actually is," I lied to comfort her.

"Are you a nurse?" Julie asked me.

"A journalist," I embellished the truth about my status as a struggling, on-the-dole freelance photographer. "Where's this Drew fellow, her boyfriend?"

"Drew? His band's touring in the South till next week. I don't think Jenny and him ever got together."

"She used to give me notes to slip to him," Claire insisted. "It's so tragic!"

"Why notes?" I asked.

Claire lowered her voice as she told me, "His great-aunts who brought him up are a bit goodlivin', don't want him messin' about wi' the likes of us."

"Goodlivin'? Stuck up, more like."

"Naw!"

"Drew went to *Campbell College!*" Julie continued in a mocking tone. "Not that he made much use of it."

"He's a great singer," Claire argued.

"He's probably chasin' loads of birds round the country when he's out of the oldies' sight."

"Ack, no, Drew's not that type. He said to me once he was waiting for the right girl."

"Just being kind when he was rebuffin' your lust," Julie chided.

I ate my meal quickly and went to the counter to pay. As I left, I glanced across at the photographs of the band and the portrait of Drew. *God forgive me*, I said to myself as I reached the door, *but I know what'll be in my mind as I climb into bed tonight.*

I was drawn to the Café Capri the following Saturday night like a groupie to Glastonbury. I had in my hand in my raincoat pocket the envelope. I'd not dared to open it or even contemplate its contents since I'd picked it up from the pavement the previous week.

When I went to order some of those succulent chips and beans, Emily and Cassie smiled in recognition: I'd been in twice during the week at lunchtime. Little did they know it was to check whether or not Drew had returned from the South – and to ogle surreptitiously at the photographs of that Adonis.

I had only just begun to eat my meal when Claire and Julie arrived. I hadn't seen them since that awful night the previous week. They came over to join me, carrying their mineral drinks and pastries.

"Hello, Isabel! What about ye?" Claire said kindly.

"Fine. Yourselves?"

"Bearing up. You know Jenny died after that crash last week?"

I nodded. "I was in here earlier in the week, Cassie told me."

"Aye, she was saying she was talkin' till ye. She likes you, Isabel."

"Oh? Thanks very much…" I was interrupted by a head that popped over the high-backed seat.

"Isabel Gibb?" he barked.

"Yes?"

"Who rattled your cage, Steve?" Julie wanted to know.

"Her!" he snarled, jerking a finger in my direction, his face contorted with the intensity of his loathing.

"D'you know what she did?" He told them with narrowed eyelids, "She took photographs of Jenny lyin' dyin' and sold them to the *Belfast Telegraph*. The pictures that were in the next day's paper, they had her name on them!"

"They only used general shots of the scene, you know that. We wouldn't use anything that would impinge on her... privacy..."

"*Why* did you do that?" Claire asked, confused.

"I'm a photo-journalist. I wasn't thinking, I just saw a story and snapped away. Out of instinct, habit." I shrugged my shoulders.

"Anything for a story," Steve's disembodied face seethed from above the leather upholstery of the seatback. "Just like they did with Princess Diana."

"Hardly," Julie defended me, to my great relief. I didn't want to have to leave the café just when I felt I was about to achieve the culmination of my desires – and get to meet the beautiful, charismatic, mysterious Drew.

"Yeah, leave her alone, Steve," Claire shouted at him. "She's not that bad."

It was at that moment that I realised that the fellow who had just walked past the end of our table was the same man who was in the photographs on the wall. How many times in the past number of days had I fantasized about having him pose for me, so I could snap away as he stooped brazenly, turned ruggedly, tilted his head temptingly, smiled with those adorable lips of his? He glided towards the counter and got a bottle of ginger ale from his great-aunt Cassie. Then, he sauntered towards the jukebox to hang out with a couple of mates. *Stay calm*, I told myself, hoping the dampness at my temples wasn't noticeable.

Julie and Claire were rabbiting on about this and that. Eventually, there came a lull in their chitchat, just as Steve passed by our table, giving me the evil eye, to hang out with some rough-looking guys at the far end.

"Is Drew's band going to play tonight? I thought they sometimes played here?"

"Dunno. *Hope* so," Claire enthused. "It would cheer us up, in the circumstances. Ask him, *please*, Julie."

"Drew!" Julie hollered across the room embarrassingly. She waved at him. He excused himself, leaving the other lads to come towards our table.

Drew moved towards us as if in slow motion like the romantic hero in a corny movie. My throat felt dry, I gulped down some Fanta to steady my nerves. He was wearing blue jeans and a black tee shirt, with a stylish, colourful sweater and brand new trainers. In the flesh, Drew was the fulfilment of all that his photographs promised: golden hair, bronze skin, bulging shoulders, sapphire eyes translucent with presumption.

"Poor Drew!" Claire moaned; Julie got up to hug him as he arrived.

She knocked the table so my tall glass tipped over; my Fanta spilt towards me. It just missed my lap, but it began to drip onto the floor beside me. I mopped at the orange juice with a paper napkin.

"Here, let me," Drew said, having seized more napkins from a holder.

"It wasn't your fault," I said, as he sidled in to sit between Claire and me.

"Who're you?" he asked with deliberate cuteness.

"This is Isabel. She's a photographer."

"You must be so cut up about Jenny!" Claire interjected.

"It's the pits," he nodded. "I came back early for the funeral." He addressed us all like a mediaeval prince holding court.

"So I heard from your great-aunt," I replied.

"But at least she went fairly quickly," Julie intoned morosely.

"You don't feel up to playing tonight, then?"

"Oh, I dunno," he sighed tactfully. "Not really. Yet I find it so difficult to resist the temptation to seek solace in my music, whatever the circumstances."

"Play for us, then!" Claire suggested.

Drew asked me, "Do you think I should?"

"I've never heard you play yet," I reminded him.

On that cue, he went to round up his mates. They began with a haunting, lilting melody, an instrumental, during which Drew's saxophone wailed like a heartbroken lover. But he craftily soothed the tune into a cheerier number, until the tempo picked up. Before long, everyone was clapping and swaying to a rawer, earthier beat. Drew held aside the sax and began to sing into his microphone, clasping it in his hand as if he were touching the cheeks of a girl, about to press his lips against hers – *my* cheeks, *my* lips, I was daydreaming at that very moment; as, no doubt, were most of the females there. Everyone seemed overcome with emotion to be in his presence, carried away on the tide of his music and his voice as the rhythm permeated to the very core of one's being.

Julie and Claire shuffled up to the front and began to cavort in their high heels, dancing in the aisle. When the band took a break, the jukebox was put on so that the spell the live music had created wasn't broken. Julie and Claire danced on.

Drew returned to my table. A few more people were crammed in around me. Drew paused to speak with one of them before sliding in beside me – I saw that it was Steve. He was still staring at me nastily. Claire hurried back to us before I was able to speak with Drew on his own.

"I've no more messages fer ye, Drew," Claire whispered to him. "But my mum heard this from her auntie: Jenny was expectin'."

My jaw dropped. The chatter around us didn't cease, yet it felt as if an oasis of silence had appeared around us, that we were caught in a bubble, a vacuum that time and all external matters failed to infiltrate.

"*We* were just friends," Drew assured Claire. "It wasn't *that* serious."

"Damn right," Steve interrupted, having heard Claire's last remark. "She was fed up with the way you messed her about and was seeing *me*."

"Jenny, two-time somebody?" Claire laughed at Steve.

"The child was mine!" Steve insisted. "And my poor wee unborn child was killed by that drunken eejit along with my Jenny!" he gurgled with overweening sentimentality.

Steve took himself off, clearly upset. Claire looked askance at Drew.

"As I say, it wasn't that deep between *me* and Jenny. We were just mates."

Shocked, Claire left, then – no doubt to tell all the latest to Julie, who was being chatted up by the drummer from Drew's band.

"I didn't know her, but she seemed to be a lovely girl," I said to Drew, aware of the sheer physicality of his presence so close to me.

"Jenny was charming, but rather young for me. Not really my type. On the other hand…"

Drew didn't need to complete the sentence for me to know he

would soon try it on. Yet in the back of my mind something else was nagging. I fingered the envelope in the pocket of my raincoat, which was bunched up on the seat behind and around me.

"Besides," Drew went on, "the group and I have been doing well on the scene in Dublin. I reckon we'll end up there more permanently. Maybe even head on over to London, now that U2 are trailblazing."

"I know Claire used to deliver these to you. I found this on the pavement the night Jenny got hit by the car." I showed him the letter.

"Oh, Jenny was just one of those people who like to write notes, explore their everyday experiences on paper. She'd write to me about Steve, ask my advice, you know…"

He reached for the stained brown envelope, but I snatched it back. With a harsh thumb I ripped it open.

"It's addressed to me!" he snapped.

"Finders keepers."

When I'd read the brief, frantic message, the paper fell limply into his hand as I laughed to myself at the irony of it.

*Drew, my darling, I love you so much. Please believe that. I didn't mean to hurt you, honestly. But you weren't here often enough and you're distant so much. You make me doubt your affection for me. I've been going mad so much of the time, not knowing how you truly feel about me because you won't open up to me. Now you're going to have to. And I'm going to have to know once and for all just where I stand with you. I love you, my dearest darling Drew, but I've made a stupid mistake. I'm about two months pregnant. No, it's not a mistake, it's real. There's no way I'll get rid of it. And don't listen to them when they say I've been unfaithful to you – I know some will try to tell you that. He was chasing after me, but there was nothing between us. You're the only one I love, Drew. So, I need to know - are you going to support me? Emotionally, I mean – I'm not trying to screw money out of you. Do you love me as I love you? Please call me.*

"I don't like to speak ill of the dead, but she was a little liar," Drew announced casually.

Steve was staring intently at us both, I suddenly noticed. He grabbed the note and scanned it, nostrils flaring as he did so.

Tossing the letter aside, Steve hissed at Drew, "She told me she was over three months gone. I reckon she knew you'd ditch her like the scumbag y'are. Mess about wi' my bird, would ye?"

I could see Steve's mates were being enticed over by the commotion like a pack of wolves closing in to pounce with their fangs.

"I think I'll go," I said to Drew. "I've seen enough tragedy for one week."

Drew tried to leave, too. He was having a chin-jutting session with Steve when I ducked out the door.

As I paused on the pavement outside to button up my raincoat, I realised Drew was beside me, lighting up a cigarette. He offered me one, which I took. We began walking away from the Café Capri.

"There's no one following," I said, glancing back at the glowing front of the nondescript diner that dark night.

"Cassie bellowed at them to sit down or she'd call the cops. It's just you and me."

Staring up into those sky-blue pupils, I asked him, "What makes you think I'd be interested in you, when you were quite prepared to treat Jenny so abominably?"

Shrugging his shoulders, grinning with that bedevilling mouth of his, Drew said, "Are you prepared to take a chance?"

Sharing in his sense of humour, I smiled too. That was when he put his arm round my waist; I put my arm around his and our hot mouths fused.

# CONTRIBUTORS

**Gary Allen** is from Ballymena, Co Antrim and has had short fiction and poetry published widely internationally.

**Claire Dagger** was born and reared in Dublin but has lived in Galway since 1982. She was a member of Ireland's International Archery team in 1987, 1989 and 1991. Claire is multi-talented, being a writer of both poetry and prose. Her play, *Ruin (Secrets)* won an Oireachtas award in 1997.

**Kevin Gormley** lives in Omagh. He has published a short story pamphlet and is currently working on a novel.

**Rosemary Jenkinson** was born in Belfast and taught abroad for many years in France and eastern Europe. Her work has been published in the Northern Short Story Writers anthology (1998) from Arc Publications and won the Black Hill Books Short Story Competition (2001).

**Brian Kennedy** was born in Belfast. He is best known as a singer / songwriter / performer, and has released 6 albums. As well as writing short stories Brian has just finished a novel which he hopes to publish in the near future.

**Gerard Kinsella** is from Downpatrick. He studied film in London. He has written and directed two short films and is currently working on a screenplay

**John McAllister** is originally from Ballymena. He went to live in Armagh for two years in 1974 and is still there. He has an M.Phil in Creative Writing from Trinity College, Dublin. He is a lecturer in creative writing, and is currently finishing a novel as well as working on a collection of short stories.

**Niall McGrath** is from Antrim. His publications include: *Heart of a Heartless World* (1995, Minerva Press, London) a novel, *First Sight* (1997, Lapwing, Belfast) poetry, *Déjà vu* (1999, Poetry Monthly Press, England) poetry, *Godsong & A Matter Of Honour* (2000, BM Press, NI) transliterations. He is editor of *The Black Mountain Review* and widely published as a reviewer.

**A F McKenna** lives in Newtownabbey, Co Antrim. He has been a university lecturer and has been writing fiction for several years.

**Stephen McMurray**, from Newtownabbey, Co Antrim, has won the Crystal Magazine Prize (2001) and has had stories in anthologies from Horseshoe Press and by Eva Wiggins Trust.

**Brian McNulty** is from Newcastle, Co Down. Brian works in Local Government and has been writing for four years. Brian is a Brian Moore winner and was awarded the Royal Mail New Writer of the Year award.

**Katherine Martin** was born in St. Paul, Minnesota, lived in seven states and over fifty houses and is now settled in Belfast with her husband, Dan. She has published articles abroad and writes arts reviews for Belfast's *City Wide*. This past year, she co-ordinated the 2002 Writers' Showcase in the Belfast Literary Festival, *Between the Lines*. She is currently a student on the Creative Writing MA at Queen University, Belfast and is working on a novel entitled *Leave to Remain*. She hardly ever breaks things.

**Jim Meredith**, from Belfast, won the Brian Moore Award with his story 'The Bed Bugs Bite'

**Sam Millar** is married with three children. He won the Cork Literary Review Short Story Competition, and was a runner up in the Brian Moore and Martin Healy Short Story competitions. He is widely published in the States and Canada, and across Europe. Some of his work has been broadcast by the BBC.

**Daithí Ó Muirí** won the Cló Iar-Chonnachta Literary Award in 2001. A native of Co Monaghan, he now lives in Connemara. His selection *Cogaí* appeared from Cló Iar-Chonnachta recently. A third collection, *Uaigheanna agus Scea,* is due out this year.

**Marie O'Nolan** was born in Dublin and educated at University College Dublin, where she took an honours degree in History and English. She has written poetry, novels and short stories. She has won prizes in the James Joyce / Jerusalem Post Competition, at the Listowel Writer's Week (twice) and in the Bookstop New Writers Competition (three times). Her collection of short stories *Tales of a Long Dry Summer* was published in 1997.

**Frank Sewell** is from Belfast and is currently researching at the University of Ulster at Coleraine. He is not only widely respected for his translations of the work of Cathal O Searcaigh among other writers but also for his own poetry. He recently co-edited *Artwords*, an anthology of contemporary Ulster visual art and poetry (Cranagh Press)

**Anthony Toner** is a newspaper editor and songwriter from Portstewart. He is currently studying Irish Literature at the University of Ulster. His work has appeared in journals such as *The Black Mountain Review.*

**Csilla Toldy** was born in Budapest, but has lived in Warrenpoint, Co Armagh for several years. She is widely accredited as a scriptwriter as well a fiction writer. Her film *Choices* dealt with teenage pregnancy in Northern Ireland.

**Gordon Williams** was born in Manchester and has lived in Co Fermanagh for twenty years. He has had articles and stories published widely over the past few years.

**Howard Wright** is a fine arts lecturer with the University of Ulster. He is from Portadown, Co Armagh and has had poetry and short stories published in many journals internationally.

*The Black Mountain Press*

## The best in emerging talent from Ireland North and South

Brian Kennedy   Katherine Martin   Jim Meredith   Brian McNulty
Marie O'Nolan   Gerard Kinsella   Stephen McMurray   Kevin Gormley
Gary Allen   Csilla Toldy   Sam Millar   Gordon Williams   Howard Wright
Niall McGrath   John McAllister   A F McKenna   Rosemary Jenkinson
Daithí Ó Muirí   Claire Dagger   Anthony Toner

Cover Artwork: Miriam de Búrca

ISBN: 0-9537570-1-3
£7.50
€12.50
$12.50